Chilean New Song

J. Patrice McSherry

Chilean New Song

THE POLITICAL POWER OF MUSIC, 1960s–1973

TEMPLE UNIVERSITY PRESS
Philadelphia • *Rome* • *Tokyo*

TEMPLE UNIVERSITY PRESS
Philadelphia, Pennsylvania 19122
www.temple.edu/tempress

Library of Congress Cataloging-in-Publication Data

McSherry, J. Patrice, author.
  Chilean new song : the political power of music, 1960s–1973 / J. Patrice McSherry.
      pages cm
  Includes bibliographical references and index.
  ISBN 978-1-4399-1151-8 (cloth : alk. paper) — ISBN 978-1-4399-1152-5 (pbk. : alk. paper)
  — ISBN 978-1-4399-1153-2 (e-book) 1. Popular music—Chile—History and criticism.
2. Protest songs—Chile—History and criticism. 3. Popular music—Political aspects—
Chile—History—20th century. 4. Music and state—Chile. I. Title.
  ML3487.C55M37 2015
  782.42'15990983—dc23

                                                                    2014039778

♾ The paper used in this publication meets the requirements of the American National
Standard for Information Sciences—Permanence of Paper for Printed Library Materials,
ANSI Z39.48-1992

Printed in the United States of America

9 8 7 6 5 4 3 2 1

Contents

Foreword · The Movement of Musical Identity in Chile
(1950–1973): The River of Cultures, by José Seves S.   vii

Preface and Acknowledgments   xvii

1 *La Nueva Canción* and Its Significance   1

2 Art and Politics Intertwined in Chile: A Selected History   26

3 The Emergence of *la Nueva Canción Chilena*   52

4 *La Nueva Canción* and the Unidad Popular   86

5 Politically Committed Artists and Their Music   115

6 Musical and Political Contributions of *la Nueva Canción*   140

7 The Coup and Its Aftermath   166

8 Conclusion   180

Notes   191

Index   219

Foreword

The Movement of Musical Identity
in Chile (1950–1973)

THE RIVER OF CULTURES

The best way for me to introduce this book is to offer a condensed version of my vision, as someone integrated within *la Nueva Canción chilena*, regarding the development of popular music that took shape within the culture of the popular sectors and quickly became a musical form that recognized and strengthened the identity of large majorities of the Chilean people. This contribution aims to complement the mosaic of opinions and viewpoints of other protagonists of this movement interviewed by the author, and to add to the reflection to which this study is dedicated regarding this important cultural phenomenon. *La Nueva Canción* stirred our society, and despite the tragic period that followed, it remains a powerful force and an essential part of our identity.

Chile, in the first half of the twentieth century, was transformed by the influence of its internal diaspora, the result of migration from the South toward the capital and beyond. People came to the nitrate fields in the North and, after the mines closed, to the country's central cities. These migrants brought new languages, ways of living, customs, experiences, and art. Their music, with roots in the peasantry and popular campesino art, came to the cities with this flow of social rivers, then provoked and pressed to obtain space and recognition. For people to maintain their cultural heritage, it was imperative to make that heritage visible and recognized.

Argentina provided a clear example of the impact of these large migrations in 1949, when President Juan Perón issued the Decree of Protection of National Music, which declared that cafés and public places had to play

Argentine music at least 50 percent of the time and ordered that Argentine artists be included in live cinematography. These measures produced an explosion of artists and folk groups. Moreover, 40 percent of the music on the radio had to be national music, the study of folklore was introduced in schools, and spaces were opened for social gatherings. Together with other activities, this stimulated musical expression, achieving a movement that was extraordinary in its musical and poetic diversity and quality. Social recognition of this music was chronicled in discography registers and brought into fashion what was called "folk-rooted" or "folk projection" music, whose authors, composers, dancers, and poets represented a style that was more integrated with Argentina's popular culture.

The "folklore boom" swept through Argentina at the end of the 1950s. It also had a strong impact on Chile and the rest of the continent, breaking the dominance of English-language rock-and-roll and other commercial music and changing popular musical tastes. Groups such as Los Chalchaleros, Los Fronterizos, and Huanca Huá; soloists, composers, and guitarists such as Atahualpa Yupanqui and Eduardo Falú; and singers such as Mercedes Sosa were outstanding figures in this enormous movement. Their music began to be played on the radio, and they began to perform in Chile.

To this was added the product of Chilean folklore researchers who had traveled throughout the country carrying out investigations. Violeta Parra had already demonstrated the fruits of her labor, and, following a suggestion by her brother Nicanor, she began orienting her musical work toward the study and diffusion of authentic campesino art rather than the distorted and instrumentalized styles presented as folk music by the mass media.

Groups of prominent intellectuals and artists gathered to discuss the country's urgent needs and dreams. Many of them sought to see, from their different artistic disciplines, into the interior of the national soul as inspiration for their own work. At these gatherings, it was possible to reaffirm that there is a search for the genuine in all fields of art—just as every human being affirms himself or herself in the past. As their ancestors did, people treasure the knowledge of lived experience, of upbringing, of education, of wisdom, and of good social life that, projected from generation to generation, forms the basis of our culture.

Violeta Parra began her investigations in 1952 and soon started recording "The Folklore of Chile," a series produced by Odeon Records. The Institute of Research of Musical Folklore at the University of Chile had been functioning since 1944. With the participation of the sisters Margot and Estela Loyola, the institute released ten records that year with twenty-seven generic examples of national music. Margot Loyola then carried out an extraordinary process of creating workshops and centers of investigation on Chilean music and dance throughout the country. Her work was fundamental in strengthening research and education on Chilean folklore and served as a potent pole of influence and orientation in the gestation of the musical movement of the 1960s.

Another important musical source was Andean music, expressed in the ancient religious festivals in northern Chile and carrying the syncretism of ancient, pre-Columbian cultural events derived from Aymara cultures and vestiges of pre-Inca times that were mixed in the melting pot of *lo criollo*. [*Lo criollo* refers to the distinctive, local cultural mix of Spanish, American-born, and indigenous traditions.] All of this was diffused through migration and became known more professionally in the capital at the beginning of the 1950s through the cultural and creative figure of Calatambo Albarracín.

The wealth of folklore from other zones of Chile was still unknown, but Violeta Parra soon inspired her disciples Gabriela Pizarro and Héctor Pavez to travel to the South, to the archipelago of Chiloé to conduct research. But then, as now, the mass media provided no space for national expression. In the 1960s, the media almost exclusively transmitted commercial Anglo-Saxon music. "If you want to be a folklorist, I wouldn't advise it," Violeta Parra told an admirer in the film *Violeta se fue a los cielos*, the testimony of her son Ángel. "You're only going to have work on the eighteenth [September 18 is Chile's Independence Day]." At that time, only music from central Chile was considered "national"—that is, music of the *huaso* dressed as a farm foreman or landowner—and the songs featured romantic descriptions of the scenic countryside, and a view of women as *chinitas*, flirtatious and available to the owner. This depiction was a caricature of folklore and showed indifference, or a discriminatory attitude, toward the people and their culture. It could be described as a kind of cultural complex of the dominant elite, who saw only the foreign—especially anything that came from Europe and the United States—as superior.

The work of disseminating folklore owes much to Margot Loyola and Violeta Parra, and to their efforts and convictions regarding what was necessary to preserve and fitting to celebrate as our own, as well as their passion for the music and its value as an element of popular identity and of beauty for the spirit. These two women spread their work through their activities of education and diffusion of popular art, with the assistance of institutions that had already taken this path. The song-and-dance group Cuncumén (which means "murmur of water" in Mapudungun, the Mapuche language) was the first of its kind in Chile. Formed in 1955 by Loyola's students in the Seasonal Schools and theater workshops of the University of Chile, Cuncumén became the seed of an extensive project that combined recordings and presentations with research and educational workshops. Initially directed by Rolando Alarcón in its musical dimension and by Alejandro Reyes in dance, the group recorded nine LPs in the "Folklore of Chile" series. Víctor Jara joined later as a member and director.

The People: Cultural, Social, and Political Dimensions

There is a unity or natural empathy among those referred to as the popular sectors, whether social centers, political parties, or cultural entities:
their waters are the same, and their actions empower one another, making
it difficult to separate the cultural, the social, and the political. There we
find the presence of Latin American songs that illuminate the three fields,
and they are jewels that transcend time. One is the love song "Canto a la
Pampa" (Song of the Pampa; 1895); originally written by Tomás Gabino and
titled "Ausencia," whose lyrics were changed by the worker-poet Francisco
Pezoa to relate the tragedy of Chile's nitrate miners. Another is "Lamento
Borincano" (Puerto Rican Lament), written by Rafael Hernández in 1929,
which tells the story of shortages and hardships in Puerto Rico. Songs of the
Mexican revolution, songs of slavery in Peru (such as "A la Molina No Voy
Más"), among many others, are also clear examples of this point.

History highlights the multiple works of Luis Emilio Recabarren, the
organizer of Chile's first unions and workers' political organizations in the
early 1900s. A tireless and visionary organizer, he promoted education and
literacy, creating newspapers, organizing cultural activities, and stimulating the production of works for the theater and in music that related to and
described the lives of the workers.

On another cultural shore, *El Canto General,* by Pablo Neruda, was a
compendium of poetry and history based firmly on love for the epic of the
Latin American continent and its long struggle for justice, which navigated
an immense sea, giving sustenance and argument to cultural and political
struggles.

The Folk *Peña*: Of the Old the New Is Born

The narrow defeat of Salvador Allende in the presidential elections of 1964
convoked many artists, among them the siblings Ángel and Isabel Parra,
who had returned from Paris to support the popular leader's new campaign.
Far from unnerving supporters, the loss raised expectations that the next
contest could be won and new initiatives pursued. The creation of La Peña
de los Parra, in an old house with insufficient space for large events, was a
milestone that marked a cultural and political change that seemed to vibrate
in the air, exalting the popular essence and aspirations.

Violeta Parra, meanwhile, had continued her research, opening lodes of
original composition. Over time, her role metamorphosed from defender
of popular song to creator of folklore, speaking for her people. Her songs
accuse. They bluntly describe the reality she was witnessing. They denounce,
and they teach one to see. The five musicians of La Peña de los Parra followed

in her footsteps, constituting a center of new creativity: Rolando Alarcón, Víctor Jara, Isabel and Ángel Parra, and Patricio Manns belonged to a generation that extended the bridge between *campesino* song and the creation of a new music based in that language. They also added songs that drew on folk styles from Argentina, Bolivia, Ecuador, Uruguay, and Venezuela. Violeta Parra's children followed her example, using the *cuatro venezolano*, the *charango*, the *quena*, and other traditional instruments from beyond Chile's borders, without concern about what was purely "national" and, as a result, reaffirmed the common values of Latin America. Any instrument born in these lands served a purpose. All spoke of Latin America. All were the sound of our common history.

At La Peña, the Parra siblings became aware of campesino song through direct family transmission, as did Víctor Jara, whose mother was a popular singer. Alarcón and Manns became aware through their own sensitivity and self-education in a culturally sensitive environment. They had access to the patrimony of a popular culture that encompassed a rich variety of music, rhythms, and styles, as well as a variety of poetic structures and aesthetic content and values. Folkloric research by Gabriela Pizarro and Héctor Pavez, with their group Millaray, brought a rich variety of songs, rhythms, and dances collected in Chiloé to the cities. Their work, published in albums in the mid-1960s, introduced people to southern Chilean styles of song and dance.

The artists of La Peña de los Parra not only interpreted folk song but also created their own compositions. Each operated with his or her particular vein, inspired by popular styles, opening them to more complex musical and poetic expressions and giving them more topical political content. From there, the content and context emerged as essential parts of what would become known as *la Nueva Canción chilena*.

Haunting the songs' lyrics were the places, crafts, and experiences of Chileans' human and geographical map: descriptions of life in the countryside, as well as in the ports, the mines, and the mountain ranges; the fishermen, bandits, miners, herders, sailors, lumberjacks, and shepherds. They were songs that described human beings and their labors, as well as the unruly winds of change.

It seemed necessary to unveil every corner to recognize ourselves.

The Democratization of Culture

The next generation was both the practitioner of this gift of popular folk art and its greatest propagator. The explosion of folk-rooted music in Chilean society was brought about by two movements: *Neofolklore* and *la Nueva Canción chilena*. *Neofolklore*—whose significance was questioned by some who asked whether "new" folk or popular wisdom was possible—became widespread through radio shows and distribution in the music market. Its performers often wore tuxedos or smoking jackets. They took their repertoires from Violeta Parra, from Raúl de Ramón, and from composers of La Peña de Los Parra, especially Rolando Alarcón and Patricio Manns. Some of these musicians, such as "El Chino" Urquidi and Willy Bascuñán, also created songs about love, travel, work in the countryside, regional trades, and military exploits. The music principally consisted of vocal quartets inspired by Argentine arrangements, accompanied by guitar and *bombo* drum.

The other movement that later was named *la Nueva Canción chilena* expressed itself in hundreds of folk *peñas* and events within the framework of student organizations, social organizations, unions, and political parties. A considerable and growing number of these musicians were able to reach large audiences as they rapidly professionalized—Aparcoa, Grupo Lonqui, Inti-Illimani, Quilapayún, and so many others—although their labor was regarded with indifference by the mass media. But they were greeted with enthusiasm by the social movements that hosted them and invited them to provide an artistic moment in political meetings or social gatherings.

In general, these groups grounded themselves in the works of previous generations and embraced the global Latin American vision. This was expressed in their repertoires; in their decisions to honor indigenous cultures by taking names from the Quechua, Aymara, and Mapudungun languages; in their instrumental creation, which was enriched by Andean elements (flutes, *sicus, quenas, charangos, bombos*); and in their choice to wear stylized ponchos, the most common and egalitarian attire of the continent.

The changing aesthetic of the time was reflected in how the *peñas* were decorated, using elements from the countryside such as wagon wheels, peasant textiles, and fishing nets, as well as natural materials such as wood, sawdust, clay, and candles. This culture extended to the clothing of the young people, who adopted wool from Chiloé, woven Andean bags, sombreros, and handicraft products.

Some *peñas* were outstanding in their function and impact and carried out a formidable artistic diffusion. They became cradles for the birth and maturation of many artists who advanced to professional levels. Chile Ríe y Canta, the *peña* founded by the well-known radio personality and promoter René Largo Farías, is worth mentioning because it nurtured the development of artists such as Nano Acevedo, Grupo Chamal, the harpist Alberto Rey, and Silvia Urbina. Also important were La Peña de Valparaíso, which featured Gitano Rodríguez, Payo Grondona, and Grupo Tiempo Nuevo; university *peñas*; and the folk group at the University of Antofagasta that early on began publishing its research on the folklore of the North.

The *peña* at the Universidad Técnica del Estado (State Technical

University; UTE) in Valdivia deserves special mention, and I serve as a witness. It was at the center of dynamic activity that included radio programs, folk ballet and guitar courses, public events for the people of the countryside and in cities in the South. All of these activities were part of a project initiated by the rector of the university in collaboration with the state, to expand the network of university branches. Many students from the two universities in Valdivia, the Universidad Austral and UTE, joined in the *peña*'s work, as did high school students; Mapuche artists, such as Los Hermanos Nahuelpan; and families of artists in the port city of Corral, such as Los Hermanos Serón. Similarly, the *peña* relied on involvement by musical groups and dance companies, soloists, comics, and theater groups from the universities, who presented collective poetic works that dramatized Latin American poetry. The institution also produced spectacular events that featured Patricio Manns, Inti-Illimani, Argentina's Jorge Cafrune, Payo Grondona, Grupo Tiempo Nuevo, Margot Loyola, Piojo Salinas, Víctor Jara, and more.

These music centers proliferated so quickly in Chile that it was difficult to count them. The musicians' and dancers' participation was spontaneous, voluntary, and free, and an attitude of solidarity and trust dominated. For example, the money earned from admission fees helped to buy guitar strings, costumes, and other items essential to the *peñas*' functioning.

Interest in organizing dance groups and *peñas* spread to labor unions, as well as to student federations, which incorporated artistic endeavors into their weekend events, voluntary work activities, and community extension courses.

Only after this massive phenomenon of new popular culture began did some radio channels give more recognition to Chilean music.

The Contribution of the Academic Musical World

It seems commonplace today to say that Chile has had a different history: a new sound that was also old; a rhythmic sensation that was different from the parameters already known—and, especially that our music was a treasure from which it was possible to evolve, from which an authentic expression could be born that would carry our music into new creations at higher levels of elaboration, emulating the evolution in Europe from popular to classical music. It was equally clear that the conservatories of music had to change and leave behind their focus on forming only European-style musicians. The academy had to look within itself, to where our essence was, and search within the old language for the elements of our identity.

Based on these realizations, the emerging music received extraordinary support from the world of academic music as classical composers who watched with interest what was happening within the popular movement began working with the folk-based groups. Especially noteworthy were the musicians Luis Advis, Sergio Ortega, Celso Garrido, and Gustavo Becerra, among others. Through these initiatives, the Conservatorio Vespertino de Música was formed and became a bridge between the two musical worlds.

This conjuncture gave birth to the works known as *cantatas* and to many beautiful songs. Advis's *Cantata Santa María de Iquique* also staked a historical claim by making public knowledge the repression suffered by Chilean nitrate miners in 1907, an episode that was not included in official histories. After the creation of this *cantata*, a series of collaborations took place that strengthened the bridge between musicians who were normally opposed to one another or who had had no direct connection in the past. This, in turn, produced an unprecedented leap in the quality of musical creation, execution, and interpretation. There was a shift, a revolution characterized by the most remarkable change in Chilean music's history: *la Nueva Canción chilena.*

The cultural ferment in those years was expressed in all of the arts—in graphic design, mural painting, ballet, film, theater, literature—and it all preceded and accompanied the candidacy of Dr. Salvador Allende until his election as president in 1970. It continued as a musical and visual column for the brief three years before the Unidad Popular government was overthrown in the fascist military coup of 1973.

The sum of all of these elements that emerged during the 1950s, 1960s, and early 1970s in Chile constituted the energy that stimulated an extraordinary wave of democratic participation in all of the arts, producing enormous growth and a leap in the quality and diversity of artistic creativity in all fields. The actors in this artistic movement were a conjuncture of generations that came together in a current of continuity with deep Chilean culture and a strong complement of Latin American culture. The decision to choose art with identity crossed the continent and was implemented in each place like a necessity of connection with the earth, of continuity with the past, of recognizing oneself in the blood that unites all of us who come from diverse ethnic tributaries but share the same history.

The terms "protest song" and "revolutionary song" were used to disparage the movement; to reduce its complexity, lessen its importance, and even demonize it. It is certainly true that the movement worked in a committed way for, and enthusiastically received, Allende's victory in 1970 and that many artists belonged to or sympathized with the popular parties. But one can also say that the movement did not depend on political parties, especially when it came to art. Indeed, I can categorically assert that all matters of artistic creativity were decided freely and autonomously by individual artists. If one takes a panoramic look at the songs from this period, one can see that few were written to serve as political propaganda or to take a directly political stance, although such songs, in the moment, probably received more play than others.

Finally, and in conclusion, it is important to note that the most transcendental issue to consider is that the three aspects of national interest—the political, the social, and the cultural—coincided in the objective and expectation of locating what belonged to the people in its proper place, recognizing their culture, giving them justice and liberty within a more equal society, and guaranteeing a nation with full self-determination and autonomy to pursue its own destiny.

The military coup led by Augusto Pinochet on September 11, 1973, extinguished Chile's democracy and initiated a national tragedy that lasted seventeen years. Acts of sabotage and boycott by conservative forces in Chile, supported by U.S. military intelligence and U.S. enterprises that had been nationalized under Allende, "broke the economy," as U.S. President Richard M. Nixon had demanded, and made the country all but ungovernable.

The consequences were immeasurable: crime, repression, Nazi-like concentration camps, the elimination of all civil rights, limits to freedom, and the prohibition of all democratic activity. Signaled by book burning; the prohibition of Andean instruments; the assassination of Víctor Jara; the assassination of the orchestra director Jorge Peña Hen, who in 1964 had created the first Children's Symphonic Orchestra in Chile; and the imprisonment of the singer-songwriter Ángel Parra, the dramatist Oscar Castro, and so many other artists and democrats, a darkness fell in the cultural world.

José Seves S.

Composer, author, instrumentalist, and singer; member of Inti-Illimani since 1971 and of Inti-Illimani Histórico since 2004

January 2014

Preface and Acknowledgments

oetic, combative, lyrical, militant, romantic, committed, idealistic, inspirational, and hauntingly beautiful—*la Nueva Canción chilena*, or Chilean New Song, is all of these. This book is about how the power of music interconnects with politics. Political science as a discipline has not paid much attention to the political power of music, but the incredible communicative capacity of music and its mysterious ability to forge a sense of human interconnection, social bonding, and common cause have clear political implications. Music is nonverbal, primordial, essential. In this book I analyze the democratizing power of music and the social roles of politically committed artists as part of a movement for social and political change in Chile during the turbulent 1960s and 1970s.

In my research I explored the parallel universe of musicology, a field that has a distinct approach and a distinct theoretical literature. As a political scientist, however, I focus mainly on the questions of why *la Nueva Canción chilena* arose when it did and what political impact it had. What was the complex interaction between changes in society and the explosion of creativity during the 1950s and 1960s? What were the social and political settings that gave rise to new popular movements, including the wave of New Song? I contend that the music was born of, and expressed, the aspirations of rising popular classes and a counterhegemonic set of principles and values as Chilean society burst through the confines of antiquated structures and institutions. The era was a revolutionary time of burgeoning aspirations for many peoples of the world, of popular struggles for self-determination and liberation, and also a time of rich artistic creativity. One question that drove this research was how these empirical phenomena were related, as I perceived that they were.

The 1960s were marked by the Cold War, by revolutions in Cuba and elsewhere in the developing world, by the Bay of Pigs and the Cuban Missile Crisis, and by the Vietnam War. On U.S. soil there was turmoil, too: the powerful Civil Rights Movement; the assassinations of John F. Kennedy, Malcolm X, Martin Luther King Jr., and Robert Kennedy; the riots in major U.S. cities; the rise in massive demonstrations against the war, first led by students; and the emergence of new ideas of freedom and equality for women, people of color, and gay people. All of these dramatic events shaped the 1960s generation, as did the music of the era, which was revolutionary in its own ways. Music accompanied the deepening politicization of young people globally, as many began to develop both a deeper critique of imperialism and support for liberation struggles in the developing world.

In the early 1970s, one such struggle was taking place in Chile. Salvador Allende and his program for peaceful, constitutional socialist change—a combination that seemed improbable, even impossible, to some—captured the interest and passionate support of people worldwide. The music associated with that struggle, Chilean New Song, gradually began to filter north. The music entranced and uplifted; it was sublime and mysterious, and evoked the deepest passions and the highest ideals of humanity, even the songs without words. After the coup of 1973 in Chile, which violently overthrew Allende's government, the songs of *la Nueva Canción* evoked lost dreams and the extinguishing of many lives. But the music and the spirit of Chilean New Song, and the artists themselves, also became symbols of resistance. The exiled musicians played in enormous concerts that attracted hundreds of thousands of people worldwide, who protested the coup and the dictatorship, bought the records, and joined solidarity movements for Chile that pressured their governments to denounce the repressive Pinochet regime and call for the restoration of democracy. Today the music has become part of Chile's cultural patrimony and historical memory. The legendary artists still perform for large audiences, and concert-goers still rise to their feet when they hear "El Pueblo Unido Jamás Será Vencido" (The People United Will Never Be Defeated).

Writing this book was a challenge. First, although it is essentially a work of social science, it crosses various disciplinary boundaries. Set within a Gramscian framework, the book analyzes the New Song movement as a component of a strong counterhegemony in Chile—a challenge and an alternative to the dominant political-economic system and ideology—in which the musicians acted as organic intellectuals in Antonio Gramsci's terms. The book combines a study of Chile's political history with a narrative of its cultural development, and brief analysis of some songs (copyright constraints restricted quotations from lyrics). The book integrates oral histories by the protagonists with historical and scholarly sources, seeking not only to communicate how key participants lived and experienced the period but also to capture their memories, views, and experiences for new generations. Grounded in my Gramscian analytical framework, their testimony, which allows the reader to hear their voices directly, constitutes an important historical record in itself. This book aims to present a history of Chile that reflects all of its passion, hope, and pain. At the same time, I wanted to avoid romanticizing the era. Therefore, the book examines some of the inevitable political and musical debates and disagreements that existed in the New Song movement.

In writing this sort of broad history within a limited space, one must always make decisions about what—and what not—to include. That means that ultimately the book is somewhat selective and certainly incomplete. It would be impossible to encompass all the political, social, and cultural elements that gave rise to *la Nueva Canción chilena*, impossible to do justice to all the artists who were important. I hope the book succeeds in providing a panoramic view of the New Song movement, its roots and its political context.

Juan Pablo González, a musicologist and a friend, once said that *la Nueva Canción* is in the DNA of Chileans. For a non-Chilean, this is a somewhat daunting idea. But it is also true that the story of Chile, its history and its music, marked the lives of millions of people across the globe in the 1970s and beyond. The promise of Allende, the ideals of the time, and the terrible coup of 1973, as well as the glorious music of *la Nueva Canción* were, and are, universal, spanning frontiers and boundaries. The music emerged from a specific historical moment in a specific region of the world, but it called forth deep emotions and political interconnections among people around the globe. This book aims to make a fresh contribution to our understanding of this important cultural movement in its political and historical context.

Structure of the Book

Chapter 1 provides the conceptual framework, drawing on Gramsci and his theory of counterhegemonic movements, and presents an overview and key features of *la Nueva Canción chilena*. The chapter concludes with a brief review of the international setting. Chapter 2 schematically treats Chile's political history from independence to the late 1960s, providing some references to key cultural developments. Chapter 3 presents Chile's musical history, especially New Song's antecedents and key figures, in more depth. Although there is some chronological overlap between Chapters 2 and 3, the structure allows Chapter 3 to focus on the emergence of *la Nueva Canción* in its cultural context. Chapter 4 examines the Allende administration between 1970 and 1973, an intense one thousand days both politically and culturally, and the changes and developments in the New Song movement during the new era. Chapter 5 presents the stories of some of the politically committed artists of the time, in which they discuss both their political ideals and the significance of their music. The chapter also analyzes the lyrics of some emblematic songs of the time. Chapter 6 examines innovations of the New Song movement and the importance of collaboration among the artists, and gives an analysis of the most important musical and political contributions of New Song. Chapter 7 offers a brief discussion of the 1973 coup and some of its ramifications for Chilean politics and culture. Chapter 8 concludes the book with reflections on the significance of the period in Gramscian terms and an analysis of the reciprocal role of institutions and human agency in the New Song movement. All translations are mine, with help from Raúl Molina Mejía, a professional translator.

Acknowledgments

After I began research for this book in 2010, I spent five extended periods in Chile between 2011 and 2014 to complete the research and writing. I am grateful to the many generous Chileans who spoke with me for many hours and shared their memories and analyses of the events of the 1960s and 1970s. I met with many of them numerous times over the years, and we engaged in countless conversations, debates, discussions, and intellectual exchanges. Their testimony and the documentary material they provided were crucial for this project, as many of the records of the time were either destroyed by the military after the 1973 coup or lost. I also studied the voluminous literature, in both Spanish and English, on Chilean politics and music. Chile's National Library, the Archivo de Música Popular Chilena at the Catholic University, and the archive of the Víctor Jara Foundation were particularly valuable to my research. In addition, I spent innumerable hours immersed in, and transported by, the music of *la Nueva Canción*, a joy as well as a requirement for this sort of book.

Many of my Chilean contacts became treasured friends and colleagues who not only shared their knowledge but also offered their friendship and affection. I am privileged to know them all. I hope this book is a realistic reflection of the events as they occurred. Although some of my Chilean sources may disagree with some points of my interpretation or analysis, I am indebted to all of them for their collaboration. Any errors of fact or interpretation are, of course, my own.

I extend special acknowledgment to several friends who took an exceptional interest in this project and acted as my guides to Chile's political and cultural history. I thank Miguel Godoy and Ilia Suazo, who welcomed me into their home and introduced me to many new aspects of Chile, both geographical and political. Their affection, solidarity, and knowledge of Chile's political history opened many windows into the Chilean reality. I am grateful to Max Berrú, original member of Inti-Illimani, whose friendship and generosity were extraordinary and who supported this project in so many ways, not only by sharing his memories but also by introducing me to other key people and welcoming me into his closest circles. I thank José Seves of Inti-Illimani Histórico, for his interest in this project, for his friendship, for many hours of engrossing discussions, and for his memories and reflections, which helped re-create the era for me. In 2011, having read his perceptive, poetic essays, I asked him to write the Foreword to this book. I am grateful to Eduardo Carrasco of Quilapayún, for his permanent collaboration on this project, his analysis, and our many hours of conversation and friendly debate. I thank Horacio Durán of Inti-Illimani Histórico, whose memories and critiques enriched this book and whose sense of humor always brightened the day. I am also grateful to two outstanding musicologists and friends: Juan Pablo González, prolific chronicler of Chilean music, who invited me to present my research to colleagues at Universidad Alberto Hurtado in 2011 and 2012, and Rodrigo Torres, whose musical and political insights always helped to put things in perspective.

Because so many people provided generous support for my work, I list them below in alphabetical order. I thank the following Chilean friends and colleagues, who shared their testimony and perspectives with me and who made this book possible: the musicians Julio Alegría, Raúl Céspedes, Carlos Contreras, Jorge Coulon, Patricia Díaz, Tito Escárate, Mariela Ferreira, Fernando García, Patricio Manns and Alejandra Lastra, Roberto Márquez, Ángel Parra, Ernesto Parra, Mario Salazar, Héctor Salgado, Horacio Salinas, Silvia Urbina, Juan Valladares, and Ricardo Venegas. In the broader world of music and art, I am grateful to Jorge Calvo, Juan Carvajal, Juan Castro, Cecilia Coll, Miguel Davagnino, Joan Jara, Antonio Larrea, Vicente Larrea, Viviana Larrea, Jorge Montealegre, Marcelo Montealegre, Leo Muñoz, Alfonso Padilla, Fabio Salas, Oscar Salas, Joyce Valdebenito, Ricardo Valenzuela, Osiel Vega, Manuel Vilches, and Ruth Viscovic Corvalán. In the academic and political worlds, I thank Carolina Aguilera, Máximo Aguilera, César Albornoz, Luis Alvarado, Salvador and Marta Barra, Mónica de Berrú, Gonzalo Cáceres, the late Fernando Castillo, Eduardo and Rebeca Contreras, Alejandro del Rio, Mónica Echeverría, Ximena Erazo, Jaime Esponda, Mario Garcés, Roberto Garretón, Tomás and María Cristina Godoy, Cristián Gutiérrez, Silvia Herrera, Jorge Insunza, Miguel Lawner,

Iván Ljubetic, Lelia Pérez Valdés, Luis Eduardo Salazar and Pati Marzá, Rodrigo Sandoval, Paulo Slachevsky, Olga Ulianova, and Carlos Zarricueta.

I am grateful to Raúl Molina Mejía and Rose Muzio for reading and critiquing the book; Brian Loveman and José Seves for their critical comments on draft chapters; Nibaldo Galleguillos, Pablo Policzer, Margaret Power, Nestor Rodríguez, Greg Shank, Erica Verba, and Eric Zolov for their various expressions of support for and assistance with this project; and Vicente Larrea for contributing one of his exemplary illustrations for the cover. I acknowledge Long Island University (LIU) for providing me with Faculty Development Awards and Provost's and Dean's Grants for research trips to Chile (2011, 2012, 2012–2013, and 2013); the Fulbright Foreign Scholarship Program for awarding me a Senior Scholar Grant for research in Chile in 2011; the Institute of Advanced Studies (IDEA) at the University of Santiago for sponsoring my stay in Chile in 2011; and the American Political Science Association for providing a Small Research Grant for fieldwork in Chile in 2012. I thank all of my colleagues in the Political Science Department, especially John Ehrenberg, and in the Latin American and Caribbean Studies Program at LIU. I am grateful to my editor at Temple University Press, Sara Jo Cohen, for her faith in this project, and to the knowledgeable reviewers for the press, whose critiques helped make this a better book.

I dedicate this book to Raúl Molina Mejía, professor, human rights advocate, colleague, and husband, whose insights and critical eye have been invaluable and whose companionship has been fundamental; to the legendary musicians of la Nueva Canción chilena; and to the people of Chile and Latin America, especially the young people, in the hope that the political passion and the music of the 1960s and 1970s will continue to inspire them. I have no doubt that la Nueva Canción will live on, as will the significance of a time of important social advances in Chile.

January 2014

Chilean New Song

1

La Nueva Canción and
Its Significance

uring the 1960s and 1970s, profound political changes were taking place in Chile and in other parts of Latin America. New political and social movements of students, workers, peasants, urban shantytown dwellers, and other groups mobilized to demand rights and political inclusion along with deeper democratization and structural changes in elitist systems. The 1960s were marked by the Cuban Revolution and the war in Vietnam, and many young people in Chile, as in other countries, were strongly anti-imperialist and in favor of progressive social change. These popular movements coalesced to form a powerful force that was instrumental in electing the democratic socialist Salvador Allende president in 1970. Allende's goal was to preside over a peaceful, constitutional path to socialism in Chile. He served for three turbulent years, attempting to implement a program to reduce social inequalities, until he was overthrown in the U.S.-backed military coup of 1973.

Political and Social Context

In Chile in the early 1960s, social divisions were severe. Some 25 percent of the population had access to sewage services, and only 10–11 percent of rural populations had supplied drinking water. In 1960, 16.4 percent of the population was illiterate.[1] Tens of thousands of people had built crude, leaky shacks to live in on the outskirts of Santiago that lacked plumbing, running water, and electricity. Workers had few rights and lived in overcrowded tenements, shantytowns, or single-room company housing; miners lived in company towns near the mines, enduring harsh conditions. In the 1950s and 1960s, workers in the textile mills labored in humid, hot air full of cotton dust, with poor wages, tyrannical managers, no job security, and threats of violence by company thugs. Women were paid 30 percent less than men for the same work, and some found themselves subject to the "affections" of the boss.[2] Workers could be fired arbitrarily and lose their company rooms.

By the 1960s, *las poblaciones*—the shantytowns around Santiago—had swollen in number. Unemployed peasants and workers had flocked to the capital looking for work in several major waves of urbanization, and by the 1950s, they were organizing, demanding basic services and labor rights. Wealthy families that had ruled the provinces for generations owned huge tracts of land. Relations between the large landowners and the peasants in the countryside were semi-feudal, although capitalist mechanization was beginning to penetrate, reducing the labor necessary on the estates. In the mid-1960s, the large estates controlled 80 percent of all agricultural land, even though they made up only 7 percent of farms, while small farmers (37 percent of all farms) occupied only 0.2 percent of available land.[3] The *patrón* of the large estates provided basic housing (usually without electricity or plumbing) and a company store (with inflated prices), and sometimes a chapel, a school, or a clinic, but peasants and rural workers often were paid in scrip rather than cash. They were punished if they tried to obtain goods elsewhere. Moreover, the votes of the peasants belonged to the *patrón*, a mechanism that kept conservative politicians in power for generations.

Students and workers, increasingly militant in the 1960s, called for nationalization of Chile's natural resources. U.S. copper giants controlled the export sector, and Chile was dependent on the foreign exchange earnings provided by copper. U.S. corporations held private investments worth $1.1 billion in Chile in 1970, and the country's steel, copper, electricity, oil, and transport systems relied on replacement parts and machinery from the United States.[4] University students were also engaged in struggles to reform the university and to reorient its mission toward solving national problems, including Chile's underdevelopment and the exclusion of the popular sectors. Idealistic students traveled to remote areas of the country to share their skills in the spirit of social solidarity and political commitment. Women began to demand respect and equality and assume new roles in the political and social movements. Chile was changing, from the major cities to the most remote rural areas.

La Nueva Canción, or New Song, was born in the midst of these major social, political, and economic transformations in Chile and in the world. Young musicians created new forms of politically aware and socially conscious music, rooted in Latin American folk traditions, that spoke to the struggles and aspirations of the time. The lyrics were poetic and stirring; the music, a haunting blend of indigenous wind and stringed instruments—some dating from the ancient Inca empire—and little-known Latin American musical forms. The music was emotional, ethereal, ancient and modern at the same time, combining folk roots with original innovations. *La Nueva Canción* also embodied an alternative worldview: that of a socially just future for millions of Chileans who had long been politically and socially excluded. That is, New Song was part of, and expressed, the social reality of Chile and, more broadly, of Latin America, and the radical-democratic and socialist projects of the era. The new music first found a broad audience among politicized and socially aware students, but it soon spread to other sectors, including unionists, rural workers and campesinos, and shantytown dwellers around Santiago. New Song was enmeshed with the mobilizations and ideals of the time, both reflecting and contributing to the deep political and social change that marked the era.

In this book, I argue that *la Nueva Canción* played a key role in mobilizing and uniting people in a common cause. The music helped to motivate and sustain the political and cultural participation of hundreds of thousands of people and gave voice to the rising social demands in Chile. The art and music of the time captured the ethos of expanding counterhegemonic movements: movements that challenged entrenched power relations in Chile, the dominant, or hegemonic, system of power. This hegemonic system and its challengers are discussed below in the context of the theories of Antonio Gramsci, an Italian Marxist from the early twentieth century who wrote extensively on the importance of cultural power in maintaining exclusionary, elitist capitalist systems.

New Song musicians drew from folk rhythms and instruments of Latin America, transcending borders, to create original songwriting and musical departures: modern, complex arrangements and harmonies (including multiple voices and dissonant notes), instrumental interludes, and poetic lyrics that spoke movingly of the burning social and political issues of the day. As the musicologist Rodrigo Torres described the New Song musicians, "Their art is a dynamic art, evolving permanently; it begins with tradition and transcends it."[5] José Seves, originally of the group Inti-Illimani and then with Inti-Illimani Histórico,[6] explained that New Song was "inspired by older Chilean and Latin American musical and poetic frameworks, giving birth to a new song, more current and modern in its elements but maintaining the original essence." The musicians essentially reinvented and modernized Latin American folk music, creating new musical genres. The lives of Latin America's humble people—*el pueblo*—were highlighted, lives that had been ignored previously. The young musicians combined sounds and instruments from Bolivia, Ecuador, Colombia, Cuba, Peru, Venezuela, and Argentina, as well as Chile,[7] playing the instruments and adapting the music in ways that were, finally, distinctively Chilean. The ancient indigenous instruments from the Andean regions of South America—the bamboo flute called the *quena*; the mystical pan pipes known as *sicus* in the Aymara language (or *zampoña* in Spanish); the *bombo legüero* drum; the lute-like *charango*, made from an armadillo shell—produced one signature sound of *la Nueva Canción*: Andean music. *La Nueva Canción* also incorporated campesino styles and rhythms from Chile's countryside and other traditional music from other Latin American countries.

Most of the young musicians were talented and prolific songwriters; indeed, a central contribution of the New Song movement was the wealth of original music created by the artists, reshaping the musical culture of Chile. "You had to compose songs, write lyrics with political consciousness. This defined *la Nueva Canción*," said the singer-songwriter Ángel Parra, son of the groundbreaking folk singer and composer Violeta Parra, known as the "mother" of *la Nueva Canción,* and a giant of the movement himself.[8] "It was the political situation that stimulated us to write songs, what was happening every day in those years[;] the situation itself nurtured our songs. . . . We were like reporters, some more like 'pamphleteers,' some more poetic, some more idealistic, but we were all reporters of a social reality. . . . We realized the dream of Simón Bolívar with our music: we sang Chilean music with instruments from many Latin American countries." The musicians also wrote songs of love, of tenderness, and of hope, said Ricardo Venegas of the emblematic group Quilapayún.[9] "There were no limits in *la Nueva Canción*," he added. "We were open to various musical styles." Seves stressed that beyond the political songs, there was a "variety of themes aimed at describing more broadly the characteristics of *lo chileno* [the Chilean essence or reality] and, by extension, the Latin American. . . . [The music] constructed a self-image or self-visualization."[10] The songs spoke to people's lives, and New Song incorporated multiple instruments and developed instrumental music, something new in Chilean popular music, Horacio Durán, an original member of Inti-Illimani (now of Inti-Illimani Histórico), pointed out.[11]

The musicians were motivated by their passion for the music and by the spirit of the era; they were independent, socially and politically committed, and militant. Many musicians joined parties of the Left, especially the youth organization of the Partido Comunista Chileno (Communist Party of Chile; PC), known as Juventudes Comunistas (Young Communists) or La Jota. Chile's political system, for various decades of the twentieth century, had been relatively open to parties across the political spectrum, including Marxist parties. The PC—which so alarmed Washington in these Cold War years—had a long history of democratic participation in Chile, interrupted several times when it was proscribed by the government (in such periods, the PC operated under other names). Members of the PC had served in Congress and in government ministries. The PC had deep roots in the unionized working class and in the cultural life of the country. In the 1950s and 1960s the PC was a strong proponent of deepening Chile's democracy by incorporating excluded social sectors (shantytown dwellers, workers, peasants) and promoting a popular, democratic revolution by peaceful means.[12] The party was a strong supporter of Allende's vision of a constitutional and democratic road to socialism. Many beloved poets, intellectuals, and artists were PC members or sympathizers, including the Nobel Prize winner Pablo Neruda; the poet (or, as he preferred, anti-poet) Nicanor Parra; the musician-composers Víctor Jara and Violeta Parra; and many others. While not all of the musicians of *la Nueva Canción* were affiliated with La Jota, virtually all were of the Left. The movement was by no means monolithic, however. Just as the musicians played different styles and genres of music, they also held different political and artistic ideas. This at times led to debates and differences, both artistic and political, within the movement.

Many artists of *la Nueva Canción* criticized the increasing influence of rock-and-roll music from the United States and Europe, seen as a cultural invasion that was extinguishing Chilean traditions, as well as the "typical folk music" of Chile, a form of commercialized folk that portrayed the countryside in an idyllic light. The power of the oligarchy was reflected in this *huaso* music. (The term *huaso* [horseman] symbolized the values of the owners and foremen of Chile's large estates.) Groups such as Los Cuatro Huasos (formed in 1927) and Los Huasos Quincheros (formed in 1937) popularized this form of music. While much of it was pleasant to hear, it painted an idealized portrait of life in the haciendas, without hunger, illiteracy, disease, cruelty, or misery or any mention of the hierarchical, semi-feudal, and authoritarian power relations that existed between owner and peasant. Such "typical" folk exalted the values of the landowning class in conservative ways: male dominance (*machismo*), family, God, and country.[13] This was the Chilean music that dominated the airwaves and Independence Day celebrations in September. Until the 1960s, singers and dancers who performed this music dressed in the costumes of the landowners. The peasants were rarely visible, but when they were, they were portrayed as happy and content with their lot. The upper classes valued this "typical" Chilean folk and the refined music of Europe.[14]

The New Song movement represented a rising challenge to this hegemonic conception of life in Chile. Culture became an arena of political contestation and hegemonic-counterhegemonic struggle—that is, a struggle between the dominant, or hegemonic, political, economic, and cultural system and ascendant popular movements that challenged those relations of power—although the musicians of *la Nueva Canción* were not necessarily conscious of this.[15] In essence, *la Nueva Canción* began to contest, and reconfigure, the elite, exclusionary sense of identity that prevailed in the dominant culture. The music played a crucial role in building a broader, more inclusive vision that valorized Chile's, and Latin America's, working and peasant classes, *el pueblo*.

The Roots of *la Nueva Canción*

The media and the upper classes of Chile generally scorned the authentic music and art of Latin America's rural and working classes and indigenous peoples, deeming them of little value. As Thomas Turino points out, "The greater institutional support for, and value placed on, elite arts as opposed to popular and so-called folk arts [marks] class distinctions."[16] In the 1960s, many young people began to link this cultural domination with oligarchic rule and U.S. imperialism. The young artists also rejected the notion of music as a commodity or a commercial endeavor. Following earlier pioneers of socially conscious folk music, especially the Argentine singer-songwriter Atahualpa Yupanqui and the Chilean Violeta Parra, the New Song musicians sought their own roots among the peoples of Chile and Latin America. Their music was part of a rediscovery of the significance of Latin America and its popular cultures. New Song communicated a new set of values of popular power, solidarity, and social justice in the struggle against underdevelopment and oppression. There was an enormous sense of recognition and validation of the music among Chileans, despite the fact that New Song was largely absent from the mass media. The music and the lyrics captured the sorrows, the suffering, and the hopes that ordinary Chileans were actually living and experiencing. The songs made visible the social injustices in the rural and urban areas, incorporating the large majority of Chileans. New Song represented a novel form of political communication in the country. It reflected the rise of new social sectors and movements and the rapid transformation of Chilean society, a new society being born within the old.

Musicians such as Violeta Parra and her children Ángel and Isabel, along with Víctor Jara, Rolando Alarcón, Patricio Manns, Aparcoa, Lonquimay, Los Curacas, Tiempo Nuevo, Los Amerindios, Inti-Illimani, Quilapayún, Payo Grondona, "Gitano" Rodríguez, Tito Fernández, and Illapu, among many other soloists and groups, made up the New Song movement (although there is some debate about whom to include in *la Nueva Canción*). They were simultaneously social communicators, historians, teachers, organizers, and translators of popular aspirations. They consciously sought to recapture and renovate Chilean and Latin American traditions and music as part of an effort to build a different consciousness and way of life, an effort that grew to reflect enormous hope and energy. The very names of the musical groups, drawing from indigenous languages, and their "look"—for example, the ponchos they wore—validated the invisible history of Latin America. The lyrics of many of the songs spoke of the lives of urban and rural workers and their aspirations for freedom, self-determination, and social justice; of forgotten struggles of workers against powerful landlords or bosses; of the suffering of the marginalized. That is, the music expressed the lived human experience of large sectors of society who lacked a voice or official recognition. As the movement grew, the very act of bringing thousands of people together in stadiums and other popular venues created new forms of communication and assembly, a sense of unity, and new environments of social criticism in Chile.

Apart from the dominant culture reflecting the interests of the powerful, the campesinos, the workers, and indigenous communities had always had their own cultural expressions. Yet much traditional folk music tends to be repetitious, even monotonous; as Turino has shown, folk music was born in participatory and egalitarian cultures. The social function of the music was to encourage participation and a communal ethos.[17] The New Song musicians "urbanized" and made more complex indigenous Andean music as well as other folk forms, such as campesino music from the central and southern regions of Chile. New Song musicians created sophisticated combinations of five or six instruments and added innovative chord structures and progressions; complex forms of harmony; and changes in tempo, rhythm, or key. As Ricardo Venegas of Quilapayún noted, "The folk songs in their purest form are, let's say, musically less interesting. What has to be done is to take some elements, work with them a little, change the rhythm or the melody, add a stanza to make them more interesting. These songs are very simple, even monotonous, because people sang them that way: they were used in ceremonies or wakes, such as the song 'Rin de Angelito.' . . . Musically they were monotonous. You have to elaborate, really re-creating the songs. . . . This is what Violeta [Parra] did."[18] The New Song music communicated a connection with the authentic lifestyles of *los pueblos* of Latin America, and an alternative to the coldness of capitalist market relations.[19] Within the Chilean Left there was also a legacy of radical-popular songs from the Italian resistance and the Spanish Civil War. (Thanks to the efforts of the government of President Aguirre Cerda and the diplomat Pablo Neruda, a number of Spanish Republicans had escaped from the fascist onslaught in Spain and settled in Chile.) New Song musicians recorded some of these songs in the 1960s, along with songs from the Mexican revolution.

The folk music of Chile's countryside changed form as one traveled from the North to the South, with different variations of *la cueca*, the traditional music and dance of Chile, for example. But the unstylized music of the rural and urban working classes was not considered art until it was "discovered" in the 1940s and 1950s by forerunners of the New Song movement—especially Margot Loyola, Violeta Parra, Gabriela Pizarro, and Héctor Pavez—who collected Chilean folk songs and brought them to urban audiences. Moreover, in the 1950s and 1960s Chile's changing society provided a transformed political, social, and cultural context within which folk music and art were newly valued. Chilean folk music and dance began to be sung, performed, and recorded by individuals and groups such as Cuncumén, a music and dance troupe directed by Loyola whose name in the Mapuche language means murmuring water,[20] and Millaray, a group led by Pizarro that performed music from the island of Chiloé. In the 1950s and 1960s, emerging popular movements were hungry for authentically Latin American music and dance that spoke to their experience and evoked their roots. Keith Sawyer points out that forms that once were not considered art (e.g., folk music) can become appreciated as art when the sociocultural system changes.[21] The rise of the New Song movement and other, similar movements around the world was linked to the political spirit of the 1960s. Global transformations and new political winds were accompanied by reawakened interest in folk music and art; politically conscious movements embraced them as a means of asserting Latin American identity and resisting the barrage of U.S. cultural exports.

Interest in popular music (music of the people) and similar folk revivals were appearing throughout the Americas in this period. Atahualpa Yupanqui was an early forerunner and a giant in Argentina, despite being persecuted by the Peronist government for his communist politics. Mercedes Sosa and Armando Tejada Gómez, among others, were folk singers who founded el Nuevo Cancionero in Argentina in 1963. In Cuba, Carlos Puebla, Pablo Milanés, and Silvio Rodríguez were central figures in la Nueva Trova; in Uruguay, Daniel Viglietti and Alfredo Zitarrosa popularized Uruguayan folk music; in Brazil, Chico Buarque created a wealth of socially conscious songs. "La Nueva Canción was really a continental phenomenon," said Eduardo Carrasco, musician and director of Quilapayún.[22] "In Brazil, in Argentina, Ecuador, Cuba, [and] later in Nicaragua, there were similar movements everywhere, a new culture of protest music, political music. It was part of a larger cultural movement that included the 'Latin American boom' in literature—Julio Cortázar, Mario Vargas Llosa, Gabriel García Márquez, magical realism, Casa de las Américas. The movement became global; in fact, we had contacts with musicians in Europe, in the United States, such as Pete Seeger and many others. . . . Our roots were in Latin America as a whole." In the 1950s and 1960s in the United States, too, there was a revival of folk music that drew from the class-conscious songs of Woody Guthrie and included Pete Seeger, Joan Baez, and the early Bob Dylan.

In Chile, the New Song movement became particularly important because it was deeply fused with powerful, organized political and social movements in the struggle for structural change. The music expressed political critiques and alternative visions of the future in a popular form, critiques and visions silenced by the mass media and conservative governments. New Song helped to create, unite, and sustain political and social communities that were politically active and significant. Gradually, as the music filtered north, it entranced and inspired people in Europe and the United States, as political polarization in the Cold War, big power interventions, and spreading capitalist penetration provoked popular and leftist reactions worldwide.

The Culture of Participation

By the late 1960s, an unprecedented sense of involvement and participation was growing in Chile, in a nascent "people's culture" that was accessible to everyone, even the tens of thousands who could not read or write. Many young people were interested in folk or rock guitar, influenced by the Beatles and by Chilean rock-and-roll and popular song known as the *Nueva Ola* (New Wave).[23] The New Song musicians also helped to bring folk music and guitar playing to masses of people in Chile. Suddenly everyone was involved—or wanted to be involved—in artistic expression, creativity, singing, and collective music making, and everyone played guitar or wanted to learn. Joan Jara, a dancer who participated in the movement (and the wife of the celebrated *Nueva Canción* singer Víctor Jara) wrote: "It was an incredible upsurge of creative activity in people who had never before been encouraged to express themselves and in an age where radio and television tended to turn people into passive listeners. The song movement was now much more than a group of well-known artists. It seemed a whole people had learned to sing."[24]

José Seves described his trip to the South of Chile as a student, organized by the State Technical University (Universidad Técnica del Estado; UTE), to teach guitar to scores of students in the spirit of popular education of the time:

> It was part of the autonomy of the university to promote this sort of initiative. . . . The Technical University was a state university, with many branches throughout the country. We in Valdivia were the last center, but there was a lot of territory to the South. One of the things we did, before and during the government of the Unidad Popular [Popular Unity; UP], was to go to an *escuela de temporada* [seasonal school], as it was called, in the summer. Professors went from each of the engineering specializations, and a school was set up for a month or two. I went or someone from the *peña* in Valdivia went [*peñas*

were intimate cultural centers where folk music was played] to create a dance group or teach guitar. We taught guitar while others taught electrical repairs in the house, basic but important. The final product was the creation of a site with university programs. . . . Once we went to an *escuela de temporada* that was very isolated, near Puerto Aysén. . . . The time that we went from UTE, Valdivia, the courses were full. I remember having a class of one hundred guitar students. I spent the whole day with my hands on the guitar, teaching groups of twenty at a time. The guitars in the local music stores were completely sold out.[25]

Culture was increasingly democratized during the 1960s and under the UP government (1970–1973) as it became an arena in which masses of people could, and did, participate.

Violeta Parra, a woman of humble origins in the countryside who knew the struggles and afflictions of Chile's poor, played a crucial role in the emergence of *la Nueva Canción*.[26] She began to sing about the lives of ordinary Chileans, including the indigenous Mapuche of the South, in a way that was unusual and riveting in the 1950s. As explained by Max Berrú, an Ecuadoran by birth who moved to Chile as a student and became an original member of Inti-Illimani:

In *la Nueva Canción*, one must recognize a fundamental figure, Violeta Parra, because Violeta, after doing a long investigation of the music of the campesinos, began to compose songs of the countryside, where she speaks of the life of the rural people: their frustrations, their disappointments, their struggles. . . . She was a woman who was an incredible artist, who wrote in a way that was simple but very profound. Moreover, she taught us the rhythms of other countries. She taught us instruments of other countries. She opened up a musical world to those of us who formed part of this movement.[27]

Similarly, Horacio Salinas of Inti-Illimani (and later of Inti-Illimani Histórico) said:

La Nueva Canción has a soul, which is essential, without which one cannot imagine this movement, and that soul is Violeta Parra. . . . [W]hat she did in the 1950s and 1960s in Chile was simply to transform all song. . . . It's the testimony of an incredible artist who knows the reality of Chilean music and, through her compositions, transformed completely the idea we had of what folkloric song, the patrimonial song of Chile, is. After Violeta, a completely new page was written in the history of the music of Chile. *La Nueva Canción* cannot be imagined without this personality, without Violeta [Parra], because what she did was open the profound, huge window toward creation, departing from the music called "folklore" and introducing the life of the people, the history of the people, through the themes of her song. Until then, the music called folklore—Chilean music, in quotation marks—was *una música paisajista* [a scenic view of the countryside], bucolic music, with some songs that were very pretty, but that gave no space to the people, the history of Chile.[28]

The New Song movement continued this focus on the lives of peasants and workers and the injustices committed against them by landowners and bosses.

The emerging social-political progressive movement in the 1960s, of which New Song was a key part, had a deeply democratic view: that all people were creative; that all should have the freedom and opportunity to learn and practice music and the arts as means of self-expression and collective creativity. The music was embedded in new, egalitarian social relationships: all people were recognized as equal and valuable in an altered environment of respect and social equity, a life-changing event for peasants and workers who previously had been invisible, marginalized, and excluded. Suddenly, control of the culture and its power to reach masses of people was escaping the hands of the elite. People involved in the struggle for social change had found a means to harness the profound powers of mass communication inherent in song, as part of a counterhegemonic movement that defied the existing structures of power. The music not only empowered people who were learning to play. It also stirred the fires of resistance. It spoke of the indomitability of the human spirit and the historical ability of masses of people to create social change. The music offered a critique of the inequalities of capitalist society and the distortions of dependency and imperialism and expressed the yearning for a new socially oriented society.

The Music of Commitment

The New Song movement came "from below," arising naturally and spontaneously from multiple cultural and artistic influences and popular roots. It was not organized in any top-down way; nor was it led or directed by any entity or political party, although the PC and La Jota provided important opportunities and support for the movement. Many of the young musicians were informally trained or self-trained, although a few studied at the University of Chile's Conservatory of Music. I use the term "movement" in this book to capture the sense of a decentralized mobilization of artists, without formal leadership or headquarters, but loosely united in a recognizable and common cultural effort and political cause.

The origins of the New Song movement lay in the passion for the music among the youth of the 1960s generation, their social consciousness and political commitment, and their fascination with discovering the rich heritage of Latin American music. "There was a very deep cultural change," said Horacio Durán, "and it never was an organized movement, not at all: it was an artistic movement, undefined politically, without an organization. New Song was a very spontaneous movement. It developed like those great rivers that begin with small streams and tributaries and become a powerful flow."[29] Similarly, Jorge Coulon, another founding member of Inti-Illimani, wrote that *la Nueva Canción* had no "headquarters, departments or infrastructure, there was never a meeting or an attempt to form an organization.... Neither was the music a homogenous expression of genre or style."[30] As John Street points out, however, institutions and networks "are key to creating what can often seem to be 'spontaneous.'"[31] During the course of my research, a central area of inquiry was the relationship of the music and the New Song movement to political institutions.

Another transformative development in the 1960s was the changing social role and self-perception of that role by artists, musicians, and poets in movements for social change. Popular musicians, artists, dancers, and theater groups began to rethink their place in society and the purpose of their art. Many decided to dedicate their art to advancing the interests of *el pueblo* and representing their voices—to take their art beyond the individual and into the social domain. Most important, they decided to engage and motivate people to participate in culture themselves by learning to play an instrument, sing, paint, or act in theater troupes. Seeing themselves as intellectuals and activists as well as artists, they infused their art with social content and revolutionary commitment.[32] In the spirit of collective effort, and reflecting the socialist and radical-democratic values of anti-individualism and anti-consumerism, "people's artists" came together to bring their art to the people and create a popular culture that reshaped the identity of the nation. Víctor Jara gave up a successful career as a theater director because he realized that his songs and his guitar reached masses of people in ways the more exclusive theater did not.[33] In groups such as Quilapayún and Inti-Illimani, the presentation of the music itself reflected solidarity and a collective ethos: no one was a "star," and all sang, often in call-and-response forms, in unison, or in harmonies that included all the voices. The black ponchos of Quilapayún and the red ones of Inti-Illimani presented a dramatic, unified appearance and an egalitarian spirit. The poncho expressed Latin American identity; it was traditionally worn by the campesino, not the landowner, thus connoting unity with the campesinos and working classes.[34] The indigenous names of many of the groups were a stark contrast to the English-language names of many Chilean rock soloists and groups such as Peter Rock and Los Blue

Splendor, who often also sang in English, and of the "typical" folk groups, which often used the term "Huasos" in their names. The New Song musicians and artists participated in political activities alongside their art in ways that were massive and new in the country.

In addition, the cultural explosion of *la Nueva Canción* interested conservatory-trained classical musicians and composers such as Luis Advis, Sergio Ortega, Gustavo Becerra, Fernando García, and Celso Garrido, among others. They began working with the young people creating New Song, blending the classical and the popular for the first time, fusing elements of each together to produce an original, more complex, stirringly beautiful form of popular music in Chile. For example, Luis Advis, a composer who was not a political activist, worked closely with New Song musicians to create intricate and emblematic works such as *Cantata Santa María de Iquique* (released by Quilapayún in 1970), a set of songs, with a spoken narrative, that told the story of a massacre of miners and their families by security forces in 1907, and *Canto para una Semilla* (Song for a Seed; recorded by Inti-Illimani and Isabel Parra in 1972), a unified work that put to music Violeta Parra's autobiographical *décimas* (poetry derived from Spanish tradition, with stanzas of ten lines and specific rhyming patterns). These works incorporated symphonic, folk, and indigenous elements, producing a unique and exquisite hybrid of musical styles. This sort of collaboration was another key part of the explanation for the burst of creativity that characterized the era.[35] Overall, it was a time of optimism, joy, creativity, discovery, and experimentation; of social mobilization and public involvement; and of significant democratic advances in Chile. It seemed that the barriers to the full expression of humanity were being overcome.

The New Song movement became closely linked to socialist Salvador Allende's presidential campaign in 1969–1970 and the impressively broad UP coalition, which united a number of leftist and center-leftist parties. "Culture Won't Be for a Few—It Will Be for All" was a slogan of the Allende campaign. Allende's "Forty Measures"—the first points of his political program—contained a clause (number 40) on the new concept of culture for the masses of people. The New Song movement played an important role in popularizing Allende's program and his candidacy.

Analyzing the New Song Movement

What was the relationship between global and state-level structures that were in a state of flux and the explosion of creativity that took place, particularly in Chile but also around the world in the fields of art and music? This book explores the relationship between the political transformations of the 1950s and 1960s and the appearance of new cultural forms—not only *la Nueva*

Canción but also experimental projects in theater, dance, poetry, literature, painting, and playwriting that reached large numbers of people. There was a veritable explosion of creativity in the 1960s and early 1970s in Chile, and I argue that the splintering of old social hierarchies and the rise of political actors "from below" was linked to the emergence of new forms of creativity and of popular culture. These interrelated phenomena were the result of rapidly changing global and national political-economic structures and new democratic openings pushed "from below" by people in many walks of life.

The world was changing rapidly in the 1950s and 1960s. The Cold War reflected deep ideological and political divisions and produced many "proxy wars" in the developing world. The Cuban Revolution of 1959 awakened a passion for radical social change, especially among young Latin Americans. Rapid technological change was transforming societies, as well. Television provided national and global visual links for the first time, connecting the world's nations ever closer and increasing awareness of events in other countries. (Television came to Chile in 1962.) Faster means of communication and transportation became available worldwide, producing new globalized trading and investment patterns and facilitating travel for individuals. Multinational corporations seeking natural resources and new markets spread worldwide. A number were engaged in rebuilding Europe after a large influx of public money via the Marshall Plan; many were already strategically placed in the developing world. In Chile, as elsewhere, shifting power structures opened opportunities for actors "from below" to express themselves and transform their societies.

Cultural expression is closely bound to democracy and liberty, and in the 1960s fresh winds of freedom were blowing. In Chile, the reformist government of Eduardo Frei Montalva was in power—unlike in nearby countries such as Argentina, Brazil, and Bolivia, where military coups and regimes marked the 1960s—resulting in more openings for political participation and protest. In addition, the spirit of collaboration and collective effort and rejection of individualism, identified with capitalist competition, of the 1960s stimulated the creative surge of the time. Political parties in Chile—especially the centrist Christian Democrats and the leftist Communist Party and Socialist Party—influenced and provided infrastructure and organizational resources to emerging social and political movements. As formerly excluded social sectors were freer to participate, speak, read, communicate, protest, and organize, the creativity of ordinary people was unleashed. Workers, shantytown dwellers, peasants, and students demanded entry into the elitist political system and gradually gained a larger political voice. At the same time, there was a burst of cultural and artistic innovation.

Antonio Gramsci, the Italian Marxist cultural analyst, noted that passions are stirred in an era of social mobilization—and passions are a crucial source of creativity. Gramsci's writings and insights provide a useful framework for understanding the New Song movement. I draw on his ideas in this book as a means of understanding the political power of culture and how cultures can be transformed. How is cultural change related to economic and political change?[36] Gramsci was interested in the questions of how knowledge is produced and how certain ideas become "normal" or "common sense" in society. He saw that new artists appeared through the stirring up of "passions and human warmth" and that they would "be born from the movement."[37] Gramsci linked, for example, the rise of the opera and the novel "with the appearance and expansion of national-popular democratic forces" in Europe in the eighteenth century.[38] Similarly, I argue that the rise of New Song was linked to the surge of popular power and participation in the 1960s.

In my interviews, a number of New Song artists and musicians said that they had only reflected the dramatic conditions they were experiencing, that they themselves were not catalysts for change.[39] I find this assertion to be overly modest, however. Indeed, I see the musicians as crucial agents of cultural change. The New Song movement was a significant democratizing force, a key component of the larger organized popular movements for social and political transformation in Chile. The movement opened new channels for political participation and expression of demands "from below." The power of the musicians to attract masses of people, reach across class lines, tap human emotions and reach rational minds, and create a sense of unity and social bonding, combined with their representation of an egalitarian ideal and an alternative future, changed people's hearts and minds and helped to build a powerful movement. Their "music of commitment" made a socially just society seem attainable and possible. All of these elements demonstrated the innate political power of music. Gramsci's theories, presented in the next section, shed more light on the significance of that power.

The musical presentations and concerts of *la Nueva Canción*, large and small, were a unique part of the political history of the era. They did not simply reflect or articulate the politics of the time; they helped to *create* the politics of the time, and embody it. As John Street notes, the Woodstock music festival not only reflected the times in the United States; it created history—it was a seminal political event in itself.[40] He also argues that politics and music are inextricably linked: music "forms and shapes the feelings and passions which animate political action."[41] That is, the New Song musicians were political as well as cultural actors, creating collective experiences and political unity through their music. The music was a catalyst for social change and political action; it expressed new, counterhegemonic norms and values.

Under Allende, some of the emblematic soloists and groups, such as Víctor Jara, Inti-Illimani, Quilapayún, and Isabel Parra, became semiofficial cultural ambassadors, performing throughout the world to communicate through their music Chile's bold social experiment. The musicians were an organic part of the broader progressive movements of the era that succeeded in changing—if only partially and temporarily—the system of domination in Chile. After the 1973 military coup, the musicians in exile, who were prohibited from returning, became actively engaged in opposition to the Pinochet regime. They traveled worldwide, performing in massive concerts, keeping alive the memory and promise of the UP, and communicating the horrors of the dictatorship, thus helping to inspire an important international solidarity movement.

In discussions of the roots of the cultural innovation of this epoch, Chilean artists and musicians pointed to a number of important causes. The photographer Antonio Larrea noted the environment of freedom and experimentation that existed as old and ossified barriers broke down.[42] The New Song musicians Ernesto Parra, formerly of Los Curacas, and Mario Salazar, formerly of Los Amerindios, separately highlighted the sense of new political possibilities in the 1960s that allowed people to hope and to dream—human emotions crucial for the creation of art.[43] Horacio Salinas spoke of the realization that "people power" might succeed in electing Salvador Allende and a government of popular unity that would transform the country.[44] José Seves described the sense of wonder and pride as the artists discovered the rich musical traditions of Latin America, its instruments and rhythms, providing people with a sense of motivation, awakening, and identity with Latin America's cultural heritage.[45] Another important source of the burst of creativity was the proximity of many artists in Santiago, allowing close working relations and collaboration. The artists collaborated freely and selflessly, without competition, composing songs together, playing, experimenting, and improvising together, searching for new talent to promote, and teaching and learning musically from one another. All of these factors are crucial and demonstrate the intertwining of structural and individual transformation, the complex interrelationships between global and national shifts and social and personal change.

I do not suggest that the *Nueva Canción* movement was the only democratizing actor during this period in Chile. There were many, as the society underwent rapid political transformation. The central question, in my view, is not which actor was most important in the broad democratization movement in Chile, but how various institutions and actors interacted, interfaced, and cooperated, producing dramatic political change. What was the relationship between the emergence of the musical movement in the mid-1960s and key institutions? This book examines the role of the *peñas*, universities, political parties, the Catholic Church, and government administrations in the sweeping sociopolitical changes of the era and, specifically, how they interacted with the New Song movement. While the musicians created the music, they were involved with and influenced by institutions, as well as by the larger environment, the ethos of the 1960s. Key institutions provided a range of opportunities and sustenance to the musicians, helping to bring them to new audiences and to diffuse the music. As suggested, one important institution was the Juventudes Comunistas, or La Jota. La Jota created a new record label to record and distribute New Song, first called JotaJota, and later Discoteca del Cantar Popular (Discothèque of Popular Song; DICAP). The label began producing records that commercial labels found too political. In a short time, DICAP became a hugely successful venture,[46] playing a decisive role in disseminating *la Nueva Canción* by building a parallel structure to bypass commercial record labels.

Ricardo Venegas of Quilapayún spoke about the reciprocal and collaborative interrelations between the revolutionary youth of La Jota and the musicians:[47]

> There were links [between *la Nueva Canción* and La Jota]. There was an intellectual approach that informed us. We were serious in our study and analysis; it wasn't unserious or "light' what we were doing. To be part of La Jota meant that one was obligated to study. . . . That militancy was important for *la Nueva Canción*, but the music was never seen as an instrument of the party. Never, no. There was a strong identification, but the musical movement was independent. Not all the musicians of *la Nueva Canción* were members of La Jota. . . . La Jota was very open. . . . The relation between La Jota and the musicians was good. It had to do with the utopia we young people dreamed of then: to change the society, to make a better world.

Gramsci: Power, Class, and Culture

While a large body of literature on music and society exists in such disciplines as musicology, cultural studies, and sociology, there is relatively little analysis of music and politics in political science.[48] Yet control of, and influence over, culture is a question of power, and culture is an arena of political contestation and hegemonic-counterhegemonic struggle, as theorists such as Antonio Gramsci and Theodor Adorno have posited.[49] Both analyzed how culture can serve as a means of social control and the manufacture of conformity and consent to elite rule. Moreover, I am interested in the counterhegemonic possibilities of music: its democratizing power and the ways in which it can create a potent sense of social unity, empathy, common cause, and political motivation among people.

There has been a resurgence of interest in Gramsci in recent years in social science.[50] While he may seem somewhat remote to readers today, Gramsci's ideas are relevant and useful in analyzing the case of Chile. Gramsci emphasized the importance of political, ideological, and cultural domination—which results in concrete, physical effects, as Kate Crehan points out—as a central method of political control by powerful elites. As a Marxist, Gramsci saw power conflicts in terms of social class. He argued that the power of states and of dominant elites resided not only in their coercive power, via military and security forces, but also through the control exercised through less visible cultural and intellectual mechanisms. That is, Gramsci saw culture as reflective of class domination. He differentiated between coercion and hegemony, the former signifying repression and violence and the latter signifying a model of cultural domination that induced the consent of the people for the existing system of power. Gramsci distinguished between

> the function of "hegemony" which the dominant group exercises throughout society and on the other hand . . . that of "direct domination" or command exercised through the State and "juridical" government. . . . The intellectuals are the dominant group's "deputies" exercising the subaltern functions of social hegemony and political government. These comprise: 1. The "spontaneous" consent given by the great masses of the population to the general direction imposed on social life by the dominant fundamental group; this consent is "historically" caused by the prestige (and consequent confidence) which the dominant group enjoys because of its position and function in the world of production. 2. The apparatus of state coercive power which "legally" enforces discipline on those groups who do not "consent" either actively or passively. This apparatus is, however, constituted for the whole of society in anticipation of moments of crisis of command and direction when spontaneous consent has failed.[51]

Dominant elites used both hegemony and coercion to maintain their control; as Gramsci put it, "Hegemony [was] protected by the armour of coercion."[52] Crehan argues convincingly that many readers misinterpret Gramsci, reducing his analysis to a sole focus on culture and ideology. In fact, Gramsci's concept of hegemony deals not simply with the realm of beliefs and ideas, or the "superstructure," she argues, but with a whole field of power that includes social class.[53] Language, books, and culture in general are mechanisms of class power, Gramsci believed.[54] Adam David Morton also delves deeply into Gramsci's writings to explain that "hegemony filters through structures of society, economy, culture, gender, ethnicity, class, and ideology." Hegemony is a form, or a component, of class rule.[55]

Gramsci argued that to produce radical structural changes in political-economic systems it was not enough to organize workers in the factories or plan to seize the state, as traditional Marxists claimed. Rather, one must contend with this ideological and political domination, present in everyday life and transmitted through schools, mass media, churches, family, and other means. This culture of domination becomes "common sense"—or, in Gramsci's terms, hegemonic, a crucial part of the system of power. "What is practice for the fundamental class becomes 'rationality,'" he argued.[56] Through this system, the powerful present their interests as universal and global, as interests that benefit everyone, to obtain the voluntary consent of the ruled for a system of power that actually excludes and oppresses them. The subordinate classes are socialized not to question their marginality or the maldistribution of wealth and resources. The system seems to represent the natural order of things. Or the excluded sectors may see the injustice of the system but believe it is impossible to change. The hegemonic culture presents the population with the message that there is no alternative; that their position in society is normal, inevitable, permanent, unchangeable. Indeed, marginalized people—especially in very individualist societies—may blame themselves for their inferior position rather than recognize that their problems are systemic and shared by millions, a realization that may lead to collective action. Traditional intellectuals play a crucial social role in diffusing this form of cultural hegemony, which benefits the powerful sectors of society, Gramsci argued, as did the material (or actual, physical) "structure of ideology": publishing houses, newspapers, journals, literature, libraries, museums, theaters, art galleries, schools, architecture, and even street names, which operate as factors or elements in the struggle over hegemony.[57]

Gramsci believed it was necessary to develop a counterhegemonic perspective formulated by "organic intellectuals" from, or allied with, the popular social classes who would articulate their genuine interests and empower them. Any revolution would be impossible without achieving a fundamental change in the worldview of the population, Gramsci thought. Organic intellectuals were charged with demonstrating that the system did not in fact benefit all and that another system was possible. Gramsci distinguished between "the notion of intellectual élites separated from the masses, and that of intellectuals who are conscious of being linked organically to a national-popular mass. . . . [The class struggle will] stimulate the formation of homogeneous, compact social blocs, which will give birth to their own intellectuals, their own commandos, their own vanguard—who in turn will react upon those blocs in order to develop them."[58]

Gramsci thought that organic intellectuals had a vital role to play in terms of illuminating the exploitative conditions that were generally taken for granted. "Critical self-consciousness means, historically and politically, the creation of an élite of intellectuals," he wrote. "A human mass does not 'distinguish' itself, does not become independent in its own right without, in the widest sense, organising itself; and there is no organisation without intellectuals, that is without organisers and leaders, in other words, without the theoretical aspect of the theory-practice nexus being distinguished concretely by the existence of a group of people 'specialized' in conceptual and philosophical elaboration of ideas. . . . The process of development is tied to a dialectic between the intellectuals and the masses."[59] The feelings of oppression that existed in the working classes "would necessarily emerge as an incoherent jumble requiring the work of intellectuals to provide it with coherence and intellectual rigor," as Crehan puts it.[60] Gramsci thought the oppressed classes were "lacking the kind of clear, rigorous insight into how local environments of oppression are located within larger economic and political realities, which is essential if a subaltern account is to have any hope of becoming genuinely counter-hegemonic."[61] He saw hegemony as a contested process rather than a fixed structure; it continually provoked acts of resistance.[62] Exploited sectors of society regularly challenged the system, but in ways that were not necessarily well organized or strategic. The role of the organic intellectual was to explain, interpret, and politically analyze the relations of power in society in ways the people could understand, to aid them in their struggle for social change. "This means working to produce élites of intellectuals of a new type which arise directly out of the masses, but remain in contact with them," Gramsci wrote.[63]

In my view, the New Song movement was one of the political actors (along with political parties and others) that played this counterhegemonic role, whether intentionally or not. The musicians were organic intellectuals in the sense of translating the hopes and aspirations of millions of Chileans in their songs, denouncing social injustice and repression, and communicating the vision of a different future. Certainly in Chile, the political vision presented by *la Nueva Canción* challenged the existing hegemonic sphere of music on radio and television, dominated by U.S. rock-and-roll, similar Chilean music (*Nueva Ola*), and "typical" Chilean *huaso* music. But beyond that, the musicians challenged the structure of power relations in Chile and Latin America that resulted in the immiseration of millions of people. The music of New Song used its poetry to cry out for social justice, equality, self-determination, and structural change. That is, the New Song movement played a key role in challenging the hegemonic system of power relations through a popular medium, in ways anticipated by Gramsci.

Along with drawing on Gramsci, this book incorporates a related historical-structural approach that recognizes and analyzes the structural and institutional constraints faced by subordinated political actors but also takes into account the ways in which those actors can change and reshape those structures and institutions. That is, I am interested in how counterhegemonies may transform social and political systems via concerted action "from below." There is a rich tradition of literature in political science that uses a historical-structural approach.[64] International and national contexts shape the conditions within which people and movements act, but those actions, reciprocally, can change the same contexts. As argued by Fernando Henrique Cardoso and Enzo Faletto, long-term structures form the parameters within which human agency operates. At the same time, while structural conditions influence, constrain, and shape, they do not *determine* actions and decisions made by states and individuals. Decision makers and people in general are presented with both opportunities and limits posed by structural conditions. Historical developments are the product of the complex, reciprocal interaction between structures—long-term power relations in political, military, and economic spheres—and human choices and action, which can also shape structures. Structures are not permanent; they can change during wars, economic crises, or when a critical mass of political opposition generates significant challenges to the existing system of power relations. I suggest that the movements for social change in Chile, which included *la Nueva Canción*, were counterhegemonic in this sense.

The International Setting

The antipathy between the United States and the Soviet Union marked the beginning of the Cold War in the late 1940s. At the same time, the postwar period saw an explosion of nationalism and anticolonialism across the less-developed world. The Cold War—which was not cold in the developing world—brought heavily ideological ways to interpret popular struggles and independence movements as the United States and the Soviet Union vied for influence. Washington made a concerted effort to establish a military presence and advocate U.S.-style capitalist development worldwide. The Truman administration created the Central Intelligence Agency (CIA) in 1947, a Cold War organization that became a clandestine paramilitary army dedicated to shaping political outcomes across the globe through covert action. The Soviet Union made efforts to support revolutionary and anticolonial movements and keep the neighboring countries of Eastern Europe in its camp as buffers against the West.

World War II had been fought, and won, as a noble struggle against the forces of totalitarianism and inhumanity personified by the Nazis and inspired by Franklin D. Roosevelt's four freedoms: freedom of speech and expression, freedom to worship God in each person's own way, freedom from want—for every person to have the economic means for a decent life—and freedom from fear, meaning worldwide arms reduction and an end of aggression.[65] After the war, people in the European colonies in Asia and Africa rose up, demanding those freedoms and their independence. Latin America's countries had already won independence in the early 1800s. But the continent was the site of new political struggles and social-political demands as people became more aware of their dependent and less-developed status and of the inequalities and injustices that permeated their societies. Major U.S. corporations controlled strategic resources and production processes in the region, such as Chile's copper mines (controlled by Kennecott and Anaconda, among others), Venezuela's oil industry (dominated by U.S. and British oil companies), and Central America's fruit plantations (controlled by United Fruit Company). Profits were repatriated without concern for the development of the host countries. In that context, new leaders arose to assert the rights of their people.

A number of social experiments and several revolutions occurred in Latin America in this period. A revolution in Costa Rica resulted in the abolishment of the army in 1948, a first in the region. The military budget was transferred to education and health care for the population. Guatemala's "democratic spring" began in 1944, and in the early 1950s, the modernizing President Jacobo Arbenz tried to raise standards of living, especially for impoverished peasants, by implementing land reform through constitutional means. His experiment sparked a confrontation with the interests of the Boston-based United Fruit Company, a large landowner, and with the Eisenhower administration in the escalating Cold War. Arbenz was ousted in a CIA operation known as "PB Success" in 1954. After the Cuban Revolution in 1959, which overthrew the anticommunist U.S. ally Fulgencio Batista, Washington assumed a hostile attitude toward Fidel Castro's government and in 1961 launched the Bay of Pigs invasion of the island, contracting Cuban exiles trained by the CIA as a covert army. The invasion and planned counterrevolution failed. Castro and Ernesto "Che" Guevara became revolutionary heroes to a generation of youth. Many people in Latin America and in the world began to identify the United States as an enemy of progress and social justice.

A sense of change and possibility was emerging throughout the world—a sense that boundaries were falling and new potential was emerging and that ordinary people were becoming protagonists and seizing control of their own destinies. In 1961, countries in the less-developed world formed the Non-Aligned Movement (NAM), proclaiming the right to remain neutral in the East–West conflict and focus on sovereignty, development, independence, and security. The NAM expressed its condemnation of racism, imperialism, colonialism, and all big-power interference in the so-called Third World. All of these developments upset existing political patterns and entrenched social hierarchies as people worldwide began to demand their rights. In Latin America, there were passionate calls for economic sovereignty, political independence, and national control of resources in the popular interest.

In 1963, John F. Kennedy was assassinated. In 1964, the Brazilian military overthrew the fiery populist President João Goulart and established a dictatorship, one of the first of the era in South America. In 1965, the United States invaded the Dominican Republic, announcing that it was taking a neutral peacekeeping role but covertly aiding the counterrevolutionary forces.[66] Meanwhile, the United States was becoming increasingly involved in the war in Vietnam. The war aroused a growing sense of outrage, especially among young people, including those in the United States, who increasingly characterized the U.S. role in the world as imperialist. The aggressive U.S. responses to movements for social change ignited an increasingly radical mood in Latin America in the 1960s. The rage against big-power domination targeting the poor and the weak was accompanied by a belief that change was possible if people mobilized. A general sense of rebellion against injustice coupled with a sense of hope and possibility was characteristic of the era. It seemed as if the mass movements of people throughout the world for social justice, equality, power, and control over decisions affecting their lives—essentially, deeper democracy and egalitarianism—were becoming unstoppable. With Allende's election in Chile in 1970, the world witnessed the first effort to move toward socialism through democratic and constitutional processes. But a series of U.S.-backed military coups halted these movements for social change: in 1963, in Guatemala and Ecuador; in 1966, in Argentina; and in 1968, in Panama and Peru (although in Peru, the political stance of the military regime was more ambiguous). In the 1970s, an even more ferocious set of coups occurred, plunging the region into repression led by brutal regimes of state terror.

Chile in the 1950s was a country undergoing rapid transformation. Its democracy was elitist but relatively modern, with liberal-democratic institutions. Advances in education and social welfare had been made during the twentieth century, although they coexisted with economic underdevelopment, extensive poverty, and striking social inequalities. Chile had an electoral democracy, but the system had been dominated by parties of the conservative upper and middle classes. In 1938, a member of the secular and moderate Radical Party, Pedro Aguirre Cerda, was elected, representing the Popular Front, which included the Communist and Socialist parties. Chile became the only Latin American country that included major Marxist parties in electoral politics, forming a multiclass coalition that supported progressive social reforms.[67]

The Chilean historian Gabriel Salazar highlights a number of factors to explain Chile's history of relatively stable—if narrow—democracy. First, there was a tradition of popular neighborhood associations and local democratic self-government in Chile.[68] Second, in contrast to other Latin American countries, the role of the military in politics had been less pronounced. Chile had a long history of constitutional rule, interrupted briefly by several coups and short periods of dictatorial rule in the 1920s and early 1930s. Ordered by civilian superiors, however, the military and the militarized police (Carabineros) had carried out numerous massacres of workers and their families, as well as protesters in the cities, over the course of the twentieth century.[69] Third, the workers' and union movements had been growing steadily since the early part of the twentieth century in Chile. With origins in the North, the area of rich copper and nitrate mines, the union movement arose alongside Chile's first socialist party, founded by Luis Emilio Recabarren and others in 1912. There was also an early anarchist movement that fought for workers' rights. These organizations were deeply involved in organizing the nitrate, copper, and coal miners, among others, especially Recabarren's party, the forerunner of the PC. Over subsequent years, the movement was able to win important concessions from the state. Fourth, Chile was relatively advanced in the field of education by the 1960s as the result of decades of popular pressure and enlightened policy. Primary and secondary schools were public, well-regarded, and free, and a relatively large part of the population was literate.

Chile, like other countries in Latin America, experienced a convergence of factors in the 1950s and 1960s: the escalating Cold War and U.S. intervention in the region; deepening capitalist modernization and globalization, in some cases propelled by the Alliance for Progress; new mass communications media (transistor radios, televisions) that were becoming widely accessible; changing conditions of life and class structure, especially in Chile under President Eduardo Frei's reformist agenda in the 1960s; growing urbanization and internal migration to Santiago; and increasing exposure to northern, especially U.S., cultural penetration. The electorate was divided roughly in thirds: Left, Center, and Right.

The 1964 presidential election was crucial in Chile. Opposed by the democratic Marxist Salvador Allende in his third attempt, Eduardo Frei of the Christian Democrat Party (Partido Demócrata Cristiano; DC) proposed a social-democratic program and "a Revolution in Liberty," pledging agrarian reform, fair conditions for workers, and new social programs. Allende had substantial support from the electorate, and his campaign drew the backing of many artists and musicians. Frei succeeded in winning the election in 1964, with a groundswell of support from many socially conscious young people—and assisted by secret U.S. funding and a CIA "campaign of terror" that portrayed Allende as an antidemocratic communist. Washington was profoundly concerned by the emerging radical-democratic and socialist movements in Chile and elsewhere and considered the DC a viable alternative. The Chilean Right was intransigently opposed to any land reform or organization of the peasantry. The pro-Allende movement alarmed conservative military forces, as well; they were being taught in inter-American military training programs that the "internal enemy" was everywhere in their societies and that they were subversives who must be repressed.

In sum, Chile, and the world, experienced a period of dramatic change in the 1950s and 1960s as new actors entered the political arena and old, ossified structures began to shift. The New Song movement helped to transform the culture of Chile, introducing original and vibrant forms of music and popularizing revolutionary ideas. The music was a harbinger of social change and a reflection of new political currents in Chile and in Latin America. The movement deepened peoples' sense of belonging to an alternative, popular force and their sense of commitment to the struggle for a different future, instilling a sense of people's power. A crucial factor in Allende's election was the unity of leftist and popular forces, and the New Song movement contributed to and cemented that unity. In Gramscian terms, a strong counterhegemony had arisen that defied existing power relations, and New Song was the music of that movement.

2

Art and Politics Intertwined in Chile

A Selected History

Analysts have pointed out that Chile has been a study in paradoxes: economically underdeveloped but with a long history of stable, constitutional rule; sharp class stratification and inequality alongside democratic politics (if narrow); strong Communist and Socialist parties that were revolutionary and Marxist but nevertheless participated in the electoral system.[1] Chile was a country of multiparty politics, with a politically tolerant society coupled with worker militancy and class consciousness, until the coup of 1973. Political and socioeconomic problems had been addressed through the political system, and it had been possible to attain moderate social and political change democratically. This tradition had important ramifications in Chile. Large masses of Chileans who supported the Unidad Popular (UP) believed that their voices would be heard and that structural change and social advances could be achieved through the political system— through popular participation and action, voting, and government policy— without civil war or revolutionary violence. This was Salvador Allende's plan with "the constitutional road to socialism."

Yet in important ways, Chile's democratic tradition was a cherished national myth. The political system was dominated by wealthy elites until the 1960s, and there were numerous cases of state-sponsored violence. Chile's democracy was narrow and oligarchic, with minimal electoral participation by popular sectors. Until the 1960s, due to restrictions written into law, only a small proportion of the population voted. Sofía Correa Sutil shows that only some 8 percent of the national population voted in the 1940s, and a small percentage of those were from the working classes. Electoral reforms expanded suffrage to women (1949) and to broader sectors of the working classes (1958, 1962). Rodrigo Baño demonstrates that the electoral rolls doubled for the 1964 election. Traditionally, there was extensive vote buying by the Right, and landowners essentially told "their" campesinos for whom they should vote.[2] In short, a wealthy minority controlled political power in Chile. These elites and their political parties resorted to political violence in the face of challenges "from below" to their power. There were numerous and frequent examples of massacres and of military and police repression of strikes, peasant protests, and student demonstrations. Governments regularly imposed states of siege and zones of emergency and outlawed left-wing parties, especially the Partido Comunista, PC.

Another factor shaping Chile's political culture was the long history of foreign ownership of key national resources, a situation that subjected the country to decisions made beyond its control to benefit foreign interests, as well as to economic crises originating abroad. Chileans were well aware of the social inequalities, repression, and outflow of wealth that had resulted from control by foreign enterprises. They had experienced the consequences of economic dependence on one vital export. The nitrate crash during World War I had devastated Chile's economy. Allende's project to fully nationalize the copper mines in 1971 was unanimously endorsed by Congress, even by right-wing anti-Allende parties. Moreover, the Chilean state played an important role in the economy; there were already numerous state enterprises by the time of Allende's election. Many UP supporters saw this as a favorable condition, one that bode well for the UP's program of nationalizations, agrarian reform, social programs, and deeper democratization. Sergio Bitar notes that by 1970, the state played a larger role in the Chilean economy than in any other Latin American country except Cuba.[3] Gradually over previous decades, pushed by an organized working class as well as by middle-class sectors, the state had increased social services and entered the production process, creating state enterprises and providing public financing for investments, wages, housing, and public works. "The state had made itself into a powerful instrument," Bitar writes, "thus providing the basis for a process of socialization."[4]

Joan Jara observed that "Chileans were class conscious and proud of it" in the decades before the 1973 coup.[5] This was largely due to the efforts of political parties of the Left, which played a central role in organizing youth, union, and workers' organizations throughout the twentieth century and were present in communities of workers and *pobladores* (shantytown dwellers). It was also due to the abysmal working conditions and exploitation suffered by urban and rural workers. Allende's project of a peaceful route to socialism was appealing because his initiatives had mass support, indicat-

ing that change was possible through democratic processes.[6] In the municipal elections of 1971, for example, the UP increased its share of the vote to
roughly 51 percent,[7] in contrast to the usual three-way split in national elections by the Right, Left, and Center.

In this chapter, I sketch the outlines of Chile's political history, with
some references to important cultural developments. I make no claim to be
comprehensive, as Chile's history is complex and space is limited. My aim
is to give readers a sense of some important historical and cultural mark-
ers and to provide a context for the origins of the political movements of
the 1960s and *la Nueva Canción*, which are examined in depth in the next
chapter.

Early Political History

Chile has been isolated historically from the rest of Latin America and the
world, flanked by a dry northern desert, by Antarctica in the South, and
by the Andes on one side and the ocean on the other. During the centuries
of Spanish rule, the southern region was home to the fierce Araucanians,
or Mapuche indigenous people, who were never defeated by the Spanish.
Indeed, the Mapuche ejected the Spaniards from their colonies south of the
River Bío-Bío between 1598 and 1612 and again in 1655.[8] Through violence
and repression, the Chilean state did manage to defeat and control these
peoples in the nineteenth century. Their social conditions continue to be
dire to this day.

After political independence was achieved in 1818, political conflicts and
several authoritarian governments followed. By the second half of the century, Chile had established a constitutional system dominated by two political
parties, the Liberal Party and the Conservative Party, that battled for influence.[9] After the War of the Pacific (1879–1883), Chile's territory expanded
by one-third. Chile annexed lands from Bolivia and Peru that were rich in
minerals—namely, nitrates and copper. Under the administration of José
Manuel Balmaceda (1886–1891) the government expanded public works as
the nitrate industry flourished, increasing foreign investment and trade. The
government modernized the country, building railroads, telegraph systems,
and schools. In the 1880s, literate men older than twenty-five won the right
to vote. The nitrate boom produced a new middle class of state employees
and commercial workers. The Radical Party, formed in 1863, represented this
rising middle class and proposed various reforms. Many mutualist societies
were also formed by working families to discuss problems, provide aid, and
pursue basic rights.[10] They were more defensive than militant organizations.

To oversimplify this complex period, suffice it to say that Balmaceda
had powerful enemies. He warned foreign owners of nitrate mines that the

state intended to tax the mines at higher rates or even take partial control of them. In 1884, two-thirds of the nitrate mines were owned by Europeans.[11] The president also had enemies in Congress and among the landowning oligarchs, who blocked his initiatives, eventually leading to civil war. The army sided with the president, and the navy sided with the conservative opposition in Congress. The civil war ended in a victory for the conservatives, and Balmaceda committed suicide. The political system was converted from a strongly presidential one to a parliamentary one that greatly restricted the power of the executive branch.

Popular songs during the Balmeceda period, many set to the music of the *cueca*, were more political than before. Some openly denounced Balmaceda's enemies.[12] There had always been songs with social content. Traditional Chilean musical forms, such as *tonadas*, *cuecas*, and waltzes, sometimes contained lyrics that pointed out social class divisions, such as impossible romances due to class differences between two people.[13] There was also a tradition of popular poets, or *payadores*, whose lineage went back to Spanish colonial times. They improvised verses that chronicled the lives of the people: their struggles, their experiences, their loves, their longings, embodying the historical memory of their communities.

In 1887, the Democratic Party (Partido Demócrata) was established. It was essentially a populist party that challenged foreign, landowning, and industrial interests and attracted anarchists, progressives, and socialists. As the mines developed, Chile was increasingly inserted into the world economic system as a producer of primary products, with an export-oriented enclave economy dominated by foreign capital. Chile became a classic example of a dependent economy.[14] The growing numbers of miners formed a powerful emerging industrial working class. The miners faced brutal and dangerous conditions. They were prohibited from meeting, forcing them to gather clandestinely, and they were required to shop in company stores with scrip provided as wages by the mines.[15] Over time, the more leftist members of the Partido Demócrata became dissatisfied with its positions. The party was drifting to the right. The socialist sector, led by Luis Emilio Recabarren, eventually left to lead militant labor organizations in the North (the nitrate and copper mines) and South (the coal mines in Lota and elsewhere). Recabarren can be seen as an organic intellectual in the Gramscian sense. He was a key labor leader and socialist organizer of an early counter-hegemonic movement of the working classes.

In 1907, some ten thousand nitrate miners and their families gathered at the Santa María school in Iquique to protest their living and working conditions and demand better wages, an end to company stores, and safety standards in the mines. Military troops were sent in; they massacred hundreds, if not thousands, of people (the figure is disputed).[16] This event was absent from Chile's official history for many years, but a song from the period memorialized the massacre. During this time, the movements of the Left—communist, socialist, and anarchist—as well as other institutions, such as the Catholic Church, changed the words to songs that were already known (known as "contrafacta," a Latin term). According to the musicologist Juan Pablo González, "The most famous song was 'Canto a la Pampa.' It was a romantic song from the early part of the century. An anarchist poet changed the words to chronicle the massacre at Santa María. Violeta Parra sang the original version after hearing it during her research in the countryside, and Quilapayún sang the politicized version later."[17] The massacre in Iquique was immortalized in Luis Advis's *Cantata Santa María de Iquique*, released by Quilapayún in 1970. In short, the historical memory of the massacre was musically documented from the beginning, forming one of the sources of *la Nueva Canción*. The early decades of the twentieth century were marked by many strikes, protests, and militant actions by workers as they gradually unionized and engaged in collective action against the mining companies. Other massacres of workers, peasants, Mapuches, and protesters occurred, such as those in San Gregorio (1921), La Coruña (1925), Antofagasta (1925), and Ranquil (1934).

The Rise of the Left

In the early twentieth century, the socialist, communist, and anarchist movements overlapped to some degree.[18] Over time, the communists became dominant within the labor movement. Recabarren founded the Socialist Workers Party in 1912 explicitly to represent the interests of workers, to organize unions, to fight for national control of resources, and to move toward a socialist society.[19] He was a strong proponent of educating the working classes and believed that they should create their own culture through popular education, as well as through art and theater. The party set up study groups and schools to teach workers how to read, write, and speak publicly.[20] A significant part of Recabarren's work was in the cultural field. He traveled from the North to the South of Chile accompanied by a theater group. He visited workers and their organizations to encourage them to fight for their rights, formed theater and music groups among the workers, and wrote plays for them to perform, works suffused with social and political content.[21] The only known surviving play by Recabarren is *Desdicha obrera* of 1921, a work that portrays the injustices faced by two struggling working-class sisters who fight oppressive conditions, as well as the lewd advances of the *patrón*.[22] An early Chilean feminist, Elena Caffarena, pointed out that "Recabarren was not only a pioneer of union organizing of the Chilean working class but also a noteworthy pioneer of the feminist movement."[23]

Recabarren's cultural innovations were a crucial way to reach workers who could not read or write, a means to educate them and involve them in collective self-expression and art. "The unions became schools for illiterate Chileans," said José Seves.[24] Joan Jara explained, "Part of Recabarren's vision, and that of the PC, was to include a cultural component in all demonstrations and acts. Theater and music were always central, to stimulate cultural expression."[25] Recabarren's cultural work was in essence an innovative form of social communication and an important precedent to *la Nueva Canción*. Joan Jara observed, "The whole cultural movement was linked to the PC from the beginning, with Recabarren. After the Spanish Civil War, with the position of Pablo Neruda [as a political and artistic figure], there was enormous inspiration for artists. . . . There was a tradition for trade unions to invite artists to May 1 celebrations, including singers and dancers."[26] Recabarren also founded workers' newspapers, such as *El Trabajo* in Tocopilla, *La Vanguardia* in Antofagasta, and *El Despertar de los Trabajadores* in Iquique, to provide an alternative to the commercial newspapers controlled by elites (such as *El Mercurio*, owned by the conservative Edwards family since 1880). Recabarren is a legendary figure among the popular classes and intellectuals of Chile as the founding father of the progressive labor movement and one who understood the importance of cultural expression. Pablo Neruda wrote about him in his epic *Canto General*, three hundred poems dedicated to the historical struggles of Latin America for development and justice. Many New Song musicians sang about Recabarren. Víctor Jara wrote "A Luis Emilio Recabarren," which appeared on his 1969 album *Pongo en Tus Manos Abiertas* (I Place in Your Open Hands), and Quilapayún dedicated its 1969 album *Basta* to Recabarren, among many other examples.

During World War I, the Germans invented synthetic nitrates, and Chile's nitrate industry collapsed, producing a social and political crisis. Middle-class sectors began demanding protections, and tens of thousands of miners were thrown out of work. The economy was "saved" by the copper industry. But by 1920, two U.S. firms, Anaconda and Kennecott, had gained control of the three most important copper mines in Chile, thus continuing the country's dependent status. The 1920s were an unstable period in Chile, but the Left began to garner significant power. Recabarren ran for president in 1920 and was elected to Congress in 1921. In 1922, inspired by the Russian Revolution, Recabarren led his party to join the Third International and rename itself the Partido Comunista de Chile.[27] Again oversimplifying the complexities of the 1920s, in 1924 the military intervened, and the parliamentary system fell. After two military juntas, Arturo Alessandri returned as president and was able to restore some powers to the presidency through the constitution of 1925. Although the military supported Alessandri, he felt compromised by that support and resigned the presidency.[28] Colonel

Carlos Ibáñez took power in 1927 and ruled with an iron fist, banning the PC and repressing workers' organizations. Nevertheless, the PC continued to win support among the workers. With the onset of the Depression and large student protests against him, Ibáñez resigned in 1931. Several short-lived governments followed, including twelve days of a socialist republic led by General Marmaduke Grove, among others. During the ensuing years, the PC and the unions were in the forefront of struggles for the eight-hour workday, the right to retirement and overtime pay, the right to unionize, and the rights of women—despite the fact that the PC could not always operate under its own name. By the 1930s, the PC had become one of the strongest communist parties in Latin America.

Alessandri was reelected in 1932 and presided over a conservative government. The constitutional system was restored for the next decades. The electorate was divided roughly into thirds among the Left, Right, and Center, and multiple political parties were represented in Congress until the 1973 coup. J. Samuel Valenzuela and Arturo Valenzuela have emphasized the importance of this multiparty system, arguing that strong parties and respect for democratic rule were key factors in Chile's democratic development. No one party could impose its will or win a majority, and the system encouraged political accommodation and the making of alliances.[29] Nevertheless, as we have seen, there were serious limits to Chile's elite democracy—specifically, the intermittent bans against the Left and frequent use of state violence.

The Popular Front Period

Adolf Hitler took power in Germany in 1933, and in 1936 the PC, the Radical Party, and the Socialist Party (Partido Socialista; PS), formed in 1933, created a Popular Front. Similar popular fronts were established in France and Spain in 1936 to resist the rise of fascism. The PS distinguished itself from the PC by its criticism of the Soviet Union and its identification with South America; it also contained a plethora of heterogeneous ideological factions, including middle-class intellectuals and professionals, anarchists, and Trotskyists.[30] Salvador Allende, a medical student at the time, was a founder of the PS, and in 1933 he became the first regional secretary in Valparaíso.[31] He was also active in creating the Popular Front. In 1936, the labor unions formed the Workers Confederation of Chile (Confederación de Trabajadores de Chile; CTCH), with the explicit goal of uniting the working class and democratizing the country.[32]

In Spain, the civil war between the socialist Republican government and the fascist forces headed by General Francisco Franco exploded in the 1930s. The war and the Republican cause evoked deep sympathy among large sectors of Chileans, and some Chileans went to Spain to fight.[33] The Popular

Front parties organized many acts of solidarity in Chile, in the National Stadium and elsewhere,[34] generating a new wave of popular culture. Spanish Civil War songs became well known. Significantly, the songs were political, mobilizing, and internationally conscious, in stark contrast to the demobilizing effect of "typical folk music" that portrayed the Chilean countryside in idealized terms. Rolando Alarcón, an early New Song singer-songwriter, recorded some of these songs in the 1960s.[35] These songs and mass concerts were forerunners of *la Nueva Canción*. Neruda, the Chilean consul in Madrid at the time, became a communist after witnessing the events in Spain. The murder of his friend, the poet Federico García Lorca, by fascist forces was a traumatic blow for him. In 1938, as a special consul for the government of Pedro Aguirre Cerda in France, Neruda smuggled thousands of Spanish refugees out of camps in France after chartering a ship, the *Winnipeg*, to take them to Chile to settle.

Aguirre Cerda, a leader of the Radical Party, had been elected president in 1938 as the Popular Front candidate, ushering in a period in which political parties of the Left became fully incorporated into the political system.[36] The Popular Front period was a time of progressive social change, at least in the cities; rural workers and peasants were essentially left out of the economic advances. Aguirre Cerda instituted a nationalist-developmentalist economic model with state-led import-substitution industrialization. He created the Chilean Development Corporation (CORFO), as well as state enterprises in electricity, textiles, and metalworking, to encourage economic diversification and industrialization. As Brian Loveman notes, however, much of the capital for CORFO came from the United States and required use of U.S. materials, machinery, and consultancy,[37] increasing Chile's dependence on Washington. Aguirre Cerda also made important concessions to the right-wing landowners—suspending the right to organize by rural workers, for example—but he refused to outlaw the PC.[38] The government built primary and secondary schools and technical training schools. Allende, at thirty, became Aguirre Cerda's minister of health in 1938, the youngest of all the ministers. Allende sponsored a reform to provide obligatory insurance to workers in the event of accidents on the job, and he worked to pass laws protecting mothers and children.[39] He was elected senator in 1945.

In the cultural field, both the state and the public University of Chile played an important foundational role in the arts in the 1940s. The Popular Front government, in conjunction with the university, created new institutions to promote Chile's culture and folklore in the academic world as part of its nationalist project. Congress established the Institute of Musical Extension, to promote musical development, in 1940, and CORFO formed the state-run ChileFilms in 1941. The Central Direction of Information and Culture, the Symphonic Orchestra and the Experimental Theater of the University of

Chile, and the Institute of Folklore Research were created in the 1940s.[40] A key figure in the founding of the orchestra and other new musical institutions was Domingo Santa Cruz, who also developed projects for musical education and choruses in working-class barrios in the 1940s.[41] Santa Cruz noted, "For the first time among ourselves and many other countries, the diffusion of musical culture is definitively recognized, by an official act of Parliament, as a public function."[42]

"There is a link between the flowering of music and the development of democracy," said the composer, classical musician, and communist organizer Fernando García. "It's the idea that art is not a market commodity but something that the state should support as a public good. Also, artists need to have the freedom and independence to create their own art. When there is a democratic political project, art grows and flourishes; when there is a regression, art also suffers."[43] One of the first, if not the first, musicians to advocate the inclusion of explicit social and political themes in music was an important classical composer and communist named Roberto Falabella (1926–1958). "For Falabella, the progressive creator had the obligation to reflect, with artistic images, the reality of the time," Fernando García wrote in 1967. "Art, and particularly music, could give support to the revolutionary process. . . . Each composer should look for the language or style that best expresses his concerns, always being conscious that the work of art should complete a social function."[44] The artists and musicians were increasingly conscious of the importance of art to the movement for social change.

Neruda joined the PC in 1945 and became a communist senator that year. The renowned poet exercised a sweeping and formative influence on the young musicians who would become important in *la Nueva Canción*. Neruda was a prolific writer who celebrated simple things ("Ode to the Onion") and also composed epic poetry that documented the struggles of people in ways that were stirring, moving, and lyrical. His *Canto General* (1950) had a major impact in Chile with its poetic power and its social and political history of Latin America. Many New Song artists put his poetry to music in the 1960s (in 1970, the group Aparcoa released an album of *Canto General* poems set to music, with collaboration by the poet himself, Sergio Ortega, and Gustavo Becerra), and many were inspired by his dual role as a communist public figure and a literary giant. Neruda produced major works of art over a series of decades and won the Nobel Prize in Literature in 1971. Neruda knew Violeta Parra, Víctor Jara, and many other artists; there were connections through art and through the PC. "Neruda was a big influence on Víctor and on Patricio Bunster, too," said Joan Jara. (Bunster was her first husband, a renowned dancer and choreographer.) "Víctor recorded songs with Neruda's poetry and directed his only play in the University of Chile. . . . Neruda was a shining example, a great figure, especially his role in looking at Latin America's cultural roots. Chile had mainly looked toward Europe before Neruda."[45]

The Cold War Comes to Chile

The Popular Front dissolved in 1941 as competition between the PC and the PS and internal political disagreements deepened. In 1946, the Radical Party candidate Gabriel González Videla was elected president with the support of his party and the PC. However, despite the formation of a cabinet that included both Communists and Radicals, the hopes of the Left for a progressive presidency were dashed. In 1948, González Videla pushed, and Congress passed, the Law of Defense of Democracy—or the Ley Maldita (evil or cursed law)—which outlawed the PC and initiated a new wave of repression against parties and organizations of the workers. There had been pressure from the Chilean right wing and the United States in the emerging Cold War. The PC won 16.5 percent of the vote in 1947 municipal elections, a worrisome development for the Right. With government ministers in the González Videla administration, the legitimacy of the PC was greatly enhanced. The party organized some 358 peasant unions of 11,000 people in the ensuing period, frightening the landowners.[46]

The Ley Maldita also followed serious strikes at Kennecott's El Teniente mine, beginning in 1946. Kennecott and the U.S. State Department insisted that the government of Chile crack down on the miners' unions and the PC, which were seen as threats to U.S. economic and security interests. Spruille Braden, the U.S. assistant secretary of state at the time, was linked to the copper industry. His father had founded the Braden Copper Company in 1904; in 1915, it became part of Kennecott.[47] In one meeting, recorded in an internal memo of 1946, the president of Kennecott asked Assistant Secretary of State Braden "what further assistance can be expected by the [State] Department" to advance the company's interest in terminating labor unrest and specifically whether Washington would block Chile's access to loans and credits from the Export-Import Bank (Eximbank).[48] On the same day, Braden met with the Chilean chargé d'affaires and complained about the strike at El Teniente. He also implied that Eximbank loans and credits for Chile were at risk and expressed "a feeling of uneasiness in certain quarters at the inclusion of Communists in the Chilean cabinet."[49] The Truman administration did, in fact, block Chile's Eximbank credits to show its displeasure at the presence of Communists in the government.

In 1946, students staged demonstrations in support of striking nitrate workers. In one march called by the CTCH and supported by students and La Jota (the Young Communists), police opened fire, killing six people, including a young communist student, Ramona Parra, and wounding many others.

(Years later, in 1968, young people in La Jota formed a group of muralists and graphic artists and named it the Ramona Parra Brigade in her honor.)[50] In 1947, González Videla sent the army into the mines to crush the strikes and unrest, and many Communists and organizers were detained. A state of siege was declared in the coal region of Lota.[51] After the military quashed a strike at the Lota coal mine and sent miners to hastily established detention camps, Neruda gave a fiery speech in the Senate denouncing González Videla.[52]

The 1948 Ley Maldita made the PC illegal and banned its political activity. The PC was the third largest voting bloc in the country, after the Radical and Conservative parties, so a large proportion of the population was excluded from political participation. The three PC ministers were forced to step down. Communist senators, congressmen, and mayors were ousted from their positions, and labor strikes were criminalized. Tens of thousands of PC voters were expunged from the electoral lists. Teachers were expelled from schools if they were affiliated with, or suspected to be affiliated with, the PC. Neruda fled into hiding to escape possible imprisonment in Pisagua, a remote prison camp set up in the North that confined labor activists and communists and their families. Several labor leaders and a number of children died in the camp because of scarce food and medical care. One woman, the wife of a nitrate miner, starved during a mass hunger strike by the detainees, an episode later chronicled by Neruda in *Canto General*.[53] Augusto Pinochet—the future dictator of Chile—was the military commander of the prison camp in 1948, overseeing detentions of labor leaders and communists in the region.[54]

Like McCarthyism in the United States, the Ley Maldita imposed a draconian policy of government-sponsored anticommunism in Chile. Ironically, the law resulted in a proliferation of splits in existing parties as they scrambled to capture the votes of the PC.[55] Carlos Huneeus has characterized the impact of the Ley Maldita as deeply negative in terms of Chilean democracy and civil and political rights, contributing greatly to the polarization of society and the deterioration of democratic rules and guarantees that contributed to the coup of 1973.[56] After the law's passage, the Eximbank financed huge investments in Chile to develop a number of state industries while requiring that only U.S. capital goods be utilized in the process.[57] The result was to enhance the interests of private Chilean and U.S. investors and make Chile increasingly dependent on foreign loans and investment.

The United States in the late 1940s had moved inexorably to a position of hostility toward the Soviet Union—its ally in World War II—and most communist, leftist, socialist, nationalist, and progressive movements in the developing world. U.S. national security doctrine was a politicized vision that combined strategies of internal war and counterrevolution with fierce anticommunism. It portrayed all attempts to challenge U.S. interests, or improve the conditions of the poor and oppressed, as communist plots managed by Moscow. Clearly, U.S. economic interests were a major concern, predating the Cold War. But Washington's foreign policy was more expansive, combining economic with political and military-security interests. As one secret document put it, "The broad U.S. interests in the underdeveloped world are as follows: 1. A political and ideological interest in assuring that developing nations evolve in a way that affords a congenial world environment for international cooperation and the growth of free [i.e., noncommunist] institutions. 2. A military interest in assuring that strategic areas and the manpower and natural resources of developing nations do not fall under communist control . . . 3. An economic interest in assuring that the resources and markets of the less developed world remain available to us and to other Free World countries."[58] U.S. Cold War policy was not only an anti-Soviet enterprise but also a strategy to establish global hegemony and advance U.S.-style capitalism.

Washington was unable or unwilling to distinguish between revolutionary communist movements seeking to overthrow governments, as in the Russian Revolution, and communist parties that were participating in democratic politics, as in Chile. The U.S. government moved aggressively to pull the Latin American governments into its orbit. The Inter-American Treaty of Reciprocal Assistance of 1947, signed by the United States and nineteen Latin American states, declared that an attack against one country would be considered an attack against all. The treaty, known informally as the Rio Pact, became a pillar of the inter-American security architecture and a vehicle for the exercise of U.S. hegemony and interventionism in the ensuing decades. Dominated by Washington throughout the Cold War and increasingly geared toward the internal "subversive threat," the Rio Pact was the first regional alliance influenced by the emergent U.S. foreign policy of anticommunism.

Within the framework of the pact, the U.S. government moved to unify and reconstitute the Latin American militaries under the banner of anticommunism and establish new inter-American security structures and agreements. Continental security and defense organizations, deeply influenced by U.S. doctrine, organizational principles, and training, included the U.S. Army Caribbean School (USARCARIB; 1946), later renamed the U.S. Army School of the Americas (SOA); the Inter-American Defense Board (1948); and the Conferences of American Armies (1960). The Rio Pact marked the beginning of deep U.S. military and intelligence involvement and influence in Latin America. The Pentagon set up a network of U.S. military bases. Especially after the Cuban Revolution in 1959, national security doctrine legitimated an expansive and politicized role for the armed forces to combat "subversion" and assume a leading national role. It also legitimized the use of harsh, extralegal countersubversive methods.

Washington pressured Latin American governments to outlaw local Communist Parties and restrain unions, students, and peasant organizations. In the case of Chile, the PC was close to the Soviet Union, but it had advocated moderate policies, sought electoral alliances within the democratic system, and designed its programs based on national conditions rather than imitating foreign models. It supported a peaceful transition to socialism rather than armed struggle. Yet Washington was unwilling to countenance any sort of Communist Party in its sphere of influence.

From 1950 to 1970, 4,374 Chilean soldiers were trained at the SOA or in the United States, compared with 2,808 from the larger Argentina. The SOA trained Latin American soldiers in combat and intelligence skills and sought to convert them into anticommunist forces that shared U.S. perspectives on the threat of internal subversion and the superiority of free-market capitalism and liberal democracy (excluding Communist and Socialist parties). Chile received more military funding than any other Latin American country except Brazil between 1953 and 1972.[59] "Efforts by the United States to support anti-Communist forces in Chile date back to the late 1950s and reflect the rivalry between the United States and the Soviet Union for influence throughout the Third World," stated the CIA's so-called Hinchey Report of 2000. "Thousands of Chilean military officers came to the United States for training, which included presentations on the impact of global communism on their own country."[60] In Chile, however, there was a strong constitutionalist tradition in the military. René Schneider, the army's commander-in-chief in the late 1960s, and Carlos Prats, his second in command, were two key constitutionalists. The Schneider doctrine of non-interference in politics, coupled with the vertical military command structure, meant that there was little chance for pro-coup sectors to succeed. That changed with the assassination of Schneider in 1970—part of a U.S.-backed plot to prevent Allende from taking office—which cleared the way for seditionist officers to gain dominance in the armed forces and eventually carry out a coup (see Chapter 3). As Latin American police and military forces became more politicized and more adept in repressing civilians, there was a marked increase in the region of violent repression and massacres, death squads, and coups.[61]

The 1950s: New Political and Artistic Currents

In 1952, Carlos Ibáñez, the former dictator who now cast himself as a populist, was elected president. Salvador Allende was also a presidential candidate for the first time, supported by the Socialist Party and the Communist Party.

Allende traveled throughout Chile to speak about his social and political ideas. He came in fourth. In 1953—despite the Ley Maldita—the Central Única de Trabajadores de Chile (Unified Workers' Central of Chile; CUT), a union confederation with many socialist and communist leaders, was formed. The PC, in clandestinity, still had an active role in the union movement. Allende, again elected to the Senate in 1953, became vice-president of the Senate in 1954. He sponsored a bill to create a social security service, which passed. That same year, the important First Congress of Popular Poets and Singers took place, sponsored by the University of Chile.[62] Neruda was a key organizer and speaker. Margot Loyola, the renowned collector of Chile's rural folklore; Nicanor Parra, the "antipoet" and brother of Violeta; and popular artists from all over Chile participated. Neruda read a poem dedicated to the popular poets of Chile, and an important interchange took place about Chile's folklore and popular culture.[63] Ignacio Ramos Rodillo argues that the PC, through Neruda, was seeking to deepen its influence in the cultural field through this congress.[64] In the 1950s, several groups that were predecessors of *la Nueva Canción* formed, including Cuncumén, organized by Loyola, and Millaray, organized by Gabriela Pizarro and Héctor Pavez. Both groups researched and collected Chile's authentic music and dance and performed them in Chile and abroad (discussed further below). Rolando Alarcón, Silvia Urbina, and Víctor Jara were early members of Cuncumén and later became key figures in the New Song movement; Cuncumén was a bridge between Chile's traditional folklore and *la Nueva Canción*.

In 1953, Violeta Parra, who was not yet well known, created her own radio show.[65] Rebellious, defiant of conventions, prolific, sensitive, and modern, Parra was a supremely creative personality. Parra was the daughter of a schoolteacher and a campesina from a small town near Chillán. After the death of her father, the family struggled to survive. Parra never had formal training in music, but she was drawn to the guitar and other instruments and soon played at gatherings in her town. She then formed a duo with her sister. Parra's music reflected the wrenching changes occurring in Chile that began in the 1940s. Industrialization and the mechanization of farming generated large movements of peasants from the countryside into Santiago and other cities. Parra and her family experienced this process of urbanization directly. Her songs expressed a sense of loss of the traditional life, the art and music of the peasants, and the alienation of modern society.[66] Parra had begun working with the PC in 1946.[67] She dedicated herself to collecting and re-creating the popular music of the countryside, especially from the *payadores*, whose influence can be seen in Parra's songs.[68] She spent years traveling throughout Chile to research and recover the disappearing music of the rural areas. In 1955, Parra joined the Chilean delegation to the World Youth Conference in Warsaw, an event that brought together young artists and musicians, many linked to Communist Parties worldwide. The PC's global connections offered opportunities and institutional support for Parra, Cuncumén, and other Chilean artists to perform in different countries, reach new audiences, achieve professional recognition, and develop crucial social and political networks.

Radio expanded rapidly in the 1950s, with new stations from the North to the South of Chile and thousands of new listeners. Ricardo García, a radio personality at Radio Chilena who was interested in the music of Chile's countryside, invited Parra to create a program. At the time, radio was dominated by "typical" Chilean folk music, along with foreign imports such as Mexican boleros, Argentine tangos, and, increasingly, commercial rock-and-roll from the global North. García became a key figure in the musical movement to preserve and promote Chilean culture. In her radio show, Parra played the songs of many rural areas of Chile, authentic campesino songs that were not heard anywhere else. "*La Nueva Canción* was born from Violeta's work," said her son Ángel. "She received thousands of letters. People recognized their music on this show, and people wrote from all over the country, from the smallest villages."[69] Rural Chileans felt their culture was being vindicated, and many in the growing leftist movements also embraced Violeta Parra's music. Their interest in Chile's authentic musical traditions blended with their other concerns: to oppose encroaching U.S. cultural forms and political intervention, to celebrate the culture of the working classes and campesinos, and to demand a national project of development and democratization. Folk music experienced a revival in the country. Violeta Parra also represented a bridge between Chile's cultural traditions and emerging counterhegemonic movements.

Parra received a prestigious prize, the Caupolicán Award for Best Folklorist, in 1955. She began to receive more invitations, to Finland, the Soviet Union, and other socialist countries; she also traveled to Paris. Parra founded the Museum of Popular Art in Concepción in 1958 and crisscrossed Chile gathering folk songs. She lived for years in Paris (1955–1957, 1962–1965) with her children Ángel and Isabel, singing in small clubs such as L'Escale and making recordings. Fernando Ríos writes that the Parras first heard Andean music in Paris. When they returned to Chile, they brought the Venezuelan *cuatro* and the Bolivian *charango* with them. Ríos has highlighted the importance of Paris in these years as a cultural magnet for Latin American (and other) artists.[70] He has traced the ways in which Andean music was brought to Paris in the early 1950s by groups such as Los Incas (whose members were mainly Argentine) and Los Guaranís (Paraguayans). Andean music was known in Argentina and in Bolivia, Peru, and Ecuador (where it originated) long before it became popular in Chile via *la Nueva Canción*. "In the 1960s, the separation with Peru and Bolivia was very strong," said Horacio Salinas of Inti-Illimani Histórico.[71] "The flow of information was poor, not like today; there was little knowledge of Andean music in Chile." Similarly, Horacio Durán commented that the indigenous people in the North, such as the Aymara people, who played the *charango*, the *quena*, and the *sicus*, were very remote, far from Santiago and urban culture at the time.[72] The music scene in Paris was quite apolitical, however; the Parras wanted to express their social and political concerns through song, which led to Ángel and Isabel Parra's founding in Santiago of La Peña de los Parra and Violeta Parra's formation of La Carpa de la Reina (see Chapter 3).

Violeta Parra began to compose her own songs in the late 1950s. Many of them were about the experiences and difficulties of ordinary Chileans; others were love songs, and some were explicitly political songs, such as "Yo Canto la Diferencia" (I Sing the Difference; 1960) and "La Carta" (The Letter; 1962).[73] In "Yo Canto la Diferencia," Parra sang of her motives for singing and her rejection of song as a commercial or frivolous undertaking:

> *I sing in the style of Chillán*
> *If I have to say something.*
> *And I don't pick up the guitar*
> *To receive applause.*
> *I sing about the difference*
> *That exists between truth and lies,*
> *Otherwise I don't sing.*[74]

Víctor Jara's "Manifiesto" (1973)—one of his best-known songs—contained echoes of this song. ("I don't sing for love of singing / Or because I have a good voice / I sing because my guitar / Has both meaning and reason. . . . My song has found a purpose / As Violeta would say / Hardworking guitar / With a smell of spring.") Jara's lyrics, like Parra's, communicated the significance of song as a source of truth and consciousness, a perspective deeply associated with *la Nueva Canción*.

Along with music and poetry, Parra produced paintings, masks, and *arpilleras* (hand-sewn textile pictures) that she had rescued from Chilean folk art tradition. Some of them were exhibited at the Louvre in 1964.

The Emergence of New Social Actors

In 1952, statistics show, more than two million Chileans—one-third of the population—had no housing or poor housing, living in shantytowns, tenements, or urban slums. Large migrations of campesinos and former miners and their families had entered the outskirts of Santiago, creating ramshackle settlements without plumbing, electricity, or sanitation services.

These marginal barrios were afflicted with periodic epidemics and inadequate nutrition. The first *toma*, or seizure of land by the *pobladores*, had occurred in 1947, when the settlement La Legua Nueva was created. In 1955, the *pobladores* joined a general strike called by CUT, as did the growing student movement. In 1957, another major land takeover took place when *pobladores* and PC organizers established the settlement La Victoria.[75] These impoverished communities, hungry and desperate for a decent life and a place to live, became increasingly important as a new, organized political actor in the 1950s.

In 1949, Margot Loyola had become head of the folklore area of the University of Chile's extension program. One group of her students, in Cuncumén, along with Millaray, formed a current of folk music that became known as *proyección folklórica* (folk projection) to show that the groups performed authentic, unembellished folk music of the rural people, unchanged, in contrast to that of the *huaso* groups. Women and men sang and danced together in Cuncumén, in contrast to earlier, all-male *huaso* groups.[76] "We were all equal," former member Silvia Urbina commented, adding that Cuncumén "was a school for future folk singers. There was a great mystique in the group; we were close friends, and we trained many other groups as well."[77] Both groups were close to the PC, although some members were of the Left but not the PC, and they traveled to the Soviet Union and other socialist countries, as well as to other Latin American countries, to participate in cultural festivals. Loyola and Violeta Parra knew each other, and Loyola was the godmother of one of Parra's daughters. Loyola was a traditionalist, presenting authentic folk songs but not composing her own music. Parra was more experimental, modern, and creative, using the instruments and rhythms of folk music as a basis for her original songs. *Proyección folklórica*, with its Chilean roots, deeply influenced the young musicians who would later create *la Nueva Canción*.

In 1957, the Christian Democrat Party (Partido Demócrata Cristiano; DC) was formed, drawing on elements of the Falangists, which had emerged in the 1930s. The DC presented itself as an alternative to both socialism and free-market capitalism, offering a socially conscious route to development through moderate structural change and a Christian orientation. It was heavily influenced by the social doctrine of the Catholic Church. While the DC was officially anticommunist, it attracted many idealistic young people inspired by the church's doctrine of social justice. Over time, several progressive factions emerged within the party that called for a "noncapitalist development path."[78] The DC grew quickly and offered a candidate, Eduardo Frei, in the 1958 presidential elections. Allende ran for president in 1958 for the second time, supported by the Popular Action Front (Frente de Acción Popular; FRAP), a new coalition of leftist parties formed in 1958. The FRAP included the PC (re-legalized in 1958 when the Ley Maldita was repealed), the PS, and the Partido Socialista Popular, as well as several other small parties.[79] The FRAP was an anti-imperialist and anti-oligarchy coalition. Its program called for the nationalization of basic resources, agrarian reform, and the redistribution of wealth to benefit the working masses, among other demands.[80] Again, Allende traveled throughout the country to speak directly with workers, peasants, women, and students. Troubled by the poverty and malnutrition he witnessed, especially affecting children, he advocated a policy of a liter of milk a day for every child.

The results of the 1958 election caused shock waves in Chile: Jorge Alessandri, a conservative independent, won, with 389,909 votes. But Allende was a close second, with 356,493.[81] It appeared that the Left—and Allende, in particular—as the second largest force in the country's politics had a real chance to win the presidency. It was this near-victory that sparked fear among Chile's elite and in Washington, DC. The CIA began to channel substantial funds to the DC as a way to prevent the future election of Allende and forestall the growing power of the Left.

The 1960s: Political Polarization

In the 1960s, Chile featured many characteristics of a dependent Latin American economy, with land concentration (in 1965, 2 percent of the large estates held 55.4 percent of the land) and copper mining concentration (three foreign companies controlled the copper industry).[82] The Alessandri government implemented an orthodox liberal economic policy based on free markets, wage ceilings, the private sector, and foreign investment. Alessandri did little to improve the welfare of the large masses of people left out of the economic model. The government faced growing opposition from newly mobilized sectors of society, which demanded more action to overcome widespread malnutrition, poor housing, illiteracy, and desperation among the popular sectors.

In 1959, the Cuban Revolution transformed the thinking of both the Left and the Right in Latin America. Suddenly, questions of land reform and social justice became urgent issues for elites who feared "another Cuba." On the Left, the successful armed revolution was an inspiration and a model for many. As a response to the Cuban Revolution, the United States proposed the Alliance for Progress, a reformist program designed to dilute the attraction of revolutionary change. As John F. Kennedy said in 1962, "Those who make peaceful revolution impossible will make violent revolution inevitable." Washington sought to prevent more Cubas by offering a reformist path to improved living conditions for the populations of Latin America, and pressured the Alessandri government to enact a limited agrarian reform law in 1962. But at the same time, the United States initiated new counterinsurgency programs for the Latin American militaries, as we have seen, that were essentially incompatible with its vision of economic progress. The elite and anticommunist sectors, empowered by strengthened anticommunist militaries, were viscerally opposed to land reform and changes in the political and economic structures that were the foundation of their wealth and power. Loveman notes that agrarian reform was "the single policy most bitterly resisted by the Chilean Right during the previous thirty years."[83] Moreover, the Latin American militaries, increasingly focused on "internal enemies," considered workers, peasants, students, and intellectuals to be actually or potentially subversive.

The 1964 elections marked a turning point in Chile. Two coalitions dominated the political system: the FRAP from the Marxist Left and the DC from the Center, displacing the Radical and Conservative parties. Both coalitions rejected neoliberal capitalism but proposed very different responses. Eduardo Frei, the DC candidate, offered a "Revolution in Liberty" to attract the newly active peasant and working-class sectors (and distinguish himself from his opponent Salvador Allende, whom he implied would be an antidemocratic communist). Frei's program, based on the Alliance for Progress, consisted of an expanded agrarian reform (which alarmed the landowners), organization of peasants and agrarian workers, and "Chilenization" (buying a majority share) of U.S.-owned copper mines. The DC endorsed the social doctrine of the Catholic Church, which decried the misery of workers and peasants but also feared and rejected communist ideas. But the church also was beginning to change during the 1960s. At the Vatican II (1962–1965) and Medellín (1968) conferences, the church adopted a "preferential option for the poor" and commitment to the oppressed, changing its long-time identification with elites and the status quo. Catholic liberation theologists wrote about the institutionalized violence created by human exploitation. There began to be a dialogue and a growing consensus between Catholic and Marxist sectors regarding social issues. A former DC student leader, Jaime Esponda, said:

> Vatican II was very important. The new concern about social problems was a huge influence on the development of the DC. In fact, the DC's rapid growth had to do with the new social concerns, coming from the renovation in the church, the change from a conservative church to a church in favor of change. . . . The church had a major influence on the agrarian reform. It began its own agrarian reform in Talca, with the Jesuits, giving away land to the peasants, and later in Santiago. . . . By the 1970s, half of the priests had moved to the *poblaciones* to make the revolution![84]

The DC also attracted support within the unions, becoming the principal competition for the PC.[85] Clotario Blest, from the Christian Left, was the first president of CUT. The church itself developed conservative and radical wings; conservatives tended to dominate the upper levels of the hierarchy.

Meanwhile, the FRAP, with its deep roots in the industrial working class, again named Allende as its presidential candidate. Explicitly Marxist, the FRAP called for radical transformation of structural ownership patterns (e.g., full nationalization of copper) and redistribution of wealth to benefit the working and peasant classes: not a reform of capitalism, but a transition to socialism. But significantly, both political forces demanded substantial change in the model of economic development for Chile. The question of which socioeconomic system would better meet Chile's needs became a central public issue.

As the election drew closer, a number of events occurred. First, by 1963, the DC became the largest party in the country. In 1964, the youth wing of the DC organized a huge march from cities throughout Chile, to converge in Santiago. Thousands of young people participated in the so-called Marcha de la Patria Joven (March of the Young Nation) and gathered for an enormous rally in favor of Frei. The DC demonstrated its ability to motivate and energize young people, as did La Jota for more radical leftist youth. The church's influence was significant within the largely Catholic population.

But there was another source of the growing organizational strength of the party. Washington, perceiving the DC as a viable alternative to communist and socialist movements, secretly funded the party as part of its anticommunist strategy. The Staff Report of the Select Committee to Study Governmental Operations with Respect to Intelligence Activities (Church Commission Report) of 1975 noted, "The CIA spent more than $2.6 million in support of the election of the Christian Democrat candidate. . . . CIA assistance enabled the CD to establish an extensive organization at the neighborhood and village level."[86] The Church Commission documented a final total of $3 million to influence the 1964 elections. In fact, Frei's campaign was financed by the CIA—which covered one-half of all of its expenses—but the candidate was not informed about the source of this funding. A number of U.S. multinational corporations with large holdings in Chile, including International Telephone and Telegraph, also offered to contribute funds to prevent Allende from being elected. Chile was selected to be the showcase of the Alliance for Progress, largely to counteract the massive support for the socialist and communist parties. More than $1 billion was directed to Chile by the Alliance for Progress between 1962 and 1969, more aid per capita than any other Latin American country received.[87]

Moreover, Washington covertly financed a "terror campaign" before the election to undercut Allende's candidacy. Right-wing Chileans enthusiastically collaborated with the terror campaign. The conservative newspaper *El Mercurio* relentlessly portrayed Allende's programs in a sinister light. There was an enormous barrage of black propaganda on radio; thousands of cartoons and press ads were published in newspapers; and numerous wall posters and murals appeared on city walls.[88] Allende was portrayed as a secret Soviet agent. The campaign instilled fear, lies, and hatred in Chilean society. Women were explicitly targeted and warned that their families would be destroyed by the communists.[89] Ángel Parra recalled that posters and murals suddenly appeared all over Santiago displaying Soviet tanks in front of La Moneda Palace.[90] Volodia Teitelboim, a communist intellectual, wrote that "the country [was] made ill by injections of deadly tons of rancor from afar."[91] Neruda wrote, "The campaign of the candidate that triumphed over Allende was carried out on the basis of unprecedented anticommunist violence, orchestrated with press notices and radio ads that attempted to terrorize the population. That propaganda made one's hair stand on end: nuns would be shot; children would die skewered by bayonets wielded by bearded men who looked like Fidel; children would be separated from their parents and sent to Siberia."[92]

On July 19, 1964, the Defense Council of the Chilean military told Alessandri that they would be willing to carry out a coup if Allende won. After the message was transmitted to the U.S. Embassy, the U.S. government strongly objected.[93] Interestingly, the U.S. decision not to support a coup at this time showed its power, as the hemispheric hegemon, to deter military action. Conversely, it underlined the importance of the U.S. role in encouraging coups (as Washington did in Chile between 1970 and 1973).

The terror campaign was not the only U.S. covert intervention in Chile in these years. In 1963, a counterinsurgency project presented as a sociological study and financed by the U.S. Army was brought to Chile by two academics deeply involved in behavioral psychology.[94] The project, called "Camelot," had been conceived by U.S. Army planners and was funded by the Special Operations Research Organization (SORO), an entity based on university campuses in the United States both to use scientific research carried out in the fields of sociology, anthropology, and psychology and to camouflage its Pentagon sponsorship. Camelot was aimed at "predicting and influencing" processes of social change and spotting signs of insipient revolution.[95] The real nature of the project was discovered when a concerned scholar, Johan Galtung, alerted colleagues in Chile. Soon an outraged Chilean Congress took up the issue. Communist Deputy Jorge Montes declared that Camelot "reveal[ed] the determination on the part of U.S. foreign policy to intervene in any country of the world where popular movements might threaten its interests."[96] The Pentagon abruptly canceled the project in Chile in 1965. But "a similar project was uncovered in Brazil less than two weeks later and others were launched in Colombia (Project Simpatico) and Peru (Operation Task), sponsored by SORO and funded by the DOD [Department of Defense]."[97] Chile and Latin America were key targets of U.S. Cold War policy.

Intensifying Mobilization and Disappointment with Frei

The 1964 elections, a two-way contest between the Left and Christian moderates in the DC, were exceptionally important historically. Unlike other elections in preceding decades, the electorate was not divided into thirds; the traditional right-wing parties had dwindled in size and influence. The Right decided to throw its support to Frei and the DC to prevent the election of Allende. Progressive artists and musicians of Chile became involved in the Allende campaign to a greater degree than ever before. Ángel and Isabel Parra returned from Europe to lend their support, followed shortly thereafter by Violeta. Many musicians, including the Parras and Víctor Jara, performed at rallies for Allende.[98] This blending of music and politics was an important impetus for the founding in 1965 of La Peña de los Parra, a cultural center and gathering place for people interested in the new, politically aware music, which rapidly became an epicenter of New Song and the Left (see Chapter 3).

Osvaldo "Gitano" Rodríguez, an important figure who would become a leading soloist of *la Nueva Canción*, explained how he, and other leftist youth of the time, embraced an early "song of commitment" that questioned the religious approach of the DC and the Catholic Church. The song, by the Argentine folk singer Atahualpa Yupanqui, was "Preguntitas sobre Dios" (Little Questions about God):

> *One day I asked*
> *Grandfather, where is God?*
> *My grandfather became sad*
> *And answered me nothing. . . .*
> *My father died in the mine*
> *Without doctor or protection*
> *The gold of the patrón*
> *Has the color of a miner's blood.*[99]

After an intense campaign, Frei won the election with 55.5 percent of the vote, as opposed to Allende's 39.5 percent. Frei's program and his promise of a "Revolution in Liberty" awakened high hopes among Chileans for improvements in their lives. The Frei government promoted an agrarian reform and unionization of peasants and the rural poor as a means of modernizing agriculture—and competing with the Left.[100] But the land reform—which Frei had stated would benefit 100,000 people—finally reached only 20,000, and only 15 percent of Chile's agricultural lands.[101] Nevertheless, landowners fiercely resisted the reform. Under the Frei government, a massacre occurred in 1969 in Puerto Montt when Carabineros attacked homeless families who had taken over land for a settlement. This event awoke public outrage and was memorialized in a song by Víctor Jara. Chilenization did not meet its stated goals, either. The government did buy 51 percent of one copper company, but the largest mines remained under U.S. corporate control.[102] There was increasing social pressure for immediate and more extensive social and economic change. The government's programs to organize marginalized popular sectors had the unexpected result of further politicizing and mobilizing them for more radical change. Even the youth of Frei's own party, the DC, were disappointed, looking toward the Cuban Revolution as a model and angered by the war in Vietnam. "We were becoming more and more radicalized," said Esponda, "and finally the rupture was inevitable. We had moved to the left, influenced by world events and by our study of Marxism, and we no longer wanted to be in a centrist party. Some 90 percent of the youth of the DC joined the Unitary Movement for Popular Action [Movimiento de Acción Popular Unitario; MAPU]."[103]

In 1965, students at the University of Concepción formed the Revolutionary Left Movement (Movimiento de Izquierda Revolucionaria; MIR), an organization greatly influenced by the Cuban Revolution, the figure of Che Guevara, and anti-imperialism. The members of MIR were dissatisfied and frustrated by the electoral strategy of the PC and the PS. They rejected the parliamentary, gradualist approach of forging class alliances with the bourgeoisie and participating in the system.[104] They believed that the recalcitrance of the oligarchies that dominated the country, and the repressive impulses of the military toward popular struggles, indicated that peaceful structural change would not be possible. They also highlighted the importance of the *pobladores*—the urban shantytown dwellers—as a major new social actor. MIR's disagreements with the PC mirrored the strategic and ideological differences between the world's communist parties close to the Soviet Union and leftist sectors who believed that the Cuban Revolution offered an alternative model to the traditional Marxist view of stages in the class struggle. Indeed, during the late 1960s there was some tension between the Cuban government and the PC of Chile regarding tactics and strategies for revolutionary change in Chile.

The MIR believed that armed struggle was inevitable and that the national bourgeoisie was not a potential ally; the institutional path was not viable, in its view. MIR believed that it was necessary to prepare for a revolutionary conflict to seize the state. At the same time, MIR rejected terrorism against civilians and worked to organize sectors of the *pobladores* and working classes. Interestingly, top leaders of MIR had extended discussions with Allende, who was always open to all parts of the Left. Andrés Pascal Allende, a leader of MIR, was Salvador Allende's nephew, and Allende's daughter Beatriz was part of the revolutionary wing of the PS and close to MIR. Miguel Enríquez, the leader of MIR, had regular political debates with Allende.[105] In 1969, as polarization in society increased, MIR formed a clandestine leadership to pursue military preparation for what it saw as the coming internal conflict. After Allende's election, MIR adopted a position of critical support for the UP government, not joining the UP coalition but also not opposing it. MIR organized and participated in land seizures with peasants and *pobladores* and wildcat strikes with workers, actions that created divisions within the Left. The PC characterized MIR as ultraleftists and adventurers whose actions and demands set back the struggle, undermined Allende and the UP government, and damaged the chance for real change in Chile. MIR considered the PC reformist and overly conciliatory toward middle-class and conservative sectors. This division within the Left had large consequences, as this book presently documents.

The University Reform

In the 1960s, the student movement also grew in strength as politicized students demanded major reform in the university. The Christian Democrat Youth (Juventud Demócrata Cristiana; JDC) and, to a lesser degree, La Jota were strong forces within the universities and secondary schools. The JDC led the Student Federation of Chile (Federación Estudiantil de Chile; FECH) until 1969. The university reform movement can be traced to the early 1960s. In 1961, a rebellion had broken out at the State Technical University (Universidad Técnica del Estado; UTE) when students and professors were not consulted about the appointment of a new director of the Mining School in Copiapó.[106] The rebellion spread to all of the university campuses of the UTE, from Antofagasta in the North to Valdivia in the South. The students demanded "their right to full and active participation in deciding the destiny of the university" and the right to elect teachers and administrators.[107] The student mobilization was successful. The appointed director of the Mining School was removed, and the students had a voice in naming the new director. Also, a commission was formed to study reform of the university, with the inclusion of students. For the next years, leadership of the student movement at the university was contested among student representatives of the Christian Democrats, FRAP, and Juventud Radical (Radical Youth).

In 1965, the Left won the university elections at UTE, and until the coup, La Jota held the presidency of the powerful student organization. Its major initiative was to launch the Universidad para Todos (University for Everyone) campaign, demanding more resources for UTE and an expansion of its enrollment.[108] University for Everyone became a national movement. Students demanded the right to higher education for the children of workers and peasants, along with new curricula that responded to the country's underdevelopment. The student leadership held workshops and seminars with students to discuss the problems of the university and the country. In 1968, an election was held for the rector of UTE using the new democratic system of 65 percent of the vote for professors, 25 percent for students, and 10 percent for administrators.[109] Enrique Kirberg, a founder of UTE, was elected rector. He was a PC member, sympathetic to the students; he later played an important role with the cultural movement of *la Nueva Canción.*

At the Catholic University in Valparaíso, the reform erupted in 1966 when students—most of them from conservative DC families—protested against conservative church authorities and, more important, called for a university committed to social change.[110] The movement spread to the Catholic University in Santiago—the most elitist in the country—and in 1967, a progressive rector, Fernando Castillo, was elected.[111] Students had 20 percent of the vote allotted to them at the Catholic University as a result of the reform movement. In 1968, the Music Conservatory of the University of Chile opened to everyone, and many working-class students entered. The conservatory had been very elitist previously.[112] Many of the young musicians of the emerging New Song movement were university students who were deeply involved in the student mobilizations. After Ángel and Isabel Parra created the first *peña* in 1965, students created others on university campuses throughout the country. The young musicians played their songs at all student events and demonstrations. "In spite of the difficulties, it was a glorious time to live, to be young," said Jaime Esponda. "Chile was a celebration for young people in those years—even though later I was taken prisoner—and the music was a central part of that celebration."[113] The struggle to reform the university caused deep changes in Chile, democratizing education and generating the participation of thousands of students in decision making in their institutions. Young people had become significant political actors.

The dramatic international events of the 1960s shaped the political context, as well, intensifying the radicalization of Chilean society. In 1965, the United States intervened in the Dominican Republic. In 1967, Che Guevara was captured and killed in Bolivia. The MIR organization at the University of Chile, Valparaíso, called for revolution after Che's death.[114] On the Right, with the disappearance of the Conservative Party, right-wing individuals formed the National Party in 1966. The National Party wanted to end all state involvement in social and economic areas and reestablish a free-market model. It harbored authoritarian sectors with close ties to the military and represented the traditional, powerful oligarchies of Chile. It became a driving force behind the coup of 1973.

Disillusionment was growing with the Frei government. Sectors within the DC began to diverge amid internal conflicts. Jacques Chonchol, Rodrigo Ambrosio, and many other leaders left the party in 1969, denouncing the betrayal of Frei's Revolution in Liberty, to form the leftist social Christian organization MAPU, which for the first time united Marxists, Christians, and Social Democrats.[115] This split had significant electoral consequences: MAPU joined the Unidad Popular, thus helping to elect Allende in 1970. Another group within the DC was led by Radomiro Tomic, a progressive social Christian who also ran for president in 1970. His program was very similar to Allende's—calling for full nationalization of copper, for example. When he came in third in the elections, he called on his allies to shift their support to Allende, a crucial step.

In sum, Chilean society experienced a tumultuous, radically democratic period in the 1960s as new social actors found their political voices. For the first time, there was mass participation in politics, not only through voting but also in grassroots organizations, assisted by both the DC government and parties of the Left. The Right found itself faced with a counterhegemonic popular movement that was poised to elect a government that would favor its interests and challenge those of the wealthy and powerful. Large sectors of society held high expectations for profound structural change. New opportunities were arising for masses of people who had been excluded from the political system and who endured harsh conditions. Mass movements challenged rigid class barriers and began to overcome them. The social movements and opposition parties converged to demand a new, more just socioeconomic and political system that would serve the interests of all sectors of society. *La Nueva Canción* was born, and was an organic component, of this counterhegemonic movement.

3

The Emergence of
la Nueva Canción Chilena

Patricia Díaz has noted that *la Nueva Canción* can be divided into three distinct phases.[1] The first was from the mid-1960s to 1970, when the movement emerged from the grassroots, grew rapidly, and in 1969 became closely linked to the campaign to elect Salvador Allende. The second was during the government of Unidad Popular (UP), when the music became identified with the government. And the third was after 1973, when the music was repressed in Chile, but musicians in exile continued to develop it and helped to build an international solidarity movement.[2]

La Nueva Canción emerged in the midst of social and political ferment and as part of the democratization movement "from below" in the 1960s in Chile, as we have seen. It provided musical documentation of the aspirations and experiences of the era and gave voice to the counterhegemonic movement that was growing in strength. Young people, politicized and militant after a decade of social movements and struggles to make Chilean politics more inclusive, rebelled against the domination of music from the North and its inherent messages and sought to recover authentic Latin American music and art. Indeed, Eric Zolov has shown that the U.S. Information Agency directly sponsored rock-and-roll in Soviet bloc countries and elsewhere as part of a pro–United States strategy, stating that "music will often make friends, open doors, influence opinion."[3] In the increasingly politicized climate of Chile, many felt that Latin America's cultural identity was being lost. Jorge Coulon, a founder of Inti-Illimani, explained the widespread view of Chile's young leftists at the time:

The situation in Chile was, from my point of view, a very, very depressed cultural situation. We were a colony of the record companies based in Mexico and in the United States. We did not have Chilean music on the radio at that time or in the media. We discovered, at that time, the work of people like Violeta Parra, Víctor Jara, and many others who were for many years working with popular music in Chile in the complete underground. Violeta Parra, at that time, invited to Chile some musicians from different parts of Latin America. For us it was a revelation to discover the music from the Andes, from Bolivia, to discover music from Venezuela, and also, at the time, there was a big movement of popular music in Argentina. We began to play music with these roots and it was an explosion. The audience was ready for that. This is the origin of the group. We began to learn to play instruments like *quena*, panpipes, and the *charango*. We discovered in Colombia the *tiple*, which is a smaller steel stringed guitar. We began to blend all these sounds. The response of the public, among the university students and among the musical underground in Chile, was enormous.[4]

Víctor Jara, among other musicians, rejected the original characterization of the movement as "protest song" as narrow and dismissive. Much of the new music portrayed the lives of the people, their trials and joys, their resistance to social injustice, their tragedies and aspirations. "For our people it is clear that *la Nueva Canción chilena* is committed to the history, the combat, the life of the workers and the youth," he said. "They know that it is a song of solidarity with our continent and with all the peoples that struggle to be the owners of their own destiny."[5] He explained the rise of *la Nueva Canción* this way: "In Latin America young people began to mobilize due to the social reality of their own countries. They began to rebel, to unite themselves with the workers—of the countryside, of the city—to manifest this rebellion together with the workers in a type of protest against the system, what we can say concretely is an imperialist system, which directs our wealth and resources and, essentially, our lives. Thus, in our continent a type of rebellious song was born."[6]

This chapter presents a brief chronology of the music of the 1950s and 1960s in Chile, from *la Nueva Ola* (New Wave) to *Neofolklore* and *la Nueva Canción*. In Chapter 4, I examine the New Song movement during the UP government. Quite rapidly in the 1960s, the New Song movement became a powerful political force, the cultural expression of the flourishing Left and the hopes of hundreds of thousands of people. "Song reaches into the soul of the people, even though it isn't on television or radio," noted Horacio Durán of Inti-Illimani Histórico. "It is carried there because song contains a seed that represents a great number of people who identify with it. This is what *la Nueva Canción* did."[7] In 1969, the musicians of *la Nueva Canción*, along with the muralists of the Ramona Parra Brigade, dancers and theater directors, and visual artists, enthusiastically joined the movement to elect Salvador Allende and were a crucial component of his presidential campaign, bringing through art and music his message of social change to the far corners of Chile.

La Nueva Ola and Neofolklore

In the 1950s, Mexican boleros, Argentine tangos, orchestra music, and, increasingly, English-language rock-and-roll filled Chile's radio waves. For politicized youth in the 1960s, the flood of foreign music was "cultural imperialism," especially driven by the United States. "Rock was seen like Coca-Cola, part of the imperialist invasion," said the musicologist Rodrigo Torres.[8] The Chilean music on the radio was "typical" or "*huaso*" folk, as we have seen, which presented a particular, narrow picture of Chilean identity. Patricio Manns—soon to become a fundamental figure in *la Nueva Canción*—explained:

> When Los Huasos de Chincolco, a vocal and instrumental group, initiated its radio activity, very few people realized then—no one, to be exact—that what was coming from the radio was not the voice of the peasant, as we were told, but the voices and the guitars of the landowners. . . . Song, from this perspective, is completing a demobilizing role[;] it can be conceived as a balm that will obscure, if not cure, the social wounds. . . . It functions to provide a paternal and kind image of the landowner, which perpetuates the tradition of the "servant families" that are born, live, and die on the patriarchal haciendas. . . . Not only does this disarm the campesinos ideologically to inconceivable levels, but even today such songs are sung in all the celebrations, urban or rural, and are practiced by choruses in schools.[9]

Interestingly, Manns was echoing Gramsci's analysis of the political-ideological impact of elite culture as a means of social control.

In 1958, a new musical current emerged in Chile, *la Nueva Ola*—that is, rock-and-roll and pop music sung by Chileans, first in English, then, increasingly in Spanish. *La Nueva Ola* essentially replicated the new styles from the United States and Europe but "Chilenized" them. RCA and other record companies saw a commercial opportunity in the popularity of Elvis Presley and other rock-and-roll singers and contracted young Chileans who sang the popular songs. Often the Chilean singers gave themselves English names (for example, Peter Rock, Danny Chilean, Los Carr Twins, Los Macs, Los Blue

Splendor). A record producer named Camilo Fernández played a key role in promoting *la Nueva Ola*.[10] He recognized talent and saw that the rise of the youth culture had commercial potential. Later, ironically—as he was anti-Allende—he played an important role in promoting *la Nueva Canción*. *La Nueva Ola* soon swept Chilean society, and in the 1960s young people began to buy records and new music magazines. The music industry was becoming globalized, a youth culture was emerging, and radio was increasingly important in Chile. New radio shows played Chilean versions of hits by the Beatles and other rock-and-roll groups. Chilean singers such as José Alfredo "El Pollo" Fuentes became teen idols. But the music was also criticized for its commercialism and for imitating "Anglo-Saxon" rock-and-roll.[11]

In the early 1960s, there were few openings on the radio for *proyección folklórica*, the authentic Chilean folk music that had been passed down for generations in the countryside and sung at festivals, weddings, and wakes. This music was being collected from villages and remote areas by Margot Loyola, Violeta Parra, Gabriela Pizarro, and Héctor Pavez, among others. A group of Loyola's students in Cuncumén performed Chilean folklore of the central valley without flourishes or modern touches, as we have seen. Mariela Ferreira of Cuncumén noted that radio personality Ricardo García—who had invited Violeta Parra to host her own show in the 1950s—also played a key role in providing airtime for Cuncumén to sing on his show. In the early 1960s, radio shows were open to the public. People would attend on Sundays to listen to the music live. "This was important for authentic folk music, the kind we sang, because most radio and television were not interested in our music," Ferreira explained.[12] Millaray, directed by Gabriela Pizarro, also performed on García's show.

An important cultural moment came when the rock group Los Ramblers sang—in Spanish—the theme song for the 1962 World Cup soccer game, held in Chile that year. It was a classic Elvis-style rock-and-roll song—the title was "El Rock del Mundial" (World Cup Rock)—but the fact that it was in Spanish was new and exciting, inspiring pride among Chileans after years of hearing English lyrics in *la Nueva Ola*. "That was very important in the musical history of Chile," commented José Seves. "The song reflected the spirit and identity of Chile."[13] After 1962, *Nueva Ola* singers began to sing in Spanish more frequently.[14]

During the early 1960s another genre of music appeared, called *Neofolklore* (a contradiction in terms, as many Chileans have pointed out). This music departed from that of the *huasos* and the *patrones*. The influence of Violeta Parra, Patricio Manns, and Rolando Alarcón was noticeable. There was also a strong influence from Argentina, where a "boom" in folk music was taking place. In 1949, as part of a nationalist project, Juan Perón's government had mandated that 50 percent of the music in concerts and on the radio had to be Argentine. The proportion was increased to 70 percent in 1971, with an equal division among modern, folk, and urban music.[15] The policy stimulated a revival of folk music in Argentina that also had ramifications in Chile. The Argentine Atahualpa Yupanqui, beginning in the early 1950s, had written political and socially conscious songs that were eagerly embraced by politicized young Chileans, and the *Nuevo Cancionero* movement appeared in 1963 in Argentina.[16] In the early 1960s, Argentine groups such as Los Chalchaleros, Los Fronterizos, and Los Trovadores, with new harmonies and modern styles, became popular and influential in both countries.[17] The music of Los Fronterizos had some Andean elements, as did the songs of another popular singer, Raúl Shaw Moreno, a Bolivian whose career began in the early 1950s and who was known in Chile; these were other early influences on the emerging generation of New Song musicians.[18]

Neofolklore was important because it attracted popular interest and opened new spaces in the mass media for a different kind of folk-based music. Two important *Neofolklore* groups were Los Cuatro Cuartos (elegant young men dressed in smoking jackets, with a style influenced by Argentine groups such as Los Trovadores and Los Huanca Huá) and Las Cuatro Brujas (young women in jewels and fancy dresses), a female version of Los Cuatro Cuartos. Both groups sang songs by Parra, Manns, and Alarcón in the early 1960s, as well as "modernized" versions of folk-based songs. The songs of Chilean *Neofolklore* portrayed conditions in the countryside more realistically, although the music did not make pointed political commentary. "*Neofolklore* was more 'lite' [than *la Nueva Canción*]," Seves observed.[19] The groups added stylized flourishes and modern vocalizations. (Los Cuatro Cuartos typically included a chorus singing "bum bum bum" in their songs.) With their pleasant voices, usually accompanied by one guitar, and their evoking of Chilean folk music, these groups achieved commercial success.

Patricio Manns was a journalist in the early 1960s. In fact, he accompanied Allende as a journalist during his campaign for the 1964 election.[20] His song "El Bandido," among others, was adapted and sung by Los Cuatro Cuartos. The singer-songwriter Rolando Alarcón composed songs for the two groups, as well. Because these key figures of *la Nueva Canción* were thus involved with *Neofolklore* in the early and mid-1960s, some analysts described New Song as emerging from *Neofolklore*. Others disagreed. The debate is interesting and important because the different currents of music reflected different political orientations and values, marking the more defined political positions emerging in Chile. While *Nueva Ola* was very popular among young Chileans, it generated criticism from the social movements and politicized youth as representing an imitation of rock from the North and an example of cultural imperialism. *Neofolklore* was a commercialized and stylized version of folk music, especially compared with *proyección folklórica*. *La Nueva Canción*, which was beginning to emerge in 1965, reflected a deeper social and political consciousness: it was committed as well as beautiful music.

The Relationship between
Neofolklore and *la Nueva Canción*

Two songs from 1965—Alarcón's "Si Somos Americanos" (If We Are Americans), which expressed pan-Americanism and solidarity among the countries and foundational races of Latin America, African, indigenous, and European; and Manns's "Arriba en la Cordillera" (High in the Mountain Range), the story of an impoverished family and a father who was shot for stealing cattle—came before *la Nueva Canción* was clearly defined and in the context of *Neofolklore*. But today both songs are seen as early classics of New Song. Indeed, the radio personality Miguel Davagnino characterized "Arriba" as the song that marked the beginning of *la Nueva Canción*.[21] These were not "protest songs" but songs that told of the humble people of Latin America and communicated a vision of unity and solidarity.

The music journalist Manuel Vilches has posited that one cannot understand *la Nueva Canción* without *Neofolklore*.[22] Vilches considered Manns and Alarcón as *Neofolklore* artists who moved into *la Nueva Canción* later: "*Neofolklore* prepared the terrain for New Song, much like Frei did for Allende."[23] Similarly, the musicologist Alfonso Padilla noted that soloists such as Manns and Alarcón sang at the same concerts as *Neofolklore* groups between 1963 and 1966 or so, and provided songs to those groups, before they moved into *la Nueva Canción*. He, among others, observed that the clear division between the two musical currents did not appear until the late 1960s, when political discrepancies widened, especially during the Allende campaign in 1969. *Neofolklore* musicians were more conservative and diverged from the increasing radicalization and political lyrics of *la Nueva Canción*.[24] Torres pointed out that in the mid-1960s, the artists were known for their work; the various currents of music were unnamed as yet. In 1969, this changed when Ricardo García organized the First Festival of New Song with the Catholic University and defined the name and the concept of the new politically conscious music.[25]

Others disagreed with the thesis that *la Nueva Canción* emerged from *Neofolklore*. Mariela Ferreira of Cuncumén noted that while the musicians of *Neofolklore* sang songs by Manns, Alarcón, and Parra, that did not mean that these composers were part of *Neofolklore*.[26] "There is a huge difference between the type of music performed by Los Cuatro Cuartos and *la Nueva Canción,*" she observed. Ferreira thought that *Neofolklore* artists such as Los Cuatro Cuartos and Las Cuatro Brujas did not capture the richness of traditional Chilean folk music and that some of the flourishes and stylizations they added to their songs actually impoverished the quality of the music. "I worked for many years, every summer, in the countryside and in *las poblaciones*, collecting songs," Ferreira explained. "It was incredible to see how these women—who could not read or write—would compose beautiful lyrics, songs for various occasions: the death of a child, a birthday, a wedding. These campesinas would pick up a guitar and play the most original, exquisite songs. I have profound respect for these women. For me, *Neofolklore* embellished and commercialized our traditional music in ways that diminished it."

José Seves posited that *Neofolklore* and *la Nueva Canción* arose more or less simultaneously. He did not see Manns and Alarcón as part of *Neofolklore* or agree that *la Nueva Canción* was born from it. Rather, Seves saw the two musical currents as arising in parallel, with some overlap between them.[27] Max Berrú believed that the root of *la Nueva Canción* was the authentic folk music of Chile and Latin America rather than *Neofolklore*.[28] Horacio Salinas also believed that the two currents of music arose together. "*Neofolklore* appeared a little earlier," he said:

> *Neofolklore* was influenced by Argentine groups such as los Trovadores del Norte, los Huanca Huá, who used a lot of technical devices such as singing "bum bum bum" in the background. . . . Los Cuatro Cuartos imitated that style. . . . There was a common root for both *Neofolklore* and *la Nueva Canción*: Argentine music, the groups of six or seven, instruments such as the *bombo*, guitars. . . . But in terms of content, it was ridiculous to us to sing "bum bum" like that; it was frivolous. . . . We wanted to find profound poetry, say transcendental things, and, above all, speak about reality, as Violeta did. . . . *La Nueva Canción* wasn't born from *Neofolklore*.[29]

Roberto Márquez of Illapu made a useful distinction: "*La Nueva Canción* was already germinating during the 1964 election. The Parras, Manns, Alarcón, and others were already part of the social movement. . . . *Neofolklore* was 'uncommitted' folk, music without political commitment. There began to be a separation between socially conscious folk-based music and apolitical folk music. *La Nueva Canción* sang of political realities and sought a different future. This divided *la Nueva Canción* from *Neofolklore*."[30] Indeed, Patricio Manns considered himself not part of *Neofolklore* but, rather, a founding figure of *la Nueva Canción*.[31] The interesting analytical point is that each current of music became identified with specific political tendencies.

The socially and politically conscious current of music was baptized *la Nueva Canción* at the First Festival of New Song in 1969, organized by García and the Catholic University, but interestingly, not only New Song singer-songwriters participated. Los de Ramón and others from diverse political backgrounds and styles were there, and honors were offered to Los Huasos Quincheros. Quilapayún was not invited (but Víctor Jara invited the group to come and sing with him). The point is that the musical currents were not as clear at the time as they are in retrospect. In 1966, the director of Los Cuatro Cuartos dissolved that group after one of its members died in an auto accident. Las Cuatro Brujas also dissolved, as did most of the other groups of *Neofolklore*. By the late 1960s, *Neofolklore*, as well as *la Nueva Ola*, had passed from the scene.[32]

Rolando Alarcón had directed Cuncumén for years, where he worked with Víctor Jara, Silvia Urbina, Mariela Ferreira, and others to present traditional Chilean folk song and dance. He left Cuncumén in 1963 and concentrated on his singing career. Alarcón's songs became more political in the mid-1960s, such as "Se Olvidaron de la Patria" (They Forgot the Nation), which refers to the security forces that massacred striking miners at the Salvador mine in 1966. Some of these songs were shunned by commercial radio, and Alarcón eventually had to leave his label, RCA Victor.[33] Alarcón recorded songs from the Spanish Civil War, songs dedicated to the Soviet Union, and pacifist songs. His song "¿Adónde Vas, Soldado?" (Where Are You Going, Soldier?; 1964), a *refalosa*—a traditional musical and dance style of Chile's countryside—caused an unexpected polemic known as the "battle of the *refalosas*." The song, which was recorded by Las Cuatro Brujas, lamented the role of the army in society: "Where are you going, soldier? / Where are you going? / To a war without quarter? / Return and fight for peace." Joaquín Alberto Prieto, a major in the army, who found the song offensive, composed a song in response and sent it to a record producer, Julio Gutiérrez. "La Respuesta del Soldado" (The Soldier's Response), released by Gutiérrez and sung by Los de Santiago, was very similar to Alarcón's: "Where am I going, you ask? / Where do I go? / To defend my homeland / Because I am a soldier." Alarcón responded with another song, "Oiga Usted, General" (Listen, General), which was recorded by Isabel and Ángel Parra and in which Isabel Parra reproaches the general for the death of her son in battle after she had raised him to believe in peace.[34] The battle of the *refalosas* captured the imagination of an increasingly politicized public.

Rightist critics interpreted Alarcón's song to be antimilitary, an affront to the army and the homeland. Two radio channels banned the song in a Cold War climate that was becoming more polarized in Latin America and the world. The song presaged *la Nueva Canción*. Alarcón commented, "I felt very surprised. . . . My *refalosa* was simply a pacifist song and not against the army. If it speaks of war, it doesn't refer to Chile, because we don't have a war here; it has a more universal sense. . . . I am, yes, against warrior armies, like those we see in Vietnam, against the black community in the United States and in Africa. With my *refalosa* I was calling to all of the armies of the world to convert themselves into armies of peace."[35] The battle of the *refalosas* was a fascinating moment in Chileans' cultural history. An incipient dispute between antiwar progressives and conservative military officers increasingly imbued with national security doctrine was being expressed through music, demonstrating the inherent political power of song. In effect, the songs captured a struggle between the hegemonic worldview of the conservative sectors and the counterhegemonic challenge, manifested in musical language.

La Nueva Canción Takes Shape

In the 1960s, classically trained composers from the academic world were also creating works that were new in Chile's cultural history. Fernando García, the classical composer, worked with Pablo Neruda in 1962 to produce "América Insurrecta" (America Rebelling), a piece for orchestra taken from *Canto General*. It was dedicated to the Communist Party (Partido Comunista; PC). This work, among others, reflected solidarity with the oppressed and the developing pan-American spirit, in opposition to the encroaching hegemony of the United States.[36] García, like other classical composers, was inspired by the new social movements and by the possibility of linking his art to the people of Chile in ways that were non-elitist and popular, essentially bridging class barriers and moving beyond the confines of the music conservatories. Sergio Ortega, another classically trained musician, composed an enormous range of works that extended from classical compositions and music for films to *canciones contingentes* (contingent songs or pamphlet songs) for the struggle.[37] He worked with Neruda to produce a *cantata* from Neruda's poem about Joaquín Murieta, a legendary Chilean Robin Hood-style outlaw, in the 1960s. He later worked closely with musicians of *la Nueva Canción* and composed anthems for the Central Única de Trabajadores de Chile (CUT), the Radical Party, and La Jota, and songs for artists of *la Nueva Canción*. Ortega, with Quilapayún, wrote "El Pueblo Unido Jamás Será Vencido" (The People United Will Never Be Defeated), one of the most beloved "hymns" of the Unidad Popular, among many others. Ortega and Advis in particular were important collaborators with two emblematic groups of *la Nueva Canción*, Quilapayún and Inti-Illimani.

In the mid-1960s a new flowering of popular and politically aware works began to appear. Ángel Parra wrote and recorded the album *Oratorio para el Pueblo* (Oratory for the People) in 1965, and Patricio Manns composed and performed *El Sueño Americano* (The American Dream) the same year. They were followed by works that fused classical elements with *la Nueva Canción* in politically conscious *cantatas*, including *Cantata Santa María de Iquique*, by Luis Advis (recorded by Quilapayún, 1970); *Canto al Programa* (Song to the Program), by Sergio Ortega, Advis, and Julio Rojas (Inti-Illimani, 1970); *Canto para una Semilla* (Song for a Seed), by Advis (Inti-Illimani and Isabel Parra, 1972); and *La Fragua* (The Forge), by Ortega (Quilapayún, 1972), among others. Another important work, Víctor Jara's *La Población* (The Shantytown; 1972), was not a *cantata* or classically influenced, but it was a path-breaking contribution, with a set of songs that told the story of the struggles of a *población*. All of these works were a new development in Chile; they were complete and unified, featuring a set of linked songs with an epic vision and profound social and political content. Moreover, through the *cantatas* "concert music, historically linked to elites, began to reach masses of people; and the people were the protagonists of works that before had been totally inaccessible to them."[38] Ángel Parra and Patricio Manns had launched this trend with their earlier works.

Ángel Parra's *Oratorio* was a reaction to contemporary pieces created by various Catholic musicians, such as Raúl de Ramón's *Misa Chilena* (Chilean Mass; 1965), with orthodox religious themes. The first song on *Oratorio*, "I, Sinner," called for justice on earth. "It was the product of a personal necessity, of someone searching for answers that the official Church did not give—or if it did, it was in Latin," Parra quipped.

> It was another means of making a claim against a conservative Church, and political in this sense. This was during an important moment for groups of Christians in favor of socialism. It was played during the *toma* (takeover or occupation) of the cathedral in Santiago [in 1968]; then there was the division in the DC [Christian Democrat Party] and the appearance of MAPU [Unitary Movement for Popular Action]. *Oratorio* was an instrument to accompany the social movement. . . . It had nothing to do with the commercial folkloric masses that were in style at the time, which respected liturgy and therefore clerical language in harmony with the ecclesiastical power. That wasn't my case.[39]

All of the compositions on *Oratorio* were Parra's, in contrast to his first studio album. The record melded rich, opera-like background vocals and indigenous instruments with lyrics that appealed for social justice.

Manns composed *El Sueño Americano* after the U.S. intervention in the Dominican Republic in 1965, an event that outraged many Latin Americans.[40] Manns, thinking of Neruda's *Canto General*, decided to compose a similar work in musical form. The musician "Gitano" Rodríguez characterized *El*

Sueño Americano as the first Chilean attempt "to create pan-American unity through music. It dealt with nothing less than the complete history of Latin America, from the epoch before Columbus to the struggles of our time, covering the key events of colonization, independence, slavery, and imperialism."[41] Manns recorded the work with harmonies by Voces Andinas, previewing sounds soon to be identified with *la Nueva Canción*. RCA delayed producing the record for some time, and after it was finally released, radio stations refused to play it.[42] The album was hauntingly beautiful, however, and went on to become very popular with the Chilean public.

Manns's song "Arriba en la Cordillera," written before *Sueño*, was hugely popular in 1965. Since Manns had written songs before for Los Cuatro Cuartos, the group wanted to record "Arriba," but Manns decided to record it himself, with Los Cuatro Cuartos singing backup. Manns recounted that at the time he wrote "Arriba," he had only six original songs, which he played repeatedly. He had been approached by the producer Camilo Fernández, who asked him to record on his label but hesitated when he learned that Manns had written only six songs. Manns promised Fernández a song by the next day. Working through the night, he produced "Arriba." Fernández was thrilled with the song and recorded it the same day. He passed the record to Ricardo García, who began playing it frequently on Radio Minería.[43] The song made Manns nationally famous. The story told in the song had a tremendous impact on the public: it was poignant and socially conscious, a Chilean tale of tragedy. "What 'El Bandido' did, and then 'Arriba' did, was put the outlaw at the center of the drama," Horacio Durán noted. "'Arriba' is also a song about a rustler with a tragic history. The song ends with his killing; they take this cattle rustler prisoner and kill him. His son tells the story. . . . Patricio Manns takes the bandit, the rustler, this person from the real popular classes, with his drama and his identity, and makes him universal."[44] Manns's lyrical album *Entre Mar y Cordillera* (Between Sea and Mountain Range; 1966) also became enormously popular.

Víctor Jara, another fundamental figure in *la Nueva Canción*, was a man from a humble campesino family. After the death of his father, the family moved to Santiago and struggled to survive. After his mother's death, Jara thought about becoming a priest and entered the seminary for a time, but decided not to follow that path. He also performed military service. He met Violeta Parra in 1957 and joined La Jota around the same time.[45] He also began to study theater, sing in the chorus at the University of Chile, and perform with Cuncumén as a dancer and singer. Mariela Ferreira of Cuncumén remembered what she believed was the first time Jara sang solo:

> We were on a long tour of European countries, and one night we were performing in Moscow. Silvia Urbina had problems with her

vocal cords and Rolando [Alarcón] said to Víctor, "You need to sing." Víctor was so shy; he was anxious and resistant. Finally he was persuaded to sing a traditional *tonada* that he had collected in the countryside. After he sang, it was so impressive—the applause didn't stop. People in the audience in that huge hall wanted more, even though they didn't understand the words. He sang [the *tonada*] again, and people demanded more. That night, he sang the song three times. Then in Leningrad, the same thing happened. That time, people threw flowers onto the stage. I think it made an enormous impact on Víctor. He discovered that he had a gift for reaching people with his music, his voice. He was studying theater at the time in Chile. He would dress as a campesino to sing—so shy, really lovely. . . . I think he realized the power he had to reach huge publics, not only with his music but with his presence. He had the power to enchant people.[46]

In 1966, Jara released his first studio album, *Geografía*, with RCA/Demon. One of his singles, "La Beata" (The Blessed), also released in 1966, caused an unexpected scandal. The song was traditional and popular and gently mocked a religious woman enamored of her priest. Despite the song's origins in the Chilean countryside, it outraged the Catholic Church, and the Frei government requested its removal from record stores and the destruction of the master tape. Church figures criticized Jara directly.[47] It was another case of the censorship—and the power of hegemonic institutions—confining the musicians during these years.

After completing his theater studies, Jara became a well-known theater director, working at the University of Chile to produce avant-garde plays (including Pablo Neruda's only play). He began working with Quilapayún in 1966 and became the group's musical director, mentoring the young musicians. By 1969, he had come to the decision to leave the university to dedicate himself to his singing, guitar playing, and composing. Jara discussed his motivations and the origins of the New Song movement:

> What is *la Nueva Canción*? A record by Violeta Parra appeared with songs where she speaks of the truth—the authentic, the real—of Chile. This made a huge impact in Chile. Forty years of her existence were spent collecting traditional music, singing songs of the people from all over Chile, passed down through generations. And a group of us, composers, felt this was the path we wanted to take, that we had to take in our country. We thought, enough of foreign music, of music that doesn't help us to live, that tells us nothing. . . . We began to create these types of songs, just in the moment when the workers in Chile began to unite in what would become the Unidad Popular.

. . . It was song that was born from the necessities of the country, the social movement of Chile. It wasn't song apart from that. Violeta marked the path, and we have followed. Now *la Nueva Canción* is essentially the language of the people, of the youth.[48]

Like the other composers of *la Nueva Canción*, Jara was supremely creative. His compositions drew from folk rhythms of Chile, Cuba, Colombia, and other countries, and his lyrics often used the vernacular of the countryside. His songs, like those of Violeta Parra, incorporated the miners of the nitrate mines of the North, the urban shantytown dwellers, and the peasants and the Mapuche of the South, along with the indigenous instruments of the northern *altiplano* and the rhythms of Chiloé. The music represented the whole country and encompassed social sectors that had been ignored and excluded from the "official" Chilean identity expressed in "typical folklore."[49] Jara's music, and *la Nueva Canción* in general, played a crucial role in restructuring this elitist view of Chilean identity and building a new, inclusive vision that valorized Chile's cultural diversity. Jara sang of love and of the lives of the popular classes with passionate political conviction.

Jara based his guitar playing on a campesino style but added new elements.[50] Musically, his songs, like those of the other composers of *la Nueva Canción*, transcended traditional folk music, taking it in original, experimental directions. As Rodrigo Torres notes, the New Song movement reshaped and renovated traditional Chilean folk, creating a major and revolutionary new genre.[51] "We believed that music from everywhere in Latin America belonged to us," Horacio Salinas explained. "We took rhythms, elements, and instruments from all over the region. It was not simply reproduction of folk music; we invented new music in *la Nueva Canción*. Violeta [Parra] was the first to do it. . . . We took the roots of folk without imitating that music but, instead, created new forms of music, building from authentic folklore."[52]

Personally, Jara was generous, respectful, and collaborative with other musicians. He organized sessions in which they would collaborate and experiment together.[53] "His decided stimulus and enthusiasm transmitted to us the possibility of growing more and more with folklore elements," José Seves wrote about Jara's visits to Inti-Illimani's rehearsals. "We discovered through this path new traditional instruments, unknown musical tones, and combinations of sounds that were shaping a distinct musical result and finally, an orchestra of Latin American sound."[54]

Isabel Parra deserves mention as one of the few women of *la Nueva Canción*. She had sung with her mother and with her brother Ángel since childhood. She also sang solo and in duos with others, such as Patricio Castillo, a former member of Quilapayún, and played a key role in introducing Cuban music to Chileans. She composed more than one hundred songs, including "Lo Que Más Quiero" (What I Love Most; with lyrics by Violeta Parra), which became immensely popular when Inti-Illimani recorded it. Her sensitive voice and authoritative presence created a large following.

In addition to Ricardo García, there were other important figures in the commercial music business at the time who opened many doors for the artists. René Largo Farías was a radio show producer and music promoter who played a key role in diffusing folklore and *la Nueva Canción*. In 1965, he opened the *peña* Chile Ríe y Canta and invited key musicians of *la Nueva Canción* to play there. In fact, he was the first to present Patricio Manns and Ángel Parra, the Uruguayan singer Daniel Viglietti, the Argentine Mercedes Sosa, and various Cuban artists.[55] Largo Farías also organized musical tours to the far corners of Chile. He and other key music promoters, including Rubén Nouzeilles (an Argentine and the artistic director at Odeon, who had taken an early interest in the work of Violeta Parra) and Camilo Fernández, were crucially important. It was through their efforts that the young musicians could be heard when much of the music industry was closed to them. Because commercial venues were not very accessible to the emerging New Song movement, Ángel and Isabel Parra and others decided to open La Peña de los Parra, a decision that changed the course of Chilean cultural history.

La Peña de los Parra

In 1965, Ángel and Isabel Parra opened their house at Carmen 340 in central Santiago as a musical salon where the new political songs could be heard. They were joined by Patricio Manns and Rolando Alarcón, and soon afterward by Víctor Jara. The old, traditional house rapidly became a cultural and political meeting place for people fascinated by *la Nueva Canción*. "In 1965, La Peña de los Parra opened, and it created a cultural explosion," said José Seves. "It caused a huge reaction and immediately began to be replicated in various parts of the country. The university students set them up on each campus—university *peñas*."[56] Soon unions, municipalities, factories, and other organizations began to establish their own *peñas* and invite the musicians. The *peñas* became a primary venue for New Song during this period, a network of popular institutions parallel to commercial theaters and radio stations, which were not hospitable to "committed" songs and generally did not invite the musicians to their shows. The *peñas* were special locales with a feeling of intimacy and comradeship between the musicians and the public.

La Peña de los Parra provided a place where the musicians, many of whom had worked for Allende's campaign, could come together, develop their art, and collaborate with a community of politically conscious people. It became a magnet for intellectuals, students, musicians, community residents, and artists. As Ángel Parra explained:

We created La Peña soon after the 1964 elections. There was great effervescence in Chile, excitement about Allende's candidacy. . . . We had classes in music, instruments, political education. . . . The place became the center of *la Nueva Canción*. Of course, all this was born in the 1920s, with Recabarren and other PC leaders creating theater, writers, and others. We were part of this great historical movement. *La Nueva Canción* responded to a big gap: only commercial music and the *huasos* were played in the media. . . . We wanted to create a new space in Santiago. There were all kinds of people there—middle class, yes—but our movement also began to sing for unionists and students. This place allowed us to make a living. People paid a little to come and hear the music. . . . During the forty-five-minute break, people would go into the garden for political discussions, to find out what was happening in other parts of the country. Sometimes foreigners knew more than we did.[57]

Upon entering La Peña, one received a glass of hot wine and an empanada. The small tables and chairs were rather uncomfortable, and the place was very informal and casual. Records by the new artists were available for sale, and locally made handicrafts were on display.[58] La Peña was open on Thursday, Friday, and Saturday nights, and often a long line of people waited to get in. The candlelit rooms focused the concentrated attention of the audience on the musicians. It was not a formal restaurant or a place to chat with friends; it was a place to listen to music. Max Berrú described his first visit to La Peña and the first time he saw Víctor Jara sing:

When I went for the first time to the Peña de los Parra in winter, I think it was 1965, it was full of people, Full! And full of smoke, too. I thought I'd be standing in the back, but there was a reserved seat open in the middle, and someone called to me to come over, saying someone hadn't come. So I sat down in the middle on a wooden chair at a wooden table, like a work table, with burn marks, and I received a glass of hot wine and an empanada. Then Los Curacas arrived, the group that opened the show at the Peña. They played Andean music, four or five young guys, nice music. Then out came Ángel Parra, who sang with his sister, and finally they announced Víctor Jara. I watched a guy come out, very imposing, with his guitar in his hand; with a strong walk; wearing black leather boots, striped dark-and-light-gray pants, a white shirt, and a black poncho. His head was large, imposing, and he presented us with a wide and brilliant smile. It reminded me of *choclos de mi tierra*, the big corn kernels of my land, the sweet ones. [Berrú was born in Ecuador and had moved to Chile in 1962.]

From the first moment when he began to sing, we were all in absolute silence, absolutely captivated. You couldn't hear a single sound, only his song. It was only interrupted by the applause after each song. And he would go on singing. In that moment, I felt that I was before a great artist, an artist like I'd never seen, and I felt he communicated with me so directly. I didn't know he was the theater director and knew how to perform, but the impression he made on my heart was so profound, . . . and his poetry was beautiful. When he sang "El Arado" [The Plow], . . . the song made an impression. How beautiful—it made an impact. Later I learned that the song was dedicated to his father, Manuel Jara, who was a campesino, who spent the whole day working under the sun . . . slowly plowing with oxen.

["El Arado" is] a song about exploitation but also of hope that this could change some day. I never imagined that later I would sing the song with him, with Inti-Illimani, or that of the very few interpretations of this song, the one I did with Inti was one of the most listened to. I always become emotional when I sing it. It reaches my soul. . . . I have to make an effort not to break down, because it is such a beautiful song. Well, neither did I imagine that I would be [Jara's] friend later, and even less that I would be a militant in the same cell in La Jota. Or that I would work with him at the university, or record albums with him. All of this was a marvel for me. . . . It was such a lovely friendship because Víctor was a person who inspired respect, affection. He was a hard worker, so creative, and he cracked a lot of jokes once you got to know him.[59]

There was an atmosphere of internationalism at La Peña mixed with nationalist ideals, such as Chilean control of copper. Art prints and posters decorated the walls. Foreign folk musicians such as Daniel Viglietti and Mercedes Sosa came there. Violeta Parra came and occasionally sang. (She had recently opened her own *peña* in the foothills, a large tent called La Carpa de la Reina, where she sang, cooked meals, and brought folk musicians to play.) Salvador Allende came, discreetly, to La Peña, as well.[60] Los Curacas became regular performers on Saturday nights at La Peña. Ernesto Parra of Los Curacas described the environment:

This was a very new cultural innovation. The place reflected the aspirations of the people, their social and political dreams. We denounced injustices. . . . There was a link with Cuban artists through tours by the musicians and also through Communist Parties of different countries, which organized Youth Festivals. Daniel Viglietti, Silvio Rodríguez, Pablo Milanés, Mercedes Sosa, Jorge Cafrune, los

Fronterizos, the Bolivians through Gilbert Favre: a whole network developed across Latin America. There was an awakening in terms of Latin American music, new points of cultural encounter. . . . The public at La Peña included all types of people, but probably more intellectual and political people came. Even ambassadors came. I remember after Che was killed, Cuban diplomats came to La Peña. Ángel sang a song for Che, and it was very emotional for everyone. The Cubans were very moved.[61]

In August 1965, shortly after the founding of La Peña, a new *peña* was established at the University of Chile, Valparaíso. "Gitano" Rodríguez and Payo Grondona, musicians who became popular soloists in the New Song movement, were its founders. So many people came that they soon had to find a larger location. The next year, Horacio Durán, an engineering student at the State Technical University (Universidad Técnica del Estado; UTE) in Santiago—soon to be a founding member of Inti-Illimani—set up a new student *peña* at that university called La China. Student *peñas* appeared at universities from the North to the South of Chile. "The *peñas* were essentially a focal point where you could come to hear folk songs with social content," said Max Berrú. "Also, of course, there were traditional songs. But important for the young people was the music being made by the new artists, in this new movement of *la Nueva Canción*."[62]

La Peña de los Parra became the epicenter of *la Nueva Canción*, stimulating a national trend. The young men who originally formed Quilapayún and Inti-Illimani were university students, and these two legendary groups of *la Nueva Canción* took shape at university *peñas* in Santiago.

New Song Giants: Quilapayún and Inti-Illimani

Many musical groups were present in Chilean New Song contemporaneously with Inti-Illimani and Quilapayún, including Aparcoa, Grupo Lonqui (which emerged from the earlier folk group Lonquimay), Huamarí, Los Curacas, and Tiempo Nuevo. They were well-known and popular in the 1960s and participated in the emerging movement of *la Nueva Canción*. Because of space constraints, I focus here on the two most noteworthy and groundbreaking groups: Quilapayún and Inti-Illimani. Both expanded musical frontiers with their innovations and were recognized for their political commitment and identification with the popular movements, La Jota, and, later, the UP.

Beyond incorporating all the regions of Chile and all of the popular majorities of Chile and Latin America as protagonists in their songs, the groups' use of indigenous names and instruments, along with their ponchos, signaled a deep identification with Chile and Latin America. The songs of Quilapayún in particular expressed militant opposition to imperialism and U.S. intervention, commitment to national sovereignty, and support for liberation struggles in the Third World, further broadening the scope and vision of Chilean folk music. Quilapayún's members made a dramatic impression, with their black ponchos, powerful voices, and revolutionary lyrics. Some of their songs reflected elements of Gregorian chants (one of Víctor Jara's influences), and others featured new and complex harmonization. Inti-Illimani became known for the exquisite precision of its instrumentation and the evocative beauty and delicacy of its musical arrangements. The group played many instrumentals, often Andean music, and traditional folk songs from across Latin America, including songs with social content, but was less militant in its songs, and concentrated on expressing the variety and beauty of Latin America's folk music.

The intricate instrumental language of the groups, which drew from many Latin American instruments and rhythms, provided another contrast to "typical" Chilean folk music and *Neofolklore*, which generally used only one or two guitars. Eduardo Carrasco of Quilapayún noted the spirit of internationalism that was part of the emerging movement: "There was a process of integrating values across geographical borders. . . . There was the idea of a common world. Things that had been local before, like Afro-Peruvian music, began to be adopted by *chilenos*. 'Samba Landó' by Inti-Illimani or our 'La Muralla,' which draws from Cuban lyrics and a Venezuelan (*jaropo*) rhythm, became Chilean music. There was a new mixing of styles."[63]

The rich texture of the groups' music, with multiple sounds, harmonies, and instruments, was a major departure in Chile's popular music. Referring to Quilapayún and Inti-Illimani, Torres wrote, "These groups generally have produced, on the one hand, a process of constant enrichment of instrumental resources, and on the other, a developing progress and growing mastery as interpreters of song, which have notably augmented their expressive potential. This has decisively influenced the extraordinary development of the instrumental language of *la Nueva Canción* in general, by means of profoundly exploiting the possibilities of timbres, melodies, and expressiveness of each instrument, taking advantage of the multiple instrumental colors to offer a matrix of sound that is more and more rich and varied."[64] Jorge Coulon described Inti-Illimani's process of blending various instruments this way:

When we began to play, there was in Chile, and we discovered after that the discussion was all around the world, the same discussion about the purity of folk music, and the purity of the use of native instruments. And from the beginning we wanted to be really free in this way, because for us, the only limit that we put on this is that we only use acoustic instruments. We don't blend with electric bass or keyboards, and sometimes some people can do this in a good way, but there is something different in the soul of the instruments that is difficult to blend. And we use the instruments of the Andean tradition, like panpipes and *quenas*, which are the traditional flutes. We also use the *charango*, . . . an instrument born in Bolivia after the Spanish settlement, because it's a blend, a sort of mandolin, but it's made with the shell of an armadillo. And the scale is a pentatonic scale. It's a typical "*criollo*," a mixture between Spanish and Indian culture. And we try to use these sounds in a new way, and the new thing that we do is blend these kinds of instruments, and instruments from Bolivia, Colombia, Mexico, and so on. Our bass is a Mexican bass, and we use a *tiple*, which comes from Colombia. It's a wonderful guitar with steel strings, and it has a sound similar to a harpsichord. And we blend this with a *cuatro* from Venezuela. So just like a painter, we began blending sounds and looking for different "matices" or shades of colours. And looking for different songs, to play a love song from Ecuador for instance, a song like "Dolencias," which is a very sad and romantic song, we try to use the instruments that can best express these feelings.[65]

Members of Inti-Illimani and Quilapayún pointed to the early influence of Chilean groups such as Los de Ramón—which incorporated various Latin American songs and instruments in the 1950s—as well as the Argentine groups Los Chalchaleros and Los Fronterizos on their music. The Beatles were also an influence, especially their harmonies, and Violeta Parra was extremely important as a creative inspiration and a singer committed to the people.[66]

Quilapayún first came together in 1965 when three students who liked to sing—the brothers Eduardo and Julio Carrasco and Julio Numhauser—decided they wanted to play revolutionary songs. The name of the group is derived from the Mapuche language and means "three beards." The Carrasco brothers were sympathetic to the Revolutionary Left Movement (Movimiento de Izquierda Revolucionaria; MIR) at the time; gradually, Eduardo gravitated toward La Jota (see Chapter 5). Julio eventually left Quilapayún to dedicate himself to MIR, and Julio Numhauser left, as well (he later formed a duo with Mario Salazar called Los Amerindios). By 1968, Quilapayún had a stable membership of six. The group's first artistic director was Ángel Parra. The group played at small venues until 1966, when it won a prize at a folk festival. Its members met Víctor Jara and, because Ángel Parra was no longer available, asked him to direct the group. This began a fruitful period of three years in which the group collaborated, performed, and recorded with Jara. Jara brought Quilapayún to his record label, Odeon, where the group recorded five albums.

Quilapayún began to tour internationally, visiting the Soviet Union, France, and Italy in 1967.[67] In 1968, it began preparing a militant set of songs for an album titled *Por Vietnam*. Quilapayún wanted to take the album as a gift to the International Youth Festival, at which it was going to participate in August 1968 as part of the Chilean delegation.[68] Because the material was too politicized for the group's commercial record label, Eduardo Carrasco, after conversations with a friend and fellow philosophy student, Carlos Cerda, suggested that La Jota produce the album.[69] La Jota was already helping to set up concerts through its relationships with unions and student organizations. Thus a new record label was born, first called JotaJota and then Discoteca del Cantar Popular (DICAP). Its first album was *Por Vietnam*. The album was, unexpectedly, a smashing success in Chile, selling out almost immediately. In fact, the nascent label had to keep producing more editions; each new release sold out. The success of *Por Vietnam* led La Jota to the realization that there was a large demand for *la Nueva Canción*.[70] "This first album was a one-time, informal production, we thought," said Ricardo Valenzuela, who became the record label's director. "We didn't expect so much success or expect to do another album."[71] Instead, the label became a key parallel institution for the promotion of *la Nueva Canción*.

The Birth of DICAP

"The origins of DICAP were rather spontaneous," said Eduardo Carrasco. "It was our initiative; it came from the artists; and it was an idea that La Jota found interesting. It was another way that La Jota could play a cultural and political role."[72] In the 1960s, there were many internal discussions about culture and politics within La Jota, and there was great enthusiasm for the music of *la Nueva Canción*.[73] Culture—art and music—was seen as a key channel for raising consciousness, communicating with and uniting young people, and expressing the political discontents of the time.[74] La Jota took on the project of producing records and creating new conduits to distribute the music. The commercial success of the new record label surprised the conventional record companies. Max Berrú worked at DICAP for a time as a liaison with the musicians. He also wrote press releases to notify radio stations and magazines, such as *Ramona* and *El Musiquero*, about new albums and to arrange interviews with the artists.[75] "There had been a problem with the diffusion of our music," he said. "It was only heard in live concerts. The big media didn't play this music; it wasn't on the radio. So La Jota created a label, and we recorded with them, as did many other artists."[76] Quilapayún and Inti-Illimani continued to record their less political albums with Odeon, as well, where Rubén Nouzeilles was the artistic director.

Ricardo Valenzuela explained why the name of the new label was changed from JotaJota to DICAP: "The first name was too internal, too limited. We wanted the name to be broader, to sell more and reach more people."[77] Valenzuela, who had business training, had financial and economic responsibilities in La Jota. The money earned from *Por Vietnam* allowed the new label to invite other musicians to record albums and to develop the enterprise. Another entity, the National Organization of Shows (Organización Nacional de Espectáculos; ONAE), was spun off from DICAP to set up concerts and tours by New Song artists. It also became very successful.[78] Gradually, DICAP set up offices in other Chilean cities—Antofagasta, Concepción, and Valparaíso—and, later, in Venezuela, Uruguay, Peru, and other countries.[79]

Juan Carvajal was the new label's first formal artistic director. He was asked to take the position—at the suggestion of Eduardo Carrasco—because he was not directly involved in composing and performing *la Nueva Canción*. Carvajal had studied classical music at the University of Chile's National Conservatory of Music. He had become involved in the student movement and was a member of La Jota. "JotaJota was looking for someone not directly linked to the music," he said. "Someone not directly participating was needed to give a certain objectivity or distance regarding the various musical proposals."[80]

DICAP's second album was *Por la CUT*. "We used the same scheme as *Por Vietnam*," Valenzuela said. "We approached the leadership of CUT [Central Única de Trabajadores de Chile] because a big congress was coming up. We suggested that they buy the album to hand out to all the workers. CUT liked the idea. This was a way to raise funds for DICAP."[81] As a practice, DICAP sold the records at demonstrations and political events, hand to hand, as well as in record stores. The label, like the music, was deeply intertwined with the social movements and with institutions such as CUT and La Jota.

DICAP was the first label to record Illapu, a group of young musicians from Antofagasta who came to Santiago in 1971. Ilapu became a very popular group of *la Nueva Canción*. Carvajal also produced the album *Chile en Cuatro Cuerdas*, with classical music composed by Luis Gastón Soublette and performed by Cuarteto Chile. He noted wryly that he received some criticism for that record; some thought there was too much conservatory influence. "DICAP's objectives were cultural as well as political," said Eduardo Carrasco. "It wasn't the goal to do only political work. Rather, we wanted to open spaces for artists who were blocked in commercial circles. . . . DICAP was important culturally as well as politically. The label finally won some 10 percent of the market. The label had prestige and used new distribution networks that we created, social and political networks that weren't normally used. We had to create our own distribution."[82]

Carvajal spoke frankly about the internal politics of DICAP. Reflecting the political positions of the PC—which opposed the model of the Cuban Revolution for Chile—there was some dogmatism, or self-censorship, regarding songs that exalted armed struggle or the figure of Che Guevara, he noted. In fact, in the late 1960s there was some tension between the Cubans and the PC regarding their different strategies for structural change. The Cubans had little faith in a peaceful transition to socialism. The PC was not opposed to armed struggle in theory but believed that a constitutional road to socialism was possible in Chile's case. This was also an interesting instance of discrepancies within the Chilean political movement, because vast numbers of young people in the 1960s admired the Cuban Revolution and saw Fidel Castro and Che Guevara as noble and heroic figures. Many songs were composed about Che, and the MIR, in particular, as well as the radical wing of the Socialist Party were greatly influenced by the Cuban Revolution. But young people in La Jota also admired the revolution and the figure of Che. Víctor Jara wrote "El Aparecido" (The Apparition) for Che (although he did not name Guevara in the song because of government and media censorship). Jara sang other songs, such as "A Cuba" and "Samba por Che," but at the same time he was dedicated to Allende and the UP, writing that "our Sierra is the election."[83] There was some friction between Jara and the PC for his songs about Che.[84] Quilapayún and Inti-Illimani, among many others, sang songs for Che, especially after he was killed by Bolivian and CIA forces in 1967—notably, Quilapayún's "Canción Fúnebre al Che Guevara" (Funeral Song for Che Guevara) and Inti-Illimani's "Carta al Che" (Letter to Che). In short, the Cuban Revolution had an enormous influence on *la Nueva Canción* as a whole. But as we have seen, the PC's strategy was to form broad coalitions and work through existing Chilean institutions—the Chilean path to socialism—not armed struggle. While there was creative freedom for the artists, Carvajal said, there were doubts about recording songs about guerrillas or armed struggle.

Eduardo Carrasco has related an incident that illustrates these internal dynamics. On various occasions, members of Quilapayún were called to discuss the album *Por Vietnam* with members of La Jota, who were worried that some of the lyrics might contradict the policy of the PC. "In Chile, Che was a symbol of the MIR," Carrasco writes, and there was a certain lack of confidence toward Quilapayún because of its past sympathy for the MIR.[85] However, when the issue was taken to the leadership of the PC, Luis Corvalán, the secretary-general, said that Che Guevara was a communist and ultraleftists should not be able to exclusively appropriate his image. He endorsed Quilapayún's songs as they were. It is interesting to see that the PC's leaders believed that artistic openness was more important than political control. Indeed, Corvalán had spoken publicly about his disagreements with the Soviet Union's policy of imposing conditions on artists.[86] The episode with Quilapayún illustrated that the PC leadership considered creative freedom for the artists to be primary (as opposed to the Soviet Union's policy of mandating "socialist realism"). The PC was astute enough to see that the artists needed artistic freedom and that the music and art drew masses of youth to the movement.

JotaJota and DICAP recorded very little rock-and-roll. The label never recorded Los Jaivas—a popular rock group that La Jota considered "hippie" and depoliticized—but interestingly, Los Blops, another rock group, did record with the label. Carvajal commented that he had had discussions with Los Jaivas about possibly recording an album with Illapu for DICAP, although the project never materialized. "We had no problem with rock per se," he said. "Rather, the rock groups that existed were depoliticized, hippie, commercial. Political young people didn't see them as a good model. We looked for music that captured the political moment. There was more attraction to a revolutionary attitude, the idea that young people should be committed to the cause. The Blops were more political, but most rock was apolitical. Rock-and-roll was seen as a U.S. import. There was no revolutionary rock, as there was in Argentina with [the singer] Charly García."[87] Ricardo Valenzuela made a similar point: "Our public didn't want Los Jaivas. They didn't represent combative youth. It wasn't a question of censorship. There was none. Rather, many university students and youth were revolutionary then. They associated Los Jaivas with Woodstock, hippies, marijuana. This wasn't attractive to mobilized young people committed to the struggle at the time."[88] Fans of rock-and-roll, such as the rock historian Fabio Salas Zúñiga, agreed that there was a stigma against those who liked rock music at the time. "It was politically incorrect," he said. "One was supposed to be allied with the suffering of the people."[89] Nevertheless, Los Jaivas was a very popular group in Chile, especially after its hit song of 1972, "Todos Juntos" (All Together), which combined indigenous instruments with elements of rock and a unifying message. Rock music never stopped being popular among broad sectors of young people in Chile.

Between 1968 and 1973, DICAP produced sixty-seven albums and many singles, including so-called *canciones contingentes* (contingent songs), which were issued almost like daily newsletters to comment on rapidly breaking events, Carvajal said. (These songs are analyzed in Chapter 5.) DICAP recorded other types of music besides New Song and musicians who were not part of La Jota, among them Los Blops, as noted earlier, and Margot Loyola. The label also recorded Russian, Mexican, Argentine, Cuban, and classical music.[90] Moreover, a new style of colorful and popular visual art became identified with DICAP. The graphic artists Vicente Larrea, Antonio Larrea, and Luis Albornoz designed captivating album covers and posters for the new music that became widely popular and led to new advances in Chilean art (see Chapter 6). DICAP became a bastion of *la Nueva Canción* and a key institutional conduit for the new music, which spread far and wide in Chile, a central component of the blossoming cultural life of the country. The movement had found new ways to bypass the restrictive commercial music industry and create new channels and institutions for the diffusion of *la Nueva Canción* and revolutionary popular culture. DICAP was a key counterhegemonic institution that broke through the censorship and silence imposed by the conservative cultural entities of the elite.

Inti-Illimani

Inti-Illimani was born from a group of engineering students at the UTE. (Members of Quilapayún also studied engineering there.) They began playing guitar and singing together in 1966, in Jorge Coulon's garage. "It is curious that the groups that were revolutionary in musical terms did not come out of the conservatory or the music schools; they were born in the technical universities, in academia," observed Horacio Salinas, the musical director of Inti-Illimani.[91] Horacio Durán and Salinas first formed the duo Los Dos Horacios, playing guitar and *charango* for the Enrique Kirberg campaign for rector of the UTE, part of the university reform. In 1967, the group took shape with Durán, Salinas, Max Berrú, Jorge Coulon, and Pedro Yáñez. In 1971, when Ernesto Pérez de Arce (who had replaced Yáñez) decided to return to his studies, José Seves joined the group. Coulon talked about the first years of Inti-Illimani:

> The first four years were full of such unusual intensity. Everything changed. We started playing in the *peña* at the university; we created our own *peña* and played there. . . . But quickly we began going to other university *peñas*—the University of Chile, the Catholic University—this started happening really rapidly. We began to get invitations from unions. So the group started in 1967, and by 1968 we were playing before large crowds, lots of people, something that hadn't happened before. . . . It was a phenomenon that was so strong and so rapid. When we started out, our public was mainly students, later unions, then the general public, very linked with what was happening in Chile. . . . This was a public of the people, a popular crowd. . . . In the beginning we were like Martians in rural areas, but this started changing quickly. . . . I'm from the South, and I remember

when I was a kid the campesinos were invisible people, and the owners, the *patrones*, looked at them thinking, why should I talk to the
Indians? The Mapuche were nothing. The campesinos were very sub-
jugated. But in very little time, this changed. Five years is nothing—
but in a period of five years, Chile completely changed.[92]

Seves was a university student and member of La Jota in Valdivia before
he joined Inti-Illimani. He was deeply involved in the *peña* at the UTE
branch in Valdivia and sang in a duo called Anita and José. He recalled
when he and other young musicians from the *peña* went to the countryside
to participate in events with the campesinos and to support the land reform:

We visited small villages as they were organizing Peasant Councils.
The agrarian reform was crucial, an attempt to rupture a colonial
situation, only a little better than slavery. . . . New organizations were
created, such as the Peasant Councils. The councils were an important democratic development. People were voting for their own representatives. We formed a relationship with the local representatives
of the land reform, and people from the *peña* went several times to
play at events with the campesinos, in places where they went to
cast votes. I remember people asking what we were doing there. We
explained that we had come because we were interested in our country, in their lives. No one from the university had ever come before.
. . . We played joyful songs—not protest songs—and the music broke
the ice." [93]

José and Anita knew the young members of Inti-Illimani, who traveled regularly to Valdivia to play and exchange notes with the duo. Anita and José
recorded an album with DICAP in 1970, and in 1971, Inti-Illimani invited
the duo to tour Ecuador with the group.

Inti-Illimani recorded several singles before its first solo album in 1969.
Two of its socially conscious songs, "Cueca de la CUT" and "Samba de los
Humildes" appeared on DICAP's *Por la CUT*.[94] In 1968–1969, Inti-Illimani
released three albums, with songs from various Latin American countries.
(On one, the group sang songs from the Mexican revolution, and Rolando
Alarcón sang Spanish Civil War songs.) By 1972, the group had recorded
eight albums. Between 1968 and 1970, still as students, the musicians traveled
to Argentina, Bolivia, and Peru on their vacations, to perform and to learn
from other musicians who were playing indigenous instruments, including
indigenous musicians themselves.[95] They began to be invited to play at union
halls, at student centers, and in the countryside. "At every union, we learned
something," said Max Berrú. "I went to sing but ended up learning, as well.

In 1969, with the campaign for Salvador Allende, I think the most important thing in our big concerts was to draw a large crowd for Allende, when he was going to speak. In the campaign there were events with music, dancing, theater, poetry. All the artistic expressions were programmed in these acts, for thousands of people. People could see a great show, first class. . . . I remember participating in these with so many groups, artists of every genre. Then, finally, Allende would end the event with a speech."[96] One of Allende's campaign slogans was "There Is No Revolution without Songs."

Music and Politics in the Late 1960s

In 1967, an international meeting called the First Conference on Protest Song, organized by Casa de las Américas in Havana, was held in Cuba. The meeting brought together popular, politically conscious, anti-imperialist songwriters and musicians from Europe and Latin America who were involved in the coalescing political song movement. Some fifty people from eighteen countries participated.[97] Ángel Parra, Isabel Parra, and Rolando Alarcón represented Chile. The international group discussed the best name for the new movement (although ultimately no single name was adopted, and different terms were used for the music of different countries—for example, *el Nuevo Canto* in Uruguay and *la Nueva Trova* in Cuba). A commemorative album was produced, with songs from many countries. At the end of the conference, the artists adopted a resolution that stated, among other things, "Protest song workers must be aware that song, by its particular nature, is an enormous force for communication with the masses. . . . [S]ong must be a weapon at the service of the peoples, not a consumer product used by capitalism to alienate us. Protest song workers have the duty to deepen their skills, since the search for artistic quality is in itself a revolutionary stance."[98] While the various movements never formed an organized or institutional whole—if that was a goal of the Cubans in organizing the meeting—the meeting brought the musicians together and deepened their sense of solidarity.

The periodic youth conferences in socialist countries also gave the young musicians, especially those associated with the PC, opportunities to travel, perform, and meet like-minded artists. The musicians also organized many of their own engagements in the early years. Yet the New Song musicians emphasized that their music was never an obligation or a party task. Horacio Salinas, for example, commented, "To belong to this musical movement meant to make songs of protest, songs of denunciation, to sing against injustice and for liberty. It was consistent with our militancy, yes. . . . But we formed the group not because of a party order but for artistic reasons. . . . What we did was to put our song at the service of the political cause."[99]

Beginning in 1967, the CUT organized several large national strikes to protest government cutbacks that left workers without sufficient salaries to meet the cost of living. That year La Jota organized a large march of young people from Valparaíso to Santiago (some seventy-five miles) to protest U.S. policies in Cuba and Vietnam. Thousands of young people participated, including many from other political parties. Víctor Jara slept on the dirt floors of houses belonging to campesinos along the way, like the others, and sang his songs at meetings between the marchers and villagers.[100] The university reform movement made important advances that year, illustrating the growing political power of the students. The Office of Communications of the Catholic University—crucial for the later New Song festivals—represented an achievement of the reform; it was an opening to the cultural life of Chile. In 1967, the Federación de Estudiantes (Student Federation) of the Catholic University organized a *toma*, or sit-in, at the university's main administrative building to demand changes in its elitist and authoritarian structures and commitment to the struggles of the poor. Soon afterward, the right-wing newspaper *El Mercurio* published articles and editorials that portrayed the student movement as a communist plot (most Catholic University students were Christian Democrats) and that falsely depicted acts of violence. Outraged, the students draped a huge sign on a campus building that read, "Chilean: *El Mercurio* lies!" This was a startling and historic counterhegemonic act at the conservative university, the most elite in Chile. It amazed the public and symbolized the rapid pace of political change taking place in the country.

The students' influence resulted in the election of a progressive Christian Democrat, Fernando Castillo, as rector in 1967, as noted earlier. He was the first rector at the Catholic University not named by religious authorities of the church.[101] Castillo was instrumental in democratizing the university, opening channels for student input and participation. Like Rector Enrique Kirberg at the UTE, Castillo began to listen to, and consult with, professors and students. UTE in particular began to open its doors to the working classes.[102] By 1968, the reform movement had transformed all of Chile's major universities, including Universidad Técnica Federico Santa María, Universidad de Chile, and Universidad de Concepción.

In 1968, the First Festival of Committed Song was held in Valparaíso, organized by the founders of La Peña de los Parra and the Chilean-Cuban Cultural Institute.[103] While modest in its first year, the festival marked another step in the development of the movement. The festivals were held yearly until 1973. In 1969, Ricardo García, working with the vice-rector of communications at the Catholic University, organized what would become a groundbreaking event: the First Festival of New Song.[104] García invited twelve noteworthy young composers, including several from *Neofolklore*, as well as Patricio Manns, Víctor Jara, and other politically committed song-writers. Joan Jara observed that the festival was essentially an encounter between "two different and opposing concepts of what constituted Chilean song: the new music, with songs that were critical and committed to revolutionary change, [and] the 'apolitical' songs, which gave the impression that nothing needed changing."[105] This cultural gathering gave the movement a name and an identity that distinguished it from other types of folk and popular music. Other emblematic composers and singers of *la Nueva Canción*, including Isabel Parra, Ángel Parra, Rolando Alarcón, and Quilapayún, performed at the First Festival of New Song. The university gym was full of people, and the final event of the festival—held in the Chile Stadium—was packed with thousands of onlookers, who roared their approval for Víctor Jara's song "Plegaria a un Labrador" (Prayer to a Farmer), performed with Quilapayún.[106] *La Nueva Canción* prevailed at the festival: the first prize was shared by Jara and Richard Rojas for his song "La Chilenera."

Political Unity and Political Polarization

The Soviet invasion of Czechoslovakia in 1968 caused an immediate reaction in Chile and sparked political disputes between the PC and the Socialist Party (Partido Socialista; PS). The PC was reluctant to criticize the Soviets, while the PS denounced the invasion as a violation of sovereignty. Allende criticized the invasion, characterizing it as a serious setback for popular movements. Despite these disputes and after extensive political discussions, leftist parties created the UP in 1969, possibly the broadest and most successful leftist coalition ever formed in Latin America. The UP united six progressive political parties—the Radical Party, PS, and PC, MAPU, Social Democratic Party, and Acción Popular Independiente—expanding the former FRAP (Popular Action Front) coalition. There were heated debates within the coalition about whom the various parties, and currents within the parties, wanted to nominate as the UP's presidential candidate. The radical wing of the PS, led by Carlos Altamirano (among others), considered Allende too conciliatory, even though Allende was a PS leader.[107] Altamirano's wing of the PS was moving closer to MIR and toward an openly insurrectionary stance. The PC strongly supported Allende and promoted his vision of alliance-building and a peaceful institutional path to socialism. The movements of students, workers, and peasants overwhelmingly wanted Allende as their candidate; Allende was able to unite young people across the Left.

In 1969, the massacre in Puerto Montt took place when police attacked landless families who had organized a *toma* on vacant land. Ten people were killed, igniting huge demonstrations and protests in Santiago and inspiring Víctor Jara to write his song "Preguntas por Puerto Montt" (Questions about

Puerto Montt; see Chapter 5). That same year, members of the Christian Democrats' radical wing left the party, accompanied by most of the youth, to form MAPU. It was a small party but one that came to wield important intellectual influence by combining social Christian doctrine with socialist ideas. Also in 1969, MIR began to carry out "direct action," robbing banks to accumulate resources for the organization; it went "underground" that same year. In October, an ominous event took place: an anticommunist faction of the military, led by General Roberto Viaux, staged an uprising in Tacna, locking itself into the regimental barracks. Viaux demanded higher pay for the army and the resignation of the defense minister and the army commander. The *golpista* sector of the military—secretly encouraged by the United States—was beginning to undermine Chilean democracy. Two or three civilians died—the number is still not clear—and some twenty were wounded in a firefight between loyal troops and the seditionists. The commander of the army was replaced, as Viaux had demanded. Viaux was dismissed from the army, but he remained a key seditionist actor. Several Chilean officers who later became top commanders in the coup and the Pinochet regime met with U.S. officials in late 1969 to discuss what the army would do if Allende won the election.[108]

By 1969, the PC had notably increased its political strength. One source said that during the government of Eduardo Frei, PC membership doubled from 30,000 to some 60,000 people, largely by incorporating new middle-class sectors that broadened its traditional base beyond the industrial working class. By 1973, the PC had about 200,000 militants and 100,000 more in La Jota.[109] In 1969–1970, the UP campaign was embraced by broad sectors of society. "Unidad Popular Committees" were formed in factories, businesses, schools, neighborhoods, and youth centers. Popular participation had vastly increased since the 1964 elections. This was due, in no small part, to the mobilization of youth and campesinos across the political parties, inspired by new ideals of social justice and *la Nueva Canción*, the music that represented that commitment. Alongside the music, murals with pro-Allende and revolutionary messages, painted by members of the Ramona Parra Brigade of La Jota and by muralists from other parties, blossomed on walls in Chilean cities (see Chapter 6).[110] The musicians of *la Nueva Canción* appeared with Allende, along with the muralists. The music and graphic art drew people to political campaign acts and publicized Allende's candidacy. Given the hostility of the private media in Chile, this form of mass social communication was vital for Allende's campaign. There was a fusion between popular politics and culture that was new, joyous, and exciting. Stirring songs and colorful images of social change were everywhere, and they were a means to bypass the mass media and reach people in new ways.

Allende asked MIR to desist from armed actions and cooperate with the UP, and the organization agreed to do so. MIR's leader, Miguel Enríquez, recognized publicly that Allende was the best hope for the working classes and deserved the party's support. Meanwhile, however, U.S. corporations such as International Telephone and Telegraph (ITT) and the U.S. government were plotting new ways to undermine Allende. *El Mercurio* and other media warned that an Allende government would become a communist dictatorship and would dismantle the armed forces and replace them with Cuban-style militias. Allende replied on national television that he had no intention of doing such a thing and that the military was not the enemy of the UP. He also insisted that his government would not be communist or socialist but would represent all of the forces in the UP and all of the Chilean people. In 1970, right-wing youths formed the neofascist group Patria y Libertad (Fatherland and Liberty), which carried out terrorist bombings and attacked muralists when they tried to paint urban walls. The group staged public marches, carrying banners featuring a swastika-style emblem. The U.S. government secretly financed Patria y Libertad.[111]

Washington again spent large sums of money to undermine Allende and prevent his election, directing $800,000–$1 million to CIA covert action to affect the outcome of the election.[112] The CIA used Chilean media extensively in a "spoiling campaign"—an intensive propaganda barrage—to equate the UP with violence and Stalinist repression. As it had in 1964, the terror campaign used wall posters and murals, radio and television commentary, and daily articles and editorials in the Chilean media to attack Allende. Jorge Montealegre's research shows that many comics and political cartoons of the time mocked Allende, and a number of them showed his death by suicide or by murder.[113] The Church Committee estimated that the extensive propaganda campaign reached some five million people.[114] Moreover, the CIA financed right-wing women's and civic action groups, among other organizations.[115] Among them, undoubtedly, were Acción Mujeres de Chile and Chile Joven, which were deeply involved in the terror campaign, with collaboration from and sponsorship by the right-wing press agency Andalién. Salvador Fernández Zegers, a former naval officer, headed the press agency. One of Andelién's initiatives was to send people—who presented themselves as UP representatives—into neighborhoods with a questionnaire asking them to list all their property, all members of the household, and other personal information for the future UP government and "the revolutionary cause"[116]—that is, to sow fear that their homes and families were under threat from the UP.

The Left fought back more vigorously than it had in 1964. One key episode effectively put an end to the black propaganda campaign. In July 1970, members of La Jota broke into the Andalién office and scooped up files and a briefcase. In the briefcase, they found what they were looking for: papers documenting payments to journalists participating in the terror campaign and sources of corporate financing (including Bank of America and Anaconda Copper). The members of La Jota promptly passed the material to the leftist press; the press, in turn, submitted it to Congress, which set up an investigative commission to study the psychological warfare. Margaret Power notes that Andalién did not dispute the authenticity of the documents, although it did criticize their illegal seizure. *El Mercurio* published stories from the perspective of the police and of Andalién manager Zegers. But the scandal united the Left and the Christian Democrats, as well as other key institutions (such as the Catholic Church), in outrage against the terror campaign.[117]

In August 1970, amid these dramatic developments, the Second Festival of New Song took place, again organized by Ricardo García and the Catholic University. As in 1969, a large audience filled Chile Stadium. The atmosphere was more polemical this time, charged by the passions of the presidential campaign and the right-wing offensive against Allende. Singers opposed to Allende—including some former members of the *Neofolklore* group Los Cuatro Cuartos—were subjected to catcalls from the audience, leading to a break in the relationships between the *Neofolklore* musicians and former friends on the Left such as Víctor Jara and the Parras.[118] There were several organizational changes in the festival. The organizers did not invite specific artists this time, for instance; instead, they opened a public competition and appointed a jury to choose the best compositions. Also, to distinguish the festival from those of the commercial music industry, no prizes were awarded. The festival included presentations and forums, as well as music. Some of the major exponents of *la Nueva Canción* performed, including Payo Grondona, Patricio Manns, Rolando Alarcón, Ángel Parra, Víctor Jara, and Isabel Parra. Quilapayún sang *Cantata Santa María* for the first time in front of thousands of people in the stadium. They wore street clothes and played borrowed instruments—their ponchos, equipment, and instruments had been stolen days before.[119] The *Cantata* received thunderous ovations and marked another milestone in Chilean cultural history with its blend of classical and popular forms and its dramatic account of a tragic and all-but-forgotten massacre of workers in Chile.

The musicians of *la Nueva Canción* continued to accompany Allende on his campaign trips in 1970, performing numerous times before multitudes of people. New Song, with its visions of political change and hope and its beloved "hymns"—the song "Venceremos" (We Will Win) was the UP's campaign song—became the music of the UP and the music of hundreds of thousands of Allende supporters.

Allende's Election and the Right-Wing Response

On September 4, Salvador Allende won the election with 36.63 percent of the vote (1,066,616 votes). Radomiro Tomic, the progressive presidential candidate of the Christian Democrat Party, asked his supporters in Congress to shift their support to Allende. When one includes Tomic's 28 percent (824,849 votes), the Left obtained almost 65 percent of the popular vote. The conservative candidate Jorge Alessandri won 35.3 percent (1,036,278 votes). The traditional parliamentary ratification vote was scheduled for October 24. After Allende's victory was announced, hundreds of thousands of his supporters flooded the streets in jubilation. Families congregated in downtown Santiago with banners and flags. Workers and students chanted, cheered, and sang. Demonstrations took place in all of Chile's major cities, and included large sectors of Christian Democrat youth. "It was mystical," Max Berrú recalled. "I remember the night Allende won. I went with my wife to hear him give a speech on the Alameda [Santiago's main boulevard] from the balcony of the Federation of Students of Chile, and there was such a sense of joy. It was like I could touch the stars with my hands. That night, I—a foreigner—felt profoundly Chilean. Afterward, I became a citizen, and Allende signed my documents."[120]

But right-wing forces, domestic and foreign, were still plotting to keep Allende from the presidency. In September, a shadowy terrorist group set off a series of bombs in Santiago. Right-wing members of the Christian Democrat Party and the National Party met repeatedly to discuss how to block Allende's rise to power.[121] On September 29, a confidential ITT memo, leaked several years later, discussed "efforts . . . to move Frei and/or the military to act to stop Allende. Efforts are also continuing to provoke the extreme left into a violent reaction that would produce the climate requiring military intervention. . . . [A] roadblock to Allende's assumption of power through an economic collapse should not be dismissed." John McCone, a former director of the CIA, was a member of ITT's board of directors and fully cognizant of earlier CIA intervention, such as the "campaign of terror" in 1964. Another ITT memo commented that the Chilean army "had been assured full material and financial assistance by the U.S. military establishment." The company sent a series of memos to the State Department in an attempt to accelerate U.S. government action against Allende. An ITT executive met with the CIA in Washington to discuss how to thwart Allende's inauguration.[122] The company was panic-stricken about losing its assets in Chile and possibly elsewhere in Latin America. The internal memos shifted among hysterical warnings of an impending communist dictatorship; exaggeration and falsehoods about the UP, Allende, and the situation in Chile; pleas to the U.S. government for intervention; and longing for a military coup.[123]

Meanwhile, the U.S. government mobilized its intelligence resources to impede Allende's confirmation. On September 15, President Richard Nixon and his top aides discussed how to prevent the democratic will of the Chileans from being realized. In that meeting, Nixon famously ordered his aides to "make the economy scream" and stop at nothing to "save Chile."[124] From that meeting, a series of covert operations was launched to promote a coup. There were two strategies, known as Track I and Track II. Track I was a plan involving U.S. Ambassador Edward Korry to engineer a complex institutional maneuver to persuade Congress to confirm Alessandri as president rather than Allende. Alessandri would subsequently resign, and Frei would call new elections in which he would be a candidate. Then, in a repeat of 1964, Alessandri and the Right would throw their support to the CD to block the Left. But to accomplish this, Frei would have to wrest away the votes cast for Tomic by thousands of Christian Democrats. More important, Frei refused to participate in the plan without a clear constitutional threat. General René Schneider—the constitutionalist head of the armed forces— was also opposed to the plot and had already blocked coup efforts within the military. In fact, he had warned Viaux that if he attempted any new subversion, he would be shot.[125]

The top-secret Track II gave the CIA a direct role in organizing a military coup.[126] Neither Korry nor the State Department was privy to Track II. On September 15, Nixon told top CIA officials that an Allende government was not acceptable to the United States and authorized $10 million to prevent Allende from taking office.[127] The CIA was already in contact with the seditious General Viaux and another anticommunist general, Camilo Valenzuela, as well as with Patria y Libertad. The agency was meeting with three different groups of Chilean military conspirators.[128] The *golpistas* were encouraged to carry out actions to instigate a coup. Schneider was seen as a major impediment to any coup, and the CIA knew that all of the groups of military plotters planned to "abduct" him.[129] The CIA agreed. In one secret memo, the CIA station chief in Santiago wrote, "Schneider is the main barrier to all plans for the military to take over the government to prevent an Allende Government."[130] The agency's so-called Hinchey Report of 2000 stated, "The US Government and the CIA were aware of and agreed with Chilean officers' assessment that the abduction of General René Schneider, the Chilean Army's Commander in September 1970, was an essential step in any coup plan."[131]

On October 22, General Schneider was ambushed and shot on the streets of Santiago in a coordinated operation. He was gravely wounded. The assailants escaped. Valenzuela had received $50,000 and three submachine guns, among other weapons, via the U.S. diplomatic pouch on October 22, although the U.S. Army attaché later demanded that the guns be returned and threw them—reportedly unused—into the sea. The ambush was carried out by Viaux's forces.

While various U.S government investigations have absolved the CIA of direct involvement in the Schneider plot, the pro-coup activities, intensive pressure, and logistical support of the U.S. government for the *golpistas* were abundantly apparent. Washington agreed with Schneider's abduction, and it was clear that a coup would have full U.S. support. Moreover, the CIA's method of operation is to use third parties to obscure responsibility. Nixon and National Security Adviser Henry Kissinger later claimed that they had "turned off" Track II on October 15. But on October 16, declassified documents show, the White House stated, "It is firm and continuing policy that Allende be overthrown by a coup. It would be much preferable to have this transpire prior to 24 October but efforts in this regard will continue vigorously beyond this date."[132]

Contrary to the hopes of the *golpistas*, however, the attack on Schneider did not lead to a coup. Chilean society was shocked and appalled by the violence, and Chileans came together in an impressive demonstration of sorrow and solidarity. Congress confirmed Allende as president on October 24 by a broad margin—153 to 35. On October 25, Schneider died. General Carlos Prats, his second in command and a constitutionalist general, replaced him. Viaux and Valenzuela were soon arrested and imprisoned, with other conspirators. Tens of thousands of people attended the state funeral for Schneider, where both Frei and Allende were prominent pallbearers.[133] Allende was inaugurated on November 3, 1970.

4

La Nueva Canción and the Unidad Popular

With Salvador Allende of the Unidad Popular (UP) elected president, the political context in Chile changed dramatically. The creative energy of the artists had been concentrated on electing Allende and promoting a progressive UP government to end social injustice in Chile. The cultural movement that had accompanied Allende was vitally important in popularizing his campaign and attracting multitudes of people to political events. "Culture was a very important factor in Allende's victory," commented the architect Miguel Lawner, PC member and former government official. (Lawner was the executive director of the Corporation of Urban Improvement under Allende.) "There was no speech by Allende that didn't include a cultural presentation. On the campaign trail, the musicians would sing at every stop for the crowds, and the muralists would paint the walls. . . . There was an incredible revolutionary spirit."[1] Allende's campaign incorporated the vibrant music and graphic art that had arisen in the 1960s, transmitting powerful visual and musical images of social change that evoked a tremendous reaction among the population. In the marches of hundreds of thousands of people during that time, "the only song you heard was 'Venceremos,'" said Ernesto Parra of Los Curacas. "It was mystical."[2]

Now that a progressive government was in power, there were several consequences for *la Nueva Canción*. On the one hand, the musicians shared a sense of euphoria about the possibilities for social and political transformation in Chile. The balance of power had changed, with the state now committed to the popular sectors. There were important new openings for the music, as well, both politically and artistically. On the other hand, with Allende's election there was a period of questioning—some contemporary analysts called it a crisis—within the musical movement as the artists grappled with how their music should, or should not, change to meet the new conditions. "There was a need for a paradigm shift" in the music, said the musicologist Rodrigo Torres.[3] Many musicians felt that the focus had to change from denouncing government failures and injustices to supporting the new government, deepening popular participation, and constructing a more socially just Chile. In fact, in the ensuing years, the musicians probably contributed more support to the government than the government did to the musicians. This new phase was a time of excitement and promise, and the musicians of *la Nueva Canción* were swept up in the rush of events and new possibilities with a popular government.

This chapter presents the evolution of *la Nueva Canción* and the flowering of cultural activity that occurred during the UP period, interwoven with key events that took place during the one thousand days of Allende's presidency. The first year of the UP government was notably successful as Allende began to implement his agenda, with nationalizations of major industries; deeper land reform; improvements in wages, employment and social conditions; increases in production; and impressive growth in the UP's share of the vote (from about one-third to one-half) in 280 municipal elections in April 1971. (Sources vary regarding the UP's margin, ranging from 49.7 percent to 50.9 percent.)[4] The second and third years witnessed growing polarization and violence and intensive efforts by the conservative opposition to block Allende's initiatives and sabotage his government. Throughout the years of the UP, the U.S. government continued to send millions of dollars in covert funding to the Christian Democrat Party (DC), to *El Mercurio*, and to anti-Allende business associations, and spent tens of thousands more to induce a split within the UP coalition.

Allende's Program in the First Year

The parliamentary presidential ratification vote in October 1970 took place in the wake of right-wing fear campaigns, the attack against General René Schneider, and increasing political violence and tensions. To secure the support for his ratification from the Christian Democrats in Congress, Allende agreed to sign a Statute of Constitutional Guarantees, promising to respect the political system, individual freedoms, and the existing structure of the armed forces. The PS disagreed with this concession to the DC, but Allende always believed it was necessary to form broad agreements among democratic forces. On November 3, when Allende formally took office, Santiago became the scene of an enormous popular celebration. Joan Jara wrote:

On twelve open-air stages set up in different points in the city center, in an atmosphere of festivity, non-stop performances were mounted by all the main cultural groups and individual artists. This time it was not just the politically committed who took part, but institutions like the Symphony Orchestra, the Philharmonic Orchestra, the National Ballet, the company of the Theater Institute, and poets, choirs, comics, operetta, clowns, pop singers, folk groups, and of course, the artists of the New Chilean Song Movement. . . . The streets were closed to traffic while masses of children and people of all ages strolled and looked and listened in the late spring air. Everywhere there was music, with the smell of empanadas, roasting peanuts and smoke from the barbeques, while thunderous applause echoed from one stage to another. . . . I remember when Víctor came out on stage, dedicating his songs to "our Compañero Presidente," Allende suddenly appeared on the first-floor balcony of the Moneda Palace, on the opposite side of the square, and waved a salute to him across the multitude of people. It was a celebration like no other for a new sort of president. The people felt that they had entered the Moneda Palace with him.[5]

Allende immediately set to work to implement his program (especially the Forty Measures, the first points of his program), directing himself first to economic issues. The Forty Measures were his priorities; he expected to have a full six-year term to move to other parts of his program. Allende and his economic advisers (and many leading social scientists of the time) put great emphasis on transforming the oligarchic structures of economic power in Latin America. Raúl Prebisch and the United Nations Economic Commission for Latin America and the Caribbean (ECLAC), which was based in Chile, were important intellectual influences: theories of dependency and imperialism were emerging in this period, and many analysts believed the best path to economic development lay in the state's taking on a central role in the economy.[6] The idea had almost universal support in Chile. Allende appointed a former ECLAC official, Pedro Vuskovic, as his economic minister.[7]

Allende envisioned an economic model with three broad ownership structures: state-controlled or social property (the large, wealth-producing industries of the country); private property (smaller, nonmonopolistic enterprises, which would remain numerically the largest); and mixed public-private property. In Chile at the time, 17 percent of business enterprises controlled 78 percent of all economic activity, and 2 percent of the rural landowners held 55 percent of the land. Three U.S. companies controlled the production of Chilean copper, which accounted for 60 percent of Chile's total exports.[8]

Within the category of social property, the government planned to national-ize monopolistic enterprises such as the large mines, the financial system, and strategic industrial conglomerates. The Forty Measures also pledged to reduce extravagant salaries (measure 1), among other economic reforms, and implement important social reforms.[9] Every child was to receive a daily free breakfast and a half-liter of milk in school (measures 14–15), and an emer-gency program was to provide every Chilean a house, electricity, and potable water (measure 19). Agrarian reform was to be deepened (measure 24), and free medical care was to be provided for all (measure 26). In the first months of his presidency, Allende began the nationalization of the textile industry and the banks, thus moving forward on the creation of an Area of Social Property.[10] The UP government signed an agreement with Central Única de Trabajadores de Chile (CUT) that incorporated workers in decision-making processes throughout society. In the international field, Chile declared itself part of the Non-Aligned Movement and recognized Cuba.

The government had a number of proposals for the cultural sector, as well. The UP program stated that "the social process that has been opened with the triumph of the people will develop a new culture oriented toward considering human labor as the highest value. . . . The profound transforma-tions envisioned require a people socially conscious and in solidarity, educat-ed to exercise and defend their political power, scientifically and technically adept to develop the economy in the transition to socialism, and open to mass creativity and to the enjoyment of the most varied manifestations of art and of the intellect."[11] One of the government's first acts was to nationalize a large book publisher, Editorial Zig-Zag. Since 1970, workers there had been on strike to demand the incorporation of the enterprise within the Area of Social Property.[12] The publishing house was renamed Quimantú, a Mapuche word that means "sun of knowledge." The enterprise began publishing classic and contemporary books in history, literature, and politics and selling them at very low prices, in an effort to distribute literature widely and educate the broad public. "There was a huge diffusion of universal, classical literature, in pocket format," recalled José Seves of Inti-Illimani Histórico. "The distribu-tion and sales of these books was incredible."[13] Inexpensive paperbacks and new magazines and popular journals were sold at kiosks and shops in the remotest corners of Chile, as well as at union halls and student centers. The response from the public was enthusiastic, and people began buying thou-sands of books and journals. "Riding the buses, you noticed that everyone—workers, women, students—were reading little books from Quimantú; there was a hunger to read and to learn," said the human rights lawyer Eduardo Contreras.[14] The editors of Quimantú were motivated by the UP's goals to reach all parts of the population, to build a new identity, and to deepen polit-ical and cultural consciousness in the country.

Cultural expression flourished throughout society. "During the Allende years everyone who wanted to express themselves could," said Ricardo Venegas of Quilapayún. "There were new theater groups, musical groups. Culture was democratized. It wasn't something that was financed; it was due to the interest among people, the desire to express themselves through poetry, music, theater. There was an incredible cultural effervescence. Suddenly, the campesinos and unionists had their own theaters; the university students had their own music. There were government initiatives, but there was not much money. . . . There was assistance from the government, but it was not very well organized."[15] The intense activity of the musicians and artists was largely the result of their own initiatives and links with social and political organizations. The new "people's culture" was everywhere. "The biggest preoccupation of the artists was to be able to bring cultural events to places where there had never been a concert, a play, a film—because this is a very centralized country," said Horacio Salinas. "Inti-Illimani traveled far and wide in the country, to small villages, mining communities in Sewell, La Serena, Lota. We came to know so many places. That was a key accomplishment of the cultural movement in those years. Along with the voluntary work projects, the Allende government is remembered for that."[16]

The Flourishing of Culture amid Increasing Schisms

In April 1971, a few months after Allende's term began, municipal elections were held in Chile. The UP garnered 50–51 percent of the vote, as stated, an impressive increase from the presidential election. But ominous events were occurring, as well. In June 1971, the former DC minister Edmundo Pérez Zujovic—whom Víctor Jara had specifically criticized in his 1969 song about the massacre in Puerto Montt—was assassinated. A shadowy group of supposed anarchists named Vanguard of the People (VOP), which also carried out criminal acts, claimed credit. The VOP had no relation with the Unidad Popular or with the PS or Communist Party (PC). The act was condemned by parties of the Left, including the Revolutionary Left Movement (Movimiento de Izquierda Revolucionaria; MIR), and President Allende ordered the capture and arrest of the perpetrators. But the Right blamed the government and the Left in general.[17] It was the beginning of an ever more violent period in Chile, a country that until Schneider's assassination in 1970 had not known political assassinations since 1837, when Diego Portales was murdered.

Within Congress, relations among the parties were becoming more difficult, as well. Pérez Zujovic's assassination caused an immediate reaction in the DC, which already opposed Allende. The DC moved farther from the UP, rejecting a possible alliance and calling off negotiations regarding Allende's initiatives. That the parties of the Center and the Left were not able to come to a compromise was a serious, perhaps fatal, setback for Allende's government, which was increasingly besieged by the right-wing parties, sectors of the military, clandestine fascist groups such as Patria y Libertad (Fatherland and Liberty), the wealthy classes, and the United States, all of which favored a coup.

Leftist members of the DC decided to leave and form a new organization, Izquierda Cristiana (Christian Left). The founding members were frustrated by the DC's increasing collaboration with conservative parties trying to undermine Allende. Izquierda Cristiana saw the social doctrine of the Catholic Church as compatible with Marxist ideals and supported the peaceful transition to socialism. Some members of the leftist Unitary Movement for Popular Action (Movimiento de Acción Popular Unitario; MAPU), including Jacques Chonchol, who disagreed with the party's increasing radicalization, also joined Izquierda Cristiana. MAPU was moving closer to MIR and away from Allende's "Chilean road to socialism."[18] Izquierda Cristiana formed part of the UP. In July 1971, Congress unanimously voted to approve the full nationalization of copper. In November, Fidel Castro visited Chile and traveled throughout the country for several weeks. The visit caused both excitement among UP supporters—people lined the streets to welcome him—and hatred among those on the Right. The first large anti-Allende demonstration took place in December with the "March of the Pots" by right-wing women. Organized by the conservative parties to protest Castro's visit and Allende's policies, the demonstration by conservative, upper-class women protesting in the streets was something new in Chile. The women were accompanied by members of Patria y Libertad, with their fascist symbols and banners.

The mass media operated freely during the UP government. In the 1960s, Chile had a wide-ranging set of newspapers from all political perspectives (including forty-six dailies and weeklies in English, Italian, Croatian, and Yiddish), four national news agencies, and 700 print shops.[19] There had been newspapers of all political persuasions linked to the political parties since the early twentieth century, although *El Mercurio* dominated. Chile also had extensive book production compared with other Latin American countries. While many of the national radio and television channels were in the hands of wealthy business groups (such as Radio Minería), there were also radio stations controlled by the Catholic Church, the University of Chile, and the Catholic University. Other channels were operated by the PS (Radio Corporación), the PC (Radio Magallanes), MAPU (Radio Sargento Candelaria), and MIR (Radio Nacional).[20] *El Mercurio*, the anti-Allende media empire, however, controlled a chain of ten daily newspapers and a radio network, and the UP program had called for eliminating monopolistic control of news.[21] On September 19, 1970—just two weeks after the election and before Allende's ratification by Congress—the Inter-American Press Association, until recently directed by Agustín Edwards, the right-wing owner of *El Mercurio*, had declared that press freedom in Chile "was being strangled by communist and Marxist forces."[22]

Contrary to the Right's continuing barrage of fear-mongering and warnings, however, the UP government respected freedom of the press and constitutional protection of the media. Robert Pierce has noted that "Chile had the freest media system in its history during the Allende period," despite fierce competition between the Right and the Left to publicize their messages.[23] The anti-Allende propaganda that deluged the media had major funding from the U.S. Central Intelligence Agency, as we have seen: the Church Commission reported that the CIA covertly financed "assets"—journalists who were CIA agents—in media to write thousands of anti–Unidad Popular articles and to plant articles written by the CIA. The CIA also funded extensive black propaganda, books, and radio and television programs.[24]

About twenty radio channels (out of 135 or so) supported the UP government at first, but that number declined. Ten big consortia owned the great majority of print and radio media outlets.[25] The Right's domination of the media and its extensive resources meant that the UP government was constantly struggling to have its messages heard. "We couldn't diffuse Allende's program adequately," said Max Berrú. "The private media attacked Allende constantly. . . . We didn't know how to take advantage of the national [state] newspaper *La Nación*. People didn't read it much. . . . The Right still got its message across and captured the public more, making people afraid that Chile was going to fall into the abyss. The Catholic Church also insisted that Chile was a Catholic country [and] spread insecurity among people."[26] According to one source, some 541,000 right-wing and anti-Allende newspapers were sold in 1972, compared with 312,000 that were pro-government. The right-wing newspapers used this press freedom to broadcast many sensational and propagandistic stories to attack the UP government.[27]

Meanwhile, thousands of students continued to use their vacations to go out to the shantytowns and the countryside to participate in *trabajos voluntarios* (voluntary work projects), building houses, digging wells, helping with harvests, and teaching people to read. Musicians, dancers, and artists also participated, to respond to new demands from workers and peasants to learn dance or theater and form their own groups. Joan Jara, a dancer with the National Ballet and the Dance School at the time, worked to train new dance teachers to work in the community, to teach people how to create their own choreography and plays. She realized that physical training and adequate food were also required: many of the new students suffered symptoms of malnutrition.[28] Venegas remembered *trabajos voluntarios* in which he participated: "I went to the *poblaciones* and helped build houses. We also helped after the earthquake in 1970. . . . There was no central organization. I wasn't a Jota militant then, but I was close and had a lot of friends in La Jota. We organized these things together. . . . During the truckers' strikes, many young people got involved in distributing food."[29] Seves recalled that Inti-Illimani went to the *poblaciones* when young volunteers constructed canals for water distribution to the population, among other projects. The group sang for the volunteers and sometimes joined the work teams.[30]

The tradition of voluntary work had existed for some time in Chile, but when the UP came into office, it dedicated funding and government resources to prioritize projects such as building permanent housing in the shantytowns. One such project, "Operation Winter," created some 20,000 new housing units with potable water, electricity, and paved roads. Thousands of people voluntarily joined in this effort and raised funds, collected winter clothes, and donated food to the *pobladores*. Children who were living in miserable conditions were brought to university buildings, where they could be warm and dry.[31] Víctor Jara composed one of his most tender songs, "Luchín," at this time; it was dedicated to the children who lived in the shantytown, and to one boy in particular, named Luchín. For several weeks, when the boy was ill, Víctor and Joan Jara cared for Luchín themselves.

Students took their education and skills to the communities. In journalism studies, for example, groups of students and their professors worked in union halls and *poblaciones* to create popular newspapers with the workers and shantytown dwellers. The papers compiled local news and discussed community problems; the objective was to have the local people learn how to put out the papers themselves. Over time, the students carried out fewer tasks and gradually turned over the production to the local people. The students learned more about the problems faced by these social groups and about their lives, and the local people learned to produce their own newspapers, which became self-sufficient and autonomous. Students in other fields also brought their practical training to communities throughout Chile.[32] The CUT, similarly, took the initiative to form theater groups among union workers and encouraged them to produce and act in their own plays, works that reflected national and local realities.

The Allende government nationalized the record company RCA, including its production plant. It was renamed Industria de Radio y Televisión, and Julio Numhauser, formerly of Quilapayún, became its director. Soon the enterprise was operating at 100 percent capacity (rather than 50 percent, as before). Numhauser recorded Los Jaivas, the group that combined rock with elements of folk-based music and indigenous instruments, as well as groups that played rock and electrified music, or that fused elements of New Song and rock. The record company EMI (formerly Odeon) remained private. In 1971, the government enacted a policy of price controls for records and established that 85 percent of artists in concerts and radio broadcasts should be Chilean.[33] However, the radio channels apparently did not comply.[34]

Despite the growing opposition of the Right to the UP project, cultural events continued to proliferate and involve masses of people. Víctor Jara commented at the time:

> I come to the people singing in union halls, in campesino festivals and in groups of miners. Although they may be illiterate they understand without analyzing and they become excited, in favor or against. They open up to me[;] they tell me their problems, their pain. . . . We are living a musical process that is very rich. In my recent presentations, in unions, schools, or universities, I offer the guitar to the public so that they too can say and express what they feel. Music has a magical aura of participation. And our youth needs to participate, wants to participate. The music, our folklore, our songs, are elements that are unifying, effective, and real.[35]

Mario Salazar, who worked in the presidential Office of Culture, explained the importance of the Train of Popular Culture, an initiative during the first months of the UP government. The train carried a number of popular artists, dancers, and musicians to remote villages and towns in the South of Chile and staged shows and performances where none had taken place before. Railroad workers supported the project, in solidarity with the artists. Salazar said:

> I organized this journey shortly into the UP term. The train went from Santiago to Puerto Montt. It included a classical ballet group, many writers, a philharmonic orchestra, a folkloric ballet group, painters, poets, folk and New Song musicians. Inti-Illimani was out of the country but Nano Acevedes went. The idea was to use the tour to organize Regional Cultural Committees, which didn't exist before. We went to towns where there had never been a cultural performance. And beyond the shows we did succeed in organizing some regional committees, which kept functioning. . . . All this was destroyed with the coup, and some of the greatest cultural figures were assassinated.[36]

Nano Acevedo wrote that in one month, the groups performed one hundred times in cities along the route.[37] Because the performances were free, often held in gymnasiums or stadiums or in the open air, large crowds greeted the train at every stop and were rapt audiences for the performances. It was an original and exciting way to reach people in the farthest corners of Chile, projecting the new concept of popular culture and the government's commitment to the people. Other tours to the North and South of Chile were organized by René Largo Farías, who had a radio program and directed the *peña* Chile Ríe y Canta. He helped to disseminate *la Nueva Canción* throughout the country, with groups of musicians and dancers who traveled by bus to various cities and towns.

Graphic art and murals acquired a more recognized status after Allende's election in 1970. Public mural painting as a means of social communication and participation had first erupted on the walls and public spaces of Chile during the 1964 election as a vibrant new form of popular art, and it continued to develop throughout the 1960s.[38] The murals and social art of the Ramon Parra Brigade of La Jota in particular represented graphically and colorfully the new, inclusive, and democratizing political project put forward by the UP. This original form of popular art made a deep impact on Chilean society. In 1971, the Museum of Contemporary Art hosted an exhibition of the art of the brigades, among other works. The young muralists continued to paint the walls of Chile's cities, sometimes with the assistance of famous artists, such as Guillermo Núñez and Roberto Matta. Moreover, murals were created as permanent projects. The huge mural of Gabriela Mistral that adorns the park at Santa Lucía in Santiago, painted by Fernando Daza, was inaugurated in 1971.[39] Like the musicians, the artists of the epoch wanted to respond to the needs of the people, take on a social and political role, and create new art forms. This was also reflected in the cover art that decorated *la Nueva Canción* albums (see Chapter 6).

When Fidel Castro came to Chile, he was accompanied by a group of young musicians called Manguaré. The group had won a national competition in Cuba and received funding from the government to travel and perform. The Cuban musicians spent six months in Chile to learn from the New Song musicians, particularly how to play the indigenous instruments and music of *la Nueva Canción* and take it back to Cuba. Castro also wanted to unite the countries of Latin American more closely through music and culture.[40] Inti-Illimani, Quilapayún, and Isabel Parra, among others, hosted and played music with Manguaré, and the musicians traveled throughout Chile playing Cuban *son*, *guajiras*, and rumbas for the Chilean people. Manguaré recorded an album with Discoteca del Cantar Popular (Discothèque of Popular Song; DICAP).

In 1971, a new *Nueva Canción* group from the North of Chile, Illapu, won a music contest in Antofagasta. Patricio Manns was part of the jury. He gave the group advice that proved to be extremely important, said Roberto Márquez, singer and composer of Illapu: "He congratulated us and said we had great potential. But he told us we shouldn't imitate Quilapayún or Inti-Illimani. It would be good to create something of our own. . . . Our region was rich in terms of the Andean world, the Aymara and Quechua cultures; he suggested that our music reflect that world. Patricio helped us reach our creative potential." Illapu incorporated multiple indigenous instruments from northern Chile, Bolivia, and Peru. When DICAP opened an office in Antofagasta, the label invited Illapu to prepare material to be recorded in Santiago. "We did that," said Márquez, "and if it had not been for DICAP, we never would have existed as a group. Many musical groups in the North were very good and well known, but they disappeared. Because of DICAP, we exist as a group."[41] His comment highlighted the importance of counterhegemonic institutions for the spread of New Song. Interestingly, Illapu's members were of the Left but belonged to various political parties; Márquez stressed that DICAP was very open, even though Illapu was not part of La Jota.

In late 1972, Pablo Neruda returned to Chile, having won the Nobel Prize in Literature in 1971. He had been stationed in France as the ambassador of the Allende government, and he was already sick with cancer. Víctor Jara organized a massive celebration in the National Stadium to welcome him back. Workers and miners from all parts of the country gathered in Santiago to prepare for the gala. The show was spectacular: hundreds of working people participated as actors. Jara's production included a reenactment of the massacre of Santa María de Iquique, with miners from the North who traveled to Santiago to act the parts; the participation of Mapuches, fishermen, and workers who acted in other parts; a simulation of the repressive period of González Videla; a scene in which the Ramona Parra Brigade circled the stadium to paint the walls; and the use of huge puppets to portray the oligarchy and foreign enemies.[42] Actors played Recabarren and Lenin, and the audience cheered as they were recognized. Children performed an original dance to the music of a piece titled "Homage to Pablo Neruda," written especially for the occasion by Jara.[43] The tens of thousands of people in the stands cheered when Neruda read his poetry. Neruda, emotionally moved, warned of the dangers of civil war in Chile.

During one rehearsal for the event, according to Joan Jara, Víctor Jara and Patricio Bunster, who were directing the production, glanced behind them at the contingent of military officers in the stands and encountered stares of "cold hatred and contempt that . . . produced a sensation of foreboding like an icy shower amid the warmth and enthusiasm of the rest of the rehearsal."[44] The forces of the Right were calculating how to put a stop to the political and cultural revolution in Chile.

New Opportunities for the New Song Movement

For the musicians of *la Nueva Canción*, the Allende period was an exhilarating time. The dream of building a just society fused with the sense that exciting new possibilities, political and artistic, were materializing. "The conquest of the popular government presents us with a broader path. It's opening up," said Víctor Jara. "The artists feel more free, more optimistic."[45] For the first time, the New Song musicians were invited to play at government events (which they did without compensation) and to play as semi-official cultural ambassadors of the Unidad Popular. Quilapayún, Inti-Illimani, Víctor Jara, Isabel and Ángel Parra, and others toured both within and outside Chile, and *la Nueva Canción* began to win worldwide attention, as did Allende's bold political experiment, the Chilean road to socialism. An important development for the musicians occurred in 1971 when the rector of the State Technical University (Universidad Técnica del Estado; UTE), Enrique Kirberg, and the Secretaria de Extensión y Comunicación of the university offered to contract a number of the artists, at a modest salary, to become part of the university's cultural outreach program. A component of the university reform, the initiative permitted the artists to leave aside their other tasks—whether jobs or studies—and dedicate themselves full time to music. Cecilia Coll, who had headed the La Jota's Commission of Culture, became the director of UTE's extension program, using the experience she had gained in La Jota to develop the university program.[46]

Berrú explained the importance of the contract:

> All of us were hired by UTE. We already worked as musicians, but I was also working as an engineer. One day I got a call saying, "Max, we want to contract you as a musician with X salary so you can dedicate yourself to music with your comrades in Inti-Illimani." I was amazed they were offering me a salary to do this—to enjoy myself! We were all part of the Secretaria de Extensión y Comunicación of UTE, a very important group that included Víctor Jara, the Parras, Quilapayún, we in Inti-Illimani, choruses, a symphonic orchestra, a folkloric ballet, theater groups—there were some twelve entities that were contracted. We as a group traveled to all the capitals of the provinces where the university had a branch, and there we would sing. At the same time, the university had agreements with workers' unions, campesinos, and we went to sing to them. . . . We traveled all over Chile. Once we went to Patagonia and sang for the oil workers. That was the farthest that we went south in Chile. We also went north, to Arica, Iquique, all those regions, and in fact in Iquique we practiced singing *Canto para una Semilla*, a *cantata* by Luis Advis with verses by Violeta Parra.[47]

Seves also discussed the contract with UTE: "After I entered Inti-Illimani in 1971, we were contracted by the Secretaria de Extensión y Comunicación.

For about two weeks per month we traveled to other branches of UTE throughout the country and spent three or four days in each place. We would perform at the university and at local theaters or *peñas* and talk to local groups. The rest of the time we spent doing our professional work—maybe recording or giving concerts. . . . We also toured outside the country. One long tour in 1972 was to Mexico, Ecuador, Argentina, Venezuela, Colombia, and Cuba." Seves described highlights of that tour:

> This was during the UP, and there was a strong interest through-out Latin America about what was happening in Chile. In terms of music, it was a privileged situation to travel in Latin America and look for genuine folklore. . . . One realizes that in many places it's not easy to find something genuine, something true. Like in Chile with Los Huasos Quincheros, there are viewpoints that are more superficial, not profound or with a view toward the authentic folk-lore of the people. . . . One realizes this, and one also realizes that it is due to the situation experienced in Latin American societies: the discrimination, in many places, that has existed since the days of colonization and the early republics. The same social structure still exists. It's exploitation that is impressive, the poverty. It is always the same contradiction: a continent that's rich but poor. The people live badly while a few are wealthy. . . . When we went to Ecuador—in exile, too, it was one of the countries we could visit, not Argentina or Uruguay or Brazil—it was a marvel to discover the indigenous world of Ecuador. . . . The people spoke Quechua. It was something beautiful and strong.
>
> It was a special experience to play in Ecuador before mainly indigenous audiences. For them, it was a surprise to see us, who weren't indigenous, playing indigenous music. It created strong bonds of affection. People invited us to their communities. . . . One village was a center of weavers. Many families were involved in a large enterprise to create textiles. People maintained their style of dress—the ponchos, the shoes, the colors—and their language. It's beautiful in the mountains of Ecuador, with houses of adobe. . . . There, something very special occurred. We sang, in Quechua, "El Tinku"—I understand that the word means "The Encounter" or something similar—which we had learned from Víctor [Jara]. He'd learned it from a Peruvian traveler. To sing that song there and see the kids laugh was special. . . . We didn't know the content of the song because we had learned the words phonetically! . . . For me, it made a big impact to know Latin America better, especially the pre-Columbian world: the colors, the languages, the music.[48]

Inti-Illimani's members also discussed the political situation in Chile during their travels. "There was a lot of interest in Allende and sympathy for the Unidad Popular," Seves continued. "People asked us a lot of questions. There was a lot of propaganda and many falsehoods in the media—paid by Washington, in part—and people asked whether certain claims were true. We had to counter the lies. There was a campaign to discredit Allende. We explained that it was a complicated process. It was not really a Marxist government—there were three areas of the economy, including private ownership—and the government wasn't a satellite of anyone." In an interview at the time in which the group's individual members were not identified, Inti-Illimani explained that the goal of that tour was to "cultivate Latin American music, to defend ourselves from cultural imperialism. . . . [There is] an international campaign to malign the UP government. Many people are disoriented and don't believe in the Chilean path. Particularly referring to leftist organizations, they don't know the Chilean reality: they cannot imagine that you can come to power through an election. Each time we present a recital, we end by conversing with the public. They want to know many things about Chile. We come well prepared to explain the reality, since a lot of people learn through what we communicate."[49] Clearly the musicians were functioning as organic intellectuals, as cultural and political voices of the UP and its popular agenda.

Through the UTE's contacts and agreements with CUT and the unions, the musicians presented concerts at union halls from the North to the South of Chile, as well as at hundreds of student assemblies and gatherings of campesinos in the countryside. "All of the organizations in Chile, all of the institutions, including CUT, had cultural committees," said Berrú. "The UTE's extension program had relations and agreements with CUT, with the unions and with peasant groups. An organization from the nitrate area invited us, and the leadership of CUT organized events, as well. The parties close to us were well organized. . . . This cultural work was very important, because culture is transversal. It crosses all parties and ideologies. During this period, it was very important. The cultural life grew and developed, recovering traditions that were being lost."[50] At the same time, the Organización Nacional de Espectáculos (National Organization of Shows; ONAE), run by La Jota, played a key role in setting up tours and events for the musicians, beginning during Allende's presidential campaign. "The ONAE contracted big theaters, for thousands of people, for important events and key dates," Berrú said. "Sometimes they would look for a plaza or a large outdoor space that could hold 20,000 people. At the end of the campaign [for Allende], there were 150,000 people at some events."[51] Miguel Davagnino, who headed the organization for a time, said that the ONAE worked with UTE's extension program to organize concerts at low cost. The organization developed events with popular musicians from the unions and theater groups, and other noncommercial artists, to play at different venues around the country.[52]

As the music historian César Albornoz has noted, "The musicians of *la Nueva Canción* became the visible face, easily recognizable by the mass public, of the new values" of the Unidad Popular.[53] But there was little direct support from the Allende government, according to the musicians. "We were unofficial diplomats of the government, you might say," said Jorge Coulon of Inti-Illimani, "but nothing official. We never received a peso from Allende's government or any official representation. The thing is that we were profoundly committed to the government. We traveled outside the country to play, as well. But this was due to the university program, the extension."[54] Seves further explained, "There was no payment from the government. Rather, we traveled under the auspices of the government. For example, when we traveled to Italy, where we were surprised by the coup, we had official passports. That is, in this sense we were representing the government. But the support was more indirect."[55] Horacio Durán discussed the same issue:

> You could say we were almost official, but not formally. We were with Víctor Jara, Quilapayún, then the Parras and other people. But in reality, [our role] was due to the identity our music represented. The UTE supported us by contracting all of us. . . . This created an important space for us. We had a salary, but they didn't tell us what to do. . . . The university, not the government, supported us. . . . There were government activities where we would go to play, but they were free of charge. . . . We played throughout the country, but these events were, first, because of the university, and second, because of our direct relationships with unions, the campesinos, the workers, and student activities. It wasn't the case that the government organized any of it. On the contrary: we had much more intense activities than an agency of the government could have organized. We were very autonomous, all of us. . . . This idea was born from the fact that we had such a well-defined and active position in favor of Allende and the UP, so it seemed as if we were an official part of the government.[56]

In short, accounts positing that the groups were employed directly or paid by the government are inaccurate. But the musicians did embody the soul of the Unidad Popular. "The critical mass of the UP made the difference, not only the artists. There were large sectors," said Juan Valladares, a musician who was part of Quilapayún and, later, the group Ortiga. "But the musicians became the reference for the whole movement. They were in all the big political acts. They were a strong presence. They represented the ideology, the vision; they generated political consciousness."[57] Valladares's comment on the role of the artists in creating political consciousness again recalls the theories of Gramsci.

The New Context

With Allende's election, the musicians confronted a changed context for their music. Their combative songs of denunciation under the Frei government no longer seemed appropriate. The New Song musicians wanted to support the new government and contribute to creating a peaceful road to socialism. They were profoundly committed to the promise of the Unidad Popular. The new context gave rise to some disorientation among the musicians. As Joan Jara has explained:

> Much of the work that both Víctor and I had been doing in our different spheres, against the odds, unsupported, almost subversively, suddenly became official government policy. It was as though a door against which you had been battering suddenly burst open and you found yourself on the other side. . . . It was wonderful, but it took a bit of getting used to. At first there was a momentary pause in Víctor's song making. After protesting and denouncing for so long, to have a real cause for celebration and so many constructive tasks to perform was in some ways disconcerting. He couldn't go straight on like a machine, churning out positive pamphlet songs. He had to take time to get used to the new conditions, absorb the new atmosphere. But as he started to get into gear and to become immersed in the new situation, songs began pouring out.[58]

One of Víctor Jara's first projects was the album *El Derecho de Vivir en Paz* (The Right to Live in Peace; 1971), dedicated to Vietnam and with the collaboration of Ángel Parra, Inti-Illimani, Los Blops, and others. Jara was experimenting with the fusion of different genres and sounds, including elements of rock music.

A number of the early songs produced by the musicians during the UP government period included appeals to Chileans to involve themselves in working to transform Chile. "All of the popular acts by the government had their songs to publicize them: the voluntary work projects, the nationalization of copper, the neighborhood food distribution committees," one observer noted. "It was a new and novel type of song. Everything was sung: the Unidad Popular was a government with music."[59] Some of these songs were Sergio Ortega's "La Marcha de la Producción" (The March of Production), sung by Quilapayún; Víctor Jara's "Qué Lindo Es Ser Voluntario" (How

Beautiful It Is to Be a Volunteer); Isabel Parra's "Póngale el Hombro Mijito" (Lend Your Shoulder, My Son); Ángel Parra's "La Cueca de la Organización"; Los Amerindios' "La Producción" (Production); Gitano Rodríguez's "Canto al Trabajo Voluntario" (Song to Volunteer Work); Payo Grondona's "Ahora Sí el Cobre Es Chileno" (Now Copper Is Really Chilean).[60] Quilapayún, Sergio Ortega, Víctor Jara, and others began to create many of their "contingent songs," targeting Patria y Libertad and other political enemies of the Unidad Popular.

Some of the songs began to attract some criticism—especially the contingent songs, catchy songs about current political issues.[61] A debate arose within the movement about the perennial balance between art and politics and the question of how to combine commitment to social change with high standards of artistic quality.[62] Some journalists and musicians at the time began to speak of a "creative crisis" in terms of the quality of new songs. Some pointed to the apparent decline in public interest and enthusiasm at the Third Festival of New Song in November 1971.[63] Undoubtedly, one reason for the lower attendance was that the festival was being broadcast live on Televisión Nacional and Radio Cooperativa for the first time.[64] In addition, the political climate was becoming more tense, with increasing right-wing hostility toward the UP. But many of the songs at the festival were of high quality, including Patricio Manns's "Elegía para una Muchacha Roja" (Elegy for a Red Girl) and Víctor Jara's "Obreras del Telar" (Workers of the Loom), both of which were dedicated to women in the struggle, as well as others by artists who were not part of the New Song movement.

I sought clarification of this period from the musicians, who held a variety of opinions about the so-called creative crisis. Berrú spoke about a period of disorientation after Allende's election and described a meeting that took place with a leader of the PC, Volodia Teitelboim:

> We had an encounter once with Teitelboim, who was one of the most important intellectuals in Chile. . . . He met with us and a number of other people not only from La Jota, but also from the whole movement. Some had Christian ideals; others, Radical. . . . Teitelboim met with us because we were in a crisis regarding our themes. . . . When you're under a government of the Right, you have a well-identified enemy, but with a government of the people, things get more complicated. He told us that artistic expression is the expression of freedom—they are closely related—and he could not tell us what themes to use. They had to come from within us.[65]

Seves commented, "Yes, this [disorientation] was normal, because one had to recognize the difference with a government that was dedicated to resolving the problems of the people. But at the same time just winning the presidency didn't mean that all problems were solved. You couldn't sing 'Glorias' yet! Everything was still to be done. So it was natural that this problem would appear.... Inti-Illimani's repertoire was mainly Latin American music; it was more universal, and we could continue with this. But I remember conversations about what to do next."[66] At the time, Inti-Illimani, asked about the so-called creative crisis, stated, "The number of groups and artists, the majority of them young, which are arising every day in all points of our country signal that *la Nueva Canción* is suffering not from a deadly disease but only from a childhood condition. Its future depends on the quality and artist transcendence that it achieves."[67]

Patricio Manns said at the time, "With respect to *la nueva canción* I think that the problem is the following: one cannot write for a determined objective. This would be like putting a straightjacket on artistic creation. I believe that the artist is the critical conscience of his or her time. What happened after [Allende's election on] September 4? As composers we began to write songs for the process. The idea of critical song was forgotten; many things were done of limited quality, and this brought a rejection from a great majority of the public. This happened to me, as well. Those songs where I've been carried away by 'the pamphlet,' people reject."[68] The radio personality Ricardo García wrote in 1971 that the time had come for self-criticism in the New Song movement: "Observing the production in 1971 it can be seen that the majority of the composers elected paths that were simply repetitions of others. These included pamphlet-like exaltation of the nationalization of copper, for example, or evoking events or people far afield from the current moment.... [There must be] a period of adaptation to new circumstances. And above all, there should be strong self-criticism to recognize that not all that is being done is of high quality."[69] García argued that the artists should immerse themselves more deeply in work with the popular organizations.

Gitano Rodríguez noted that the provocative lyrics of some of the contingent songs ignited a brief debate at the time.[70] The songs often mocked or criticized right-wing forces and their attempts to undermine the Allende program. (These songs are analyzed in more depth in Chapter 6.) But while there was a discussion within the movement about contingent songs, it passed quickly and never became a serious conflict. The debate formed part of the introspection and self-criticism within the movement at the time. Moreover, many of the *canciones contingentes*—while a small proportion of the multitude of new songs—were very popular with the public.

Some musicians rejected the "creative crisis" characterization. Eduardo Carrasco of Quilapayún commented, "There was never a lack of inspiration for our songs. This was a false polemic.... To call it a 'crisis' was silly, with bad intentions.... Some people said that with Allende there was no protest, but that wasn't true."[71] Carrasco felt that some journalists (although not Ricardo García) were attempting to discredit the musical movement by sentencing it to oblivion. Similarly, Horacio Durán of Inti-Illimani disputed the idea of a crisis, pointing to the enormous creative output of the artists and musicians during the UP government. *La Nueva Canción* had moved to the public plazas and the streets, he said; the festivals created by García were no longer necessary to hear the music; their original function had been superseded.[72] Durán explained that while some of the musicians (including Inti-Illimani) avoided *canciones contingentes*, there was a sense of mutual acceptance and coexistence within the New Song movement. Each group followed its own trajectory, and these songs were one element of a huge outpouring of musical creativity.

Certainly, there was a veritable explosion of creative work, with hundreds of memorable songs and albums released during the three years of the Unidad Popular government, indicating that the period of disorientation was short-lived. Víctor Jara, for example, was enormously productive, dedicating himself to both transcendent works of art—such as his conceptual work *La Población* of 1972, on the struggles of the *pobladores*—and to contingent songs denouncing the subversion of the UP government by the Right. Claudio Rolle notes that Jara did "not shy away from 'contingent' themes, as is demonstrated in the waltz 'El Desabastecimiento' [The Shortage] . . . in which he castigates the Right with decision and sarcasm, as he considers it responsible for the shortages and for conspiring."[73] During this period, Jara also adapted an acerbic song by the U.S. folk singer Malvina Reynolds, "Little Boxes," translated as "Las Casitas del Barrio Alto," caricaturing the well-off Chileans who lived in the foothills. "Some of our songs could be characterized as 'pamphlet songs,' but also I think it's a question of not being afraid of the term 'pamphlet,'" said Jara. "It could be a pamphlet with content. How many pamphlets about love do we hear every day?"[74]

La Población recounted the unwritten history of *pobladores* who seized land in a 1967 *toma* and built a community. They named their settlement Herminda de la Victoria in honor of a baby shot and killed by a Carabinero during the conflict. Jara spent long periods of time in the *población*, speaking with the people there. His pioneering work included both original songs and interviews, interspersing the music (with lyrics by a friend and collaborator, the dramatist Alejandro Sieveking) with taped recordings of the voices of the women and men of *la población* telling the history of the community. The album was an example of Jara's work as an organic intellectual and of the innovations of *la Nueva Canción*. It was a set of songs and first-person testimony combined in a novel way, telling a little-known history of the Chilean reality. The work featured the sounds of the shantytown: the voices of children, the barking of dogs, the crowing of roosters. It was also a collective work, with choruses by the groups Cantamaranto and Huamarí and vocals by Isabel Parra. José Seves also worked with Jara in the shantytown and with the female group Cantamaranto on guitar and vocal arrangements.[75] "My role was in support of the use of the instruments so that the *muchachas* could accompany themselves with guitars, *charango*, *quenas*, and percussion," Seves wrote. "It consisted of practicing rhythms and searching for different functions for the instruments."[76]

La Población was well received, and the Peasant Confederation of Ranquil invited Jara to visit Lonquimay to document the massacre of campesinos that had taken place there in 1934. "I'm thinking of continuing my experience with *La Población*; applying it to other fields," Jara said. "I think there are enormous possibilities for creative people, for musicians. . . . We could do many more works about the *pobladores*."[77] Jara traveled to Lonquimay at the end of 1972, lived with the people there, and recorded their testimonies. He found documents on the formation of the first peasant union and gathered the histories of the Mapuches who lived in the area.[78] At the same time, Jara was working on another major piece, "Los Siete Estados" (The Seven States), a ballet combining classical and popular genres. He was collaborating with the classical composer Celso Garrido and the choreographer Patricio Bunster, as well as with Inti-Illimani, members of the Symphony Orchestra, and the National Ballet Company to conceptualize this work.[79] Jara was never able to complete his work on the Ranquil massacre; the year 1973 was full of intensity, with constant public concerts, political activities, and campaign events that absorbed much of his time. He also recorded an album of popular songs titled *Canto por Travesura* (Mischievous Song).

Between 1970 and 1973, Inti-Illimani released five albums, including *Canto al Programa*, a musical version of Allende's Forty Measures, and *Canto para una Semilla*. In the group's ground-breaking LP *Autores Chilenos* (Chilean Authors; 1971), Inti-Illimani performed mainly songs by Violeta Parra and Víctor Jara for the first time, with arrangements by Luis Advis; the group's earlier LPs had featured songs, both traditional and contemporary, from across Latin America. Horacio Salinas's original song "Tatatí" was on *Autores chilenos*. (The first original song he wrote, titled "Inti-Illimani," was on a 1969 album issued by DICAP.) During the UP years, Quilapayún released five albums. After *Cantata Santa María de Iquique* (1970), Quilapayún followed with *Vivir como Él* (To Live like Him; 1971), with political songs dedicated to Vietnamese revolutionaries. Several other songs incorporated Cuban rhythms, and the group sang a hymn of the UP, "Venceremos," which had first been recorded by Inti-Illimani on *Canto al Programa*. "Venceremos" was one of the most popular anthems of the UP, along with "El Pueblo Unido." In 1973, Quilapayún released *La Fragua*, another epic *cantata* composed by Sergio Ortega that extolled the history of popular movements and the PC in Chile.[80] The group's first double album, *La Fragua* also included six contemporary *canciones contingentes* and a song performed with Manguaré. During the UP period, Ángel Parra released five LPs, many with original compositions, some of them co-written with his uncle Roberto Parra, and he continued to develop the Peña de los Parra. He also managed the group Los Curacas, who played at the *peña*, and taught them songs, techniques of Andean music, and guitar arrangements. His sister Isabel was busy traveling as part of a cultural delegation. In 1970, with Quilapayún, she traveled to Finland, the Soviet Union, Romania, Denmark, France, Germany, and Sweden. She played an important role in introducing Cuba's *Nueva Trova* musicians to the Chilean public. Isabel Parra hosted Silvio Rodríguez, Pablo Milanés, Noel Nicola, and Sergio Vitier in Chile in 1970 and recorded several albums, including "De Aquí y de Allá" (From Here and There), with original compositions and Cuban *Nueva Trova* songs, and "Recopilaciones y Cantos Inéditos de Violeta Parra" (Compilations and Unpublished Songs of Violeta Parra), putting to music poetry by her mother. In 1972, Isabel recorded an LP with Cuban musicians in Havana and attended a number of Latin American artistic festivals; in 1973, she again hosted *Nueva Trova* musicians in Chile, where they played at the Peña de los Parra.[81]

In 1971, Patricio Manns released his fifth album, *Patricio Manns*, which was directed by Luis Advis. The album included two of Manns's most haunting songs: "No Cierres los Ojos" (Don't Close Your Eyes), with its premonition of the coup, and "Valdivia en la Niebla" (Valdivia in the Fog), which mixed nostalgia for a lost love with longing for the city of Valdivia. Collaborating on this record were Inti-Illimani, Los Blops, the Symphonic Orchestra of Chile, and the Philharmonic Orchestra of Santiago, again demonstrating the ability of *la Nueva Canción* to erase boundaries among musical genres. The legendary song "La Exiliada del Sur" (The Exile from the South), also on this major album by Manns, featured lyrics by Violeta Parra and music by Manns. All of these works were only part of the output of the musicians during these years. The musicians of *la Nueva Canción* were performing constantly in Chile and in other countries, at concerts, rallies, government events, and large stadiums. In short, the three years of the UP government were an extraordinarily creative period for *la Nueva Canción*, in which the musicians produced an avalanche of unforgettable, beautiful and enduring classics.

But *la Nueva Canción* remained largely absent on private radio and television channels, and rock music, *boleros* and *rancheros*, romantic ballads, and *cumbias* remained very popular with the mass audience in Chile. There was a pair of exceptions. One was "Charagua," composed by Víctor Jara, which the national television channel used as a station-identification jingle (with Tevito, a cartoon mascot dog) between programs. "Charagua" was recorded by Inti-Illimani and became ubiquitous. Salinas's song "Tatatí," which was used by all of the media to introduce speeches by President Allende to the public, was also important during the UP. "When Allende would speak to the country by radio or television, the broadcast would begin with the sounds of the *bombo* and then the *tiple*, and then the announcer would introduce Allende," Salinas remembered.[82]

As Daniel Party has argued, though, looking at only *la Nueva Canción* and its "golden age of political song" can lead to a distorted perception of the popular music scene of the time, which remained largely apolitical and dominated by other forms of music.[83] In my investigations I asked the musicians whether *la Nueva Canción* became hegemonic at any point during the Unidad Popular. Rodolfo Parada, an original member of Quilapayún, had argued in an article published in 2009 that the music did become hegemonic during the three years of Allende's government.[84] Most of the musicians I spoke with, however, were more circumspect. "Our music never became hegemonic," said Durán. "In the '60s, we had little radio play. Our music was heard in the streets, at marches. With the Allende government, it was heard more. Perhaps we thought our music was hegemonic, but we were rather self-referential and sectarian! On the Left, our music was hegemonic, but not in the whole society. The Right hated us, and 'Preguntas por Puerto Montt' [by Víctor Jara] had offended people in the DC."[85] Max Berrú also disputed the idea that New Song became hegemonic. "The music was diffused more with the UP," he said. "But it is also true that foreign music still dominated private radio channels. . . . We only had three or four radio channels, and some magazines, in favor of the UP. The state television channel was directed by Sergio Ortega, and he was in favor. The media was run in large part by the Right. Our music never dominated."[86] Carrasco also disagreed: "*La Nueva Canción* never dominated, if that's what Parada meant by hegemonic. There was always romantic music, popular music, dance music, music from the United States, the Rolling Stones, Los Jaivas, Los Blops. They never disappeared. There was still an influence from the United States, from Argentina and Brazil. . . . We in *la Nueva Canción* never had the relevance that Chico Buarque had in Brazil."[87] Similarly, Juan Carvajal, formerly of DICAP, said, "No, *la Nueva Canción* wasn't hegemonic. Yes, it was played a lot on some pro-Allende channels. But there was a lot of other music on radio and television."[88]

The Worsening Political Climate in 1972–1973

The second two years of the UP government were increasingly difficult and tense. Hyperinflation appeared, as did shortages of food and basic products due to boycotts and hoarding by wealthy and middle-class Chileans; the covert blockade and subversion sponsored by the United States; and a convulsive social climate, with increasing strikes by workers,[89] right-wing terrorism, and land takeovers by peasants and *pobladores*, often supported by MIR. The UP government also made mistakes and policy errors, which included printing of excessive currency and a loss of control regarding increasing wage demands and wildcat strikes.[90] Allende refused to send in the police to break strikes and refused to impose draconian austerity measures. Moreover, the UP was increasingly hindered by its internal divisions. The radical Altamirano wing of the PS, and MAPU, drew closer to MIR; their insurrectionist view clashed with Allende's policy of the peaceful road to socialism, supported by the PC and others in the UP coalition. When Allende attempted to engage in dialogue with the DC—a large and critically important party—to amass democratic forces against the Right, the left wing of the UP opposed him. Allende, and the PC, believed that only a large, pro-democracy alliance among centrist and leftist parties would provide the capability to move Chile forward and counter the increasingly coup-prone Right—not an armed revolution.

In mid-1972, the right-wing opposition led an effort in Congress to impeach Allende's minister of the interior. Soon afterward, in the midst of a strike by small businessmen who closed their stores, the government declared states of emergency in Santiago and Concepción. Quimantú was bombed five times in 1972. MIR, supported by MAPU and the PS, called for abolishing Congress and setting up a People's Assembly. In September 1972, the Confederation of Truck Owners declared a strike, halting the distribution of food and basic goods throughout the country. By October, it had become a virtual lockout by the owners. The government declared a state of emergency. Thousands of university students signed up to be emergency drivers to deliver food, gasoline, and raw materials. Sometimes they had to physically fight right-wing militants who blocked warehouses and attacked professors at the university. In one episode, a convoy was blocked on the highway between Santiago and Melipilla by members of the right-wing group Patria y Libertad, who pulled the students and workers out of their vehicles. Two students were killed, and two Panamanians—whom the rightists thought were Cubans because they were black—had their arms broken by the assailants.[91] In December 1972, Allende gave a speech at the United Nations in which he said that Chile was "the victim of serious aggression" and that Chileans had "felt the effects of large-scale external pressure against us."[92]

As a way to stabilize the situation, Allende named several military ministers to his cabinet. The constitutionalist General Carlos Prats became the interior minister. The conservative opposition expressed its confidence in Prats and negotiated an end to the truck owners' strike. The government promised "to return enterprises occupied by workers during the strike and also not to nationalize the transport and wholesale trade sectors of the economy."[93] In early 1973, all eyes were fixed on the upcoming parliamentary elections. The Right hoped to gain a two-thirds majority in the Chamber of Deputies and the Senate to impeach Allende. The New Song musicians were deeply involved in the parliamentary campaign, playing at campaign stops and in public plazas for leftist candidates. "Víctor [Jara] didn't hesitate for a moment to put himself at the disposition of the campaign and together with Inti-Illimani every day, from morning until night, participate in dozens of meetings and gatherings in support of the candidates Eliana Araníbar and Gladys Marín, in the streets, the plazas, the open-air festivals of all the popular neighborhoods of Santiago with this 'door-to-door' music," wrote Coulon.[94] The outcome of the elections did not permit the Right's strategy of an "institutional coup" to take place. The opposition won 56 percent, but the UP won 44 percent, gaining two seats in the Senate and six in the Chamber of Deputies. The UP maintained a significant proportion of the popular vote. The parliamentary route to oust Allende was closed; at this point, the antidemocratic opposition concentrated all its forces on destabilizing the government, undermining its effectiveness, and preparing for a coup.

The barrage of fearful articles in the press constantly equating Allende with sinister forces, the political polarization, and the shortages and economic crises that became more frequent ate away the support of middle-class sectors for the Unidad Popular. The UP itself was more and more divided internally. MAPU and the PS argued (along with MIR) that it was time to stop attempts to negotiate with the DC and rely on popular power—the increasingly militant workers and peasants—to push forward the class struggle and establish full workers' control. There were more calls to abolish Congress as a bourgeois institution that was blocking progress toward socialism. Allende, backed by the PC and other allies, argued, in contrast, that the UP was a workers' government that represented popular power and that should be supported by all sectors of the Left. He and his allies believed that middle-class sectors should not be frightened off; that a constitutional path to socialism was still possible through an agreement among the parties; and that as an elected government, the UP should use its substantial legal and constitutional power.[95] On the Right, the National Party, now allied with the DC, continued using the institutions of the state to sabotage policy action by the government. In March, the military cabinet members withdrew. Between April and June 1973, Congress impeached four more of Allende's ministers. In May, copper workers at a major mine, El Teniente—led by a Christian Democrat[96]—went on strike, further crippling the government and the economy. Many radical students supported the strike. Workers in the industrial belts, increasingly militant, took over dozens of factories and operated them by themselves.

As shortages became more serious, neighborhoods formed so-called Juntas de Abastecimientos y Precios (Boards of Shortages and Prices). They were licensed by the government to distribute food and other goods, which were delivered by ordinary people using cars, carts, and whatever modes of transportation they could find. The musicians of *la Nueva Canción* took part in unloading supplies and distributing food in various parts of the capital. Berrú recalled, "Víctor [Jara] was incredible. When we worked together doing voluntary work, for example, trains brought food into the city. Since the workers were on strike, we had to unload. All of us—the artists—had to pick up and pass back these sacks to a store, then go back and unload again. Víctor was the only one who would carry two sacks. . . . [H]e was so passionate about it. And he'd go and drop off, return, drop off, return. It made an impact on me."[97]

In July, Arturo Araya Peters, Allende's military aide-de-camp, a constitutionalist Navy officer, was assassinated in a terrorist act: a sniper from naval intelligence, encouraged and supported by Patria y Libertad, shot him in front of his house. The sniper escaped but later was identified—and after the coup, the dictatorship pardoned all the conspirators. Allende, with the assistance of Cardinal Raúl Silva Henríquez, again attempted to hold talks with the DC. But the party was uninterested in conversations and allied with the Right at this point. Carrasco remembered the climate of violence in those months: "Quilapayún faced threats and violence many times. Once my house was painted with the word 'Jakarta.' There were many direct threats in the streets. Right-wingers recognized us."[98]

During all of these events, musical festivals, art exhibits, mural painting, and other expressions of the new culture continued. But culture was increasingly becoming a contested arena, as well, characterized by polarization and political conflict. In the Festival at Viña del Mar—normally a conservative and commercial venue—in 1972, conservatives in the crowd heckled the renowned African singer Miriam Makeba when she praised Allende.[99] Rolando Alarcón was jeered, as well, as he sang "Canción para Pablo," a song dedicated to Pablo Neruda, who had recently won the Nobel Prize in Literature—and who was also a prominent communist.[100] Around the same time, three celebrated members of the Cuban *Nueva Trova*—Pablo Milanés, Silvio Rodríguez, and Noel Nicola—visited Chile and performed in the Chile Stadium. They also visited student organizations, unions, and peasant groups. In the Fourth Festival of Committed Song in Valparaíso in January 1973, Quilapayún, Inti-Illimani, Ángel Parra, Isabel Parra, Víctor Jara, and Illapu played, as did several foreign folk singers, including Daniel Viglietti of Uruguay. The musicians also took part in a ceremony in which Allende received a donation of machinery from the East German government. The same month, at the Festival of the Huaso in Olmué, traditional, conservative folk groups such as Los Huasos Quincheros performed, and there were antigovernment commentaries, songs, and jokes from the stage.[101] In 1973, political polarization at the music festivals was even more intense. Quilapayún was invited for the first time to the Festival at Viña del Mar, but a large number of anti-Allende people in the audience threw tomatoes and carrots at the musicians.[102]

In June 1973, a large gathering called the Cultural Antifascist Offensive took place at O'Higgins Park in Santiago with the participation of many of the best-known and beloved musicians of *la Nueva Canción*, as well as theater troupes, artists, and poets. Shortly thereafter, Lieutenant-Colonel Roberto Souper led a faction of the army in a coup attempt (called "El Tanquetazo" because the seditionists drove tanks into the streets of Santiago, which fired on government offices). Patria y Libertad had pushed for the coup attempt. Some thirty people were killed. Through his control of the armed forces and his personal courage in confronting the seditionists, General Prats was able to suppress the coup attempt. But soon afterward, military squads began raiding houses in pro-Allende neighborhoods, *poblaciones*, and factories, supposedly looking for weapons. They did so under a 1972 law passed by the conservative opposition in Congress. This campaign allowed the military to collect intelligence, train for the repression of civilians, and disarm supporters of Allende (few of whom actually had guns). It was another piece of the preparation for the coup.

Critiques of the UP's Lack of a Cultural Policy

During the UP government, no well-articulated government cultural policy or effective institutional structure ever took shape.[103] The National Institute of Culture envisioned in the fortieth measure of the Forty Measures was never established, and the government's office of culture had little staff and funding. Clearly, Allende faced monumental challenges: growing political opposition and economic difficulties were urgent priorities. Another factor may have been concerns by a segment of the intellectual Left. Albornoz reviews the case of intellectuals such as Enrique Lihn, who were sympathetic to the UP but concerned about the potential danger a government-directed cultural project might pose to creative freedom. The so-called Padilla case in 1971 may also have had an effect in these circles.[104]

But other sectors of the Left and the Unidad Popular were disappointed by the UP's lack of a defined cultural policy. Víctor Jara, for example, was dissatisfied that the fortieth measure had not been carried out. "As he traveled around the country, seeing all the work that was going on in an improvised, spontaneous way, without technical help, subsidies, or planning, he saw the need for a more active and coherent cultural policy. This did not imply imposing norms and models from above, but helping in practical ways so that new values, new attitudes could emerge," wrote Joan Jara.[105] "I believe the time has come for a central organization to organize, plan and orient [the cultural work]," Víctor Jara said at the time. "Our people are enthusiastic about culture and, in fact, are producing cultural works. Confusion and anarchy could make us lose a lot of time in something that we can start now. I propose that we celebrate the third year of the UP with the First Congress of Cultural Workers, with a view to creating an Institute, Center, or Ministry of National Culture."[106]

One of the new magazines published by Quimantú was *La Quinta Rueda* (The Fifth Wheel, or Spare Tire), and the magazine itself was critical of the lack of a clear cultural policy from the Allende government. Indeed, the name of the journal was a critique of the government's lack of attention to the development of cultural policies (i.e., the idea that the fifth wheel was somehow unnecessary).[107] The magazine incorporated multiple political perspectives and points of view and included book, music, and theater reviews; essays on contemporary cultural events; news; criticism; and even comics. Mario Salazar of the PS and Carlos Maldonado of the PC were on the editorial board. The magazine attracted the interest of many leading intellectuals, who contributed to the journal, and it sold well on the newsstands. In its sixth issue, the editorial board, referring to the lack of a cultural policy, wrote, "Seven months have passed and the situation remains the same. There are varied expressions of popular cultural activity triggered by the process, but still no sign of coordination or overall stimulus."[108] Maldonado, and the PC in general, particularly highlighted the need for more action by the UP government. Volodia Teitelboim of the PC, for example, argued at the PC's National Assembly of Cultural Workers of in 1971: "The essential task of the cultural revolution is the struggle for revolutionary consciousness. And this struggle does not take place in the cold or in a vacuum, but through participation in practical work to construct a new society." He added, "We think that transformative actions in culture require a new organization of artists, writers, and intellectuals. . . . We should revive the Committees of Popular Unity."[109] Teitelboim was arguing that changing the hegemonic culture in Chile would require organized efforts—specifically, the organized efforts of the artists themselves—and sustained development. It was not a change that would happen automatically. It was a Gramscian argument, although Gramsci's work was not very well known in Chile.

While the government was unable to devote many resources to the cultural field—it simply did not have the capacity—the universities and the CUT played central roles in promoting cultural activity, as did the leftist political parties and student organizations. The artists themselves contributed their passionate enthusiasm and energy to developing a new popular culture in Chile. Overall, it was a period that saw a massive wave of creativity and brilliant works of art, a period that was unique in Chile's history.

In July 1973, both Quilapayún and Inti-Illimani left for tours in Europe. Ugly incidents and violence continued to take place throughout Chile. The truck owners declared a second national strike in July, again shutting down the distribution of vital goods. Patria y Libertad assisted the owners by throwing nails and spikes across the highways so that no transport could go through. In July, a Patria y Libertad leader announced that the group would unleash a total armed offensive to overthrow the Allende government.[110] The Church Commission Report later confirmed that the CIA had funded three business organizations that supported the owners' strike, indirectly contributing to its effectiveness. In fact, the commission determined that the second strike could not have been maintained without outside funds. The Church Commission documented constant and systematic CIA subversion of Allende's government throughout the three years he was in office. Large sums of money were sent to opposition parties and to anti-Allende media and were spent on the production of anti-Allende books, articles, and magazines. Efforts were ongoing to divide the DC and turn its more progressive sectors against Allende, and to splinter the UP coalition. The U.S. government spent some $7 million on covert action in Chile between 1970 and 1973. Richard Nixon and Henry Kissinger wanted to prevent the consolidation of the socialist, radical-democratic project of the UP and "limit its attractiveness as a model" for other countries.[111]

Meanwhile, the United States deepened its ties with the armed forces through the CIA and military attachés. Military aid from the United States grew during the UP years, while economic aid was severely cut. Nixon had told his aides to "make the economy scream" in 1970. U.S. representatives in international financial organizations used their influence (and the economic weight of the United States) to block or reduce loans and grants to Chile. In August 1973, as Allende was giving a speech, Patria y Libertad blew up strategic power lines to take him off the air, an attack that reflected a high level of technical expertise. That month, the wives of right-wing military officers protested in front of General Prats's house, insulting him and condemning his loyalty to the Allende government. Soon afterward, the Council of Generals voted to expel him. Prats resigned as defense minister. On Prats's advice, Allende appointed Augusto Pinochet—supposedly a loyal officer—to replace him as head of the army. Eduardo Frei, the president of the Senate, declared that the government was unconstitutional, opening the door to a military coup. Coup plotting was intensifying within the armed forces and the Right. Allende decided to call a plebiscite on his presidency. He planned to announce it on September 11.

In September 1973, as the national organization of business owners called for a country-wide offensive against Allende, pro–Unidad Popular multitudes gathered in Santiago on September 4 to celebrate three years of Allende's government. Some one million people marched to La Moneda and packed the plaza and its surroundings to hear Allende speak, shouting slogans such as "Allende, Allende, the people will defend you!"[112] The musicians and artists formed a large delegation, and the music of *la Nueva Canción* filled the streets. On September 9, Carlos Altamirano, secretary-general of the PS, denounced the *golpistas* and called for resisting sedition in a fiery speech. On September 11, the military carried out a bloody coup in Chile.

As the military abruptly terminated the Allende experiment, it also brutally suppressed the cultural life of the country, particularly *la Nueva Canción*. It was clear that the armed forces, and the Right, feared and hated the cultural transformations that had changed the face of Chile in such a short time. The music of *la Nueva Canción* symbolized the values of the UP government and the popular movements that had elected Allende. The military targeted the protagonists of those counterhegemonic movements and moved to erase even the memory of the period from the minds of Chileans through political terror and severe economic austerity. Before presenting a brief overview of the coup and its immediate aftermath in Chapter 7, readers hear more from the musicians themselves. In Chapter 5, I present their views on the political power of music and how they came to politics and music. In Chapter 6, I examine the creative processes of some of the artists and the importance of collaboration to their art, and summarize key political and musical innovations of *la Nueva Canción*.

5

Politically Committed Artists
and Their Music

In this chapter, I recount some of the political and artistic stories of some of the legendary artists and protagonists of *la Nueva Canción chilena*. I was interested in what led them to politics and to music and how the two intertwined, how they experienced the 1960s and the Allende period, and how they saw the role of music in the popular movements. How did the political context inspire the music? What was the role of institutions in facilitating the New Song movement, and why did so many musicians join La Jota? What moved people about the music? The lyrics? The sounds of the music itself? The emotions awakened by the songs? The political and social relationships associated with the movement? Did the musicians see the music and the songs as political tools to achieve concrete ends?

The musicians were swept up in the social movements and the political ethos of the time, as well as in new currents in music. Many were involved as students in the movement to democratize the university and open it to the working classes. Young Chileans of the 1960s generation also wanted to free themselves from conservative social mores and conventions, as in the United States and Europe; long hair and radicalism were widespread in Chile. Many musicians were inspired to play music by the Beatles, a major influence in popular culture in a rapidly globalizing world. As Eduardo Carrasco of Quilapayún explained, "The atmosphere in Chile at that time was not so different from that in the United States and Europe—the youth movement, young people who were politically committed. It had to do with the war in Vietnam, the Cuban Revolution, the guerrilla wars around the world. It was a liberated generation that wanted to break with earlier, conservative generations. That was the spirit of the era. It was an anti-imperialist movement, as well."[1]

The fact that the cultural movement in Chile was an integral part of the broader popular movements of the time led me to the work of William G. Roy, who addresses the role of music in social movements in the United States. He points out that the impact of music on political and social movements depends on the social relationships that exist or are created. His analysis is important because he goes beyond many analyses of culture that focus on symbols and meanings and how they affect individuals. Even more than the lyrics or sound of the songs, Roy argues, "The effect of music on social movement activities and outcomes depends . . . on the social relationships within which it is embedded."[2] The act of singing in unison, Roy observes, creates a unity and social cohesion among people that is "precommunicative"—deeper than conscious meaning. The very act of singing together creates profound emotions, solidarity, "the submergence of the self in the flow, the feeling of being part of a larger collectivity."[3] Roy shows that in contrast to Europe, where folk music has been associated with narrow nationalist or right-wing sentiments, U.S. folk music has been linked to leftist ideas and movements, expressing the values of equality, justice, and democracy—that is, "people's culture." Roy's key thesis is that "music is fundamentally social. Accounts and perspectives that focus solely on textual meaning or sonic qualities disregard a profound sociological dimension of how music operates in social interaction. Music is a social relationship, and glossing over the interaction of people around music clouds over the explanatory power that sociological analysis can bring."[4]

Roy's analysis is useful for analyzing New Song. In Chile, the musicians were politically active alongside their art and their music, and they wanted their art to be for the people. They deeply felt, and expressed, unity with the struggles of the oppressed and defiance of unjust authority. The musicians projected a sense of solidarity by drawing on Chilean and pan–Latin Americanist traditions (the two were not seen as contradictory). The settings of the New Song music ranged from gatherings of several dozen on street corners or construction sites to thousands of people in stadiums. The feeling of collectivity spurred by such acts bound people together in a new social relationship conducive to political awareness and collective action. Using Roy's criteria, *la Nueva Canción* was a cultural project in the sense of communicating a new set of values to the broader public, but it was also an internal culture, a means of solidifying the bonds among the people interested in, or engaged in, the movement for social change. Roy's concept of the "precommunicative" aspect of music is also evocative. Beyond singing in unison, one can employ the concept to understand the emotions provoked by songs without words. Some of the most moving songs of *la Nueva Canción* are instrumentals. The best of this music beautifully captured the hopes, the passions, and the convictions of the political movements. Víctor Jara's "La Partida" is a good example of a sublime instrumental that speaks eloquently without words. The soaring sound of the *quena* seems to project the idealism, the longing, the struggle, and the aspiration for a new society; it also summons bittersweet emotions today, when one realizes that the vision of a generation and a people for a new Chile was crushed by repression.

New Song Musicians: Coming to Music and Politics

As we have seen, social ferment was taking place throughout Latin America and the world in the 1960s and early 1970s. In Chile, President Eduardo Frei had begun an agrarian reform and partial nationalization of Chile's copper industry, the largest in the world. Unionists, shantytown dwellers, peasants, and students were pushing for social change. In the world, anticolonial and revolutionary struggles were taking place, and the Cold War was politicizing the world's peoples. Carrasco explained the international political context of the times:

> The situation in Chile, and in all of Latin America, during this time was difficult. Many countries were in situations of conflict. There were military coups—not yet in Chile—but young people felt deep solidarity; a profound political consciousness was developing as a result of the Cold War and the national crises. There was enormous social injustice, inequality—there still is today, but it was worse then—and the music, like the literature of the era, experienced a political radicalization. We began to sing songs that responded to these situations, and there was an immediate positive response from people. There was an immediate echo among students. . . . Our music did have a political role, not necessarily in transmitting an ideology, but, rather, in the sense of transmitting the spirit of the social movement. *La Nueva Canción* was part of the social movement, not apart from it.[5]

Carrasco explained how he came to music as a young man:

> I loved singing, and I loved classical music. I played music with my brothers. One day Julio Numhauser appeared. He was interested in folklore and invited us to form a group. I wasn't that convinced, I was involved in my studies at the university. Finally I did participate—and eventually I ended up being the only one who remained! Folklore interested us because it was part of the demand of the

national movement. There was growing influence of Violeta [Parra], Víctor [Jara], Argentines like Atahualpa [Yupanqui] too. We were a trio at first and we sang songs from various countries. Our roots were in Latin America as a whole. . . . The music had a powerful impact.

Max Berrú, founding member of Inti-Illimani, came to Chile from Ecuador as a youth in 1962 to see the World Cup soccer tournament. He fell in love with the country and the people and decided to stay and attend the State Technical University (Universidad Técnica del Estado; UTE) in Santiago, which was free at the time, to study mechanical engineering. How did he get involved in politics? He said:

As university students the university reform interested us very much, and we struggled for that, to produce the changes necessary for the people to be able to educate themselves, to have the possibility of a profession. The technical university was one of the most combative universities in this sense. It was the first to win a new statute for the university, to implement the reform, and it took many years to get it and to put it into place, until finally Salvador Allende signed the statute for the new university reform without any critique or any revision. He did that because of the confidence he had in the young people. . . . [T]he Cuban Revolution, the Vietnam War, the events that occurred in France—all of this strongly affected us. As young people, as students, all this greatly interested us. We supported all of these movements, with a lot of activity and a lot of presence. At the same time, this was a form of political growth. Then came the militancy of the different political parties, with different political movements of the Left—the Socialists and the Communists; the MIR (Revolutionary Left Movement [Movimiento de Izquierda Revolucionaria]) of the ultraleft was there, too, and other movements that were identified with leftist ideology. It was understandable that the youth of those years supported movements of the Left, being around Allende, a public personality who was a leader of the Socialist Party and the whole Left. He was, in a sense, a channel for all the dissatisfactions and concerns and a clear possibility to achieve a socialist government.[6]

At the same time, Berrú and other students were fascinated by the music of Latin America. He said:

In terms of song, we were interested in recuperating the cultural values of Latin America, of Chile, that were being lost because the big media didn't take them into account. The media, like television and radio and the specialized magazines, bombarded us with rock-and-roll, foreign music, and the record companies were affiliated with foreign consortia, such as Odeon and EMI. They did not consider the singers of *la Nueva Canción*, the great movement that emerged in the 1960s. It was difficult for us to be able to show what we were doing. Nevertheless, we had a very strong conviction that at some moment this could be opened up—and we did it. . . . There was a new generation tired of rightist governments, conservative governments that didn't solve the problems of the people in general. We had a clear vision that we could change things. And, of course, as a result of the personal activity of each of us— our professional work, our singing, our political work with the social organizations—we were very closely linked to this idea of achieving a socialist government. We participated in many ways, not only in the protests, the marches, but also in composing songs, telling through them what we wanted to say, and much contact above all with the workers, the students, the campesinos. This was our space.

José Seves, the historic member of Inti-Illimani, explained how he was drawn to music as a young person:

In general, I think my case is like many cases in Chile, where there is a family matrix that was very motivating. On the one hand, music was for entertainment; on the other, it was a way to gather people together, a bit like the idea of *el fogón*—people sitting together around the family hearth. In my case, as in many cases, the pleasure of the music was important, a childhood with the radio and radio programs, with a lot of different types of music. From the point of view of Latin America in the 1950s, we had cross-currents of tropical airs, mambo, bolero, and the tango in this period. This is the matrix within which one listens. . . . This motivated me to sing not only in family get-togethers and with friends. I started to receive the support of people who told me to go on radio programs, and I appeared in various talent shows. I was about fourteen then, living in Santiago. And when I was sixteen, my father gave me a guitar. I participated in student festivals, and there was a situation that I remember to be very surprising. Because I am from another generation, I was privileged in the sense of being educated in the public education system, which was of high quality then. It had been created in the 1930s, more or less, and had been extended across the country at all levels. I studied at a primary school and then a secondary school that were public and free. The extracurricular activities—putting on festivals and so forth—were part of the spirit of these institutions then. There were always cultural festivals, and where I participated it was always the case that people would come, the people from our school, to give support—it was very collective—and I remember I participated in a festival in a stadium, a basketball gymnasium that was full of people, which means two thousand or three thousand people had come. It was very important, and this was the first time I had to dare to sing, to confront what might happen on the other side—the acceptance, or not, of the audience. This was the beginning of my path to music.[7]

As a teenager, Seves won two radio contests and recorded his first song with his friend Orlando Salinas.

Berrú continued with an explanation of the impact of the musicians and how he arrived at political commitment with La Jota:

How did the artists participate, lend their support? Recording their songs, making denunciations, carrying out activities with the unions, in schools, in the countryside, with the workers, in short. This was a form of diffusion, too, a way to raise consciousness and learn at the same time. . . . Allende would end each cultural event with a speech. He always had great respect and affection for all the artistic movements, because he always said, "We are the most and the best" (*Somos los más y los mejores*). Because the Right had no such presentations, the art and music were always led by the Left. Why? I think it's because culture is important to develop in any country, because it means the growth of the people. It's something that the Right doesn't understand, because this might give the people new tools. . . . [G]iving the people education, culture—I think this is so important, and it has always been the Left that supports cultural movements, because those movements are transversal; they cross frontiers. . . .

Why did so many of us join La Jota? For one thing, it was more organized than the other parties' youth organizations. . . . It was more capable of organizing things, and it also attracted more artists—Víctor Jara, the Parras, Violeta [Parra], [Pablo] Neruda. There were a lot of important cultural figures who were part of the PC [Communist Party (Partido Comunista)]. This, too, was part of the attraction for all of us, in the moment of making a decision. It seemed more representative of the struggle of the people. Also we were interested in the Socialist Youth, but we realized that there were more intellectuals, and we thought for the functioning of the country the workers—those who produce (*los obreros*)—were the most important. We became militants in La Jota as a group. Of course, we had obligations as militants, but our collaboration was mainly in the artistic sphere. We had an agreement with various unions, organizations of campesinos, and our area of work was in these places. . . .

In the political campaigns, to accompany Communist candidates, or sometimes those who were socialist or on the Left—this was our natural work, and it was constant for the musicians of *la Nueva Canción*. We were also involved in publicity with the most important brigades, like the Ramona Parra Brigade. [Ramona Parra] was a communist who was killed in a demonstration, and the brigade was named after her. The brigade would paint walls with phrases that were simple but deep, that would have an impact on the heart of the people. They were also important in the political campaigns. I remember the last campaign we participated in, in the year 1973. In March, there were elections for Congress. We accompanied Gladys Marín [then the secretary-general of La Jota], who was a candidate for congressional deputy, and Volodia Teitelboim for senator. All through the month of February we worked—we had more than 150 performances—and each day we did between eight and ten. We'd accompany the workers at their workplaces—singing in the street, for instance, for utility workers. If there were ten workers, we'd sing there! Gladys Marín would give her greetings, and then we'd go to another place, and it was like this every day. The same thing happened when we accompanied Volodia. There was an intense itinerary. We also went to big demonstrations, but we'd go from street to street, as well.[8]

Berrú, like the other musicians, explained that neither La Jota nor the PC imposed itself on the artists or gave orders to produce certain types of songs. The artists had creative freedom in this sense:

As a group, we never had the PC tell us, "Do this." Never. We had an encounter once with Volodia Teitelboim. . . . He never said to us, "Do this." Art is the expression of liberty; artistic expression is the expression of freedom. They are closely related. He said that he could not tell us what themes to use—that these had to come from within us. This is why the Right never worried about or was interested in artistic expression. It is synonymous with freedom, and freedom, for the Right, is dangerous.

Horacio Durán of Inti-Illimani Histórico concurred regarding the role of the PC:

There was a long tradition in the PC, from the beginning, to provide cultural education to the workers, exposure to the arts. Culture and music were always present in union meetings, from the days of [Luis Emilio] Recabarren, to gather people together. Many, many intellectuals and artists were close to the PC, not only in Chile, but also in Europe—French intellectuals, [Pablo] Picasso, Neruda. The party was very relevant politically. . . . In Chile, the PC promoted art in cultural and political activities. It was very open in Chile, never trying to impose "socialist realism" in art or music. . . . But *la Nueva Canción* developed spontaneously. It was not formed by the PC. . . . We never used the music in a way to recruit people or generate militancy.[9]

As a university student at the UTE in Valdivia in the late 1960s, Seves was active as an organizer and singer at the *peña* of Valdivia and part of a folk duo named Anita y José. In Valdivia, he gravitated toward La Jota.[10] What led him to that decision? He said:

I think one fact that wasn't minor was that Pablo Neruda was a communist. Then one realized that many people you admired were communists. There's a line there of influences. The other thing is that the PC, in my interpretation, is linked from its beginnings, from its birth, to unionism—but to unionism that is centered in the masses, . . . a force that proposes, advocates, creates a leftist syndicalism and a leftist party. An important figure is Luis Emilio Recabarren, who was present at the origins of the PC and unionism. Without being a professional journalist, he created the first union newspaper and, moreover, advocated the rights of workers and created works for the theater. Finally, the union became a school for the workers, for many people who couldn't read, who were illiterate. For me, all these things are valuable; they have a value that's very important. It gives one a certain confidence, really. What I found interesting—or what motivated us—was that it was an organization that was very broad in the sense of being very large, but also in the sense of representing different strata, which meant that the information that came from it—the social structure of the organization—captured the necessities, the aspirations, and the wisdom of the people and diffused them. It was a way to know the country, as well; what was going on in the country. This is something that was powerful for me—that the party put one in touch with who we are, with our identity. Furthermore, one gained confidence as one realized that people in the party had enormous intellectual and technical capabilities; who could analyze problems; who were in touch with the problems of the country that had to be resolved; and who looked outward. For example, to analyze what was happening in the world that could help in our campaign University for Everyone. And with the capacity to provide a statistical analysis of Chile regarding what was happening with this problem. . . .

What was the role of the state? It was already somewhat a social state, with education that was free and of good quality, and the health system was quite advanced. It was necessary to have people who were technically qualified to study these problems . . . and [who could] support the campaign for higher education for all with information, analysis, arguments. . . . But also it was a period in which there were notable intellectual figures in other parties, as well.

Seves also stressed that the PC did not impose rules or demands but left the musicians free to create their songs.[11]

Ángel Parra also joined La Jota. He explained his participation:

We were almost all militants of La Jota. Rolando Alarcón was a sympathizer. . . . We identified with the PC, and we were all proud of our affiliation. . . . The party left us to do our art. There was complete creative freedom. . . . Víctor Jara was part of the leadership, but I never functioned at that level. Rather, I worked at the base, teaching music classes and so on at La Peña. . . . But *la Nueva Canción* was spontaneous and autonomous. There was no help from the state. . . . The PC was important for the diffusion of the music, but in the formation of the movement, no. . . . But the party was very important in those years. It had 21 percent of the vote and included many, many artistic figures, including Neruda. The party played a moderating role in the Unidad Popular, protecting Allende from more extreme forces on the Left, providing equilibrium in the alliance. . . . The PC was of the working class. We understood that there was a great opportunity to advance under Allende.[12]

Ricardo Venegas of Quilapayún explained why he joined La Jota:

I joined La Jota in 1973. I'd been a sympathizer before. La Jota was a very important movement in the 1960s and 1970s. Why? First, it was a movement of young people. To belong was a voluntary act, and it was a way to be incorporated in a collective that was happy, full of enthusiasm. The people in La Jota were a group of friends, not just a political group. Of course, there were norms, rules. One had to attend meetings: meetings of the cell, discussions. People educated themselves. La Jota had an educational quality. But also there was this aspect of pride in belonging. We were proud to be members. We even had shirts! They were a red color, *amaranto*. You would see people in the streets, dressed in these shirts, and it gave us a feeling of pride. Why did most of the musicians of *la Nueva Canción* participate, have such a strong relation with La Jota? I would say, fundamentally, that the people in the musical groups—not all, but most—felt a strong political identification with the movement of La Jota. It allowed us to develop our art, without imposition. The party never said we had to create this or that song. We weren't militants who went on stage to sing what the party told us to sing. Rather, we were artists. But we had a social consciousness and belonged to a party with a defined political commitment. The fact of belonging to La Jota also permitted us to gain deeper consciousness, receive information and analysis, education. . . . We all participated, in Quilapayún. We all involved ourselves in the political work.[13]

Carrasco explained why he, as a university student, moved from being closer to MIR toward La Jota:

In this era there was a vast social movement. There were many factors that played in favor of a revolutionary position: principally, the Cuban revolution, which signified a challenge, a heroic fight against the United States, with ethical leaders. Che was received in Latin America like a liberator. We were very interested in this. That's one side. The other is that there were movements demanding rights and vindication for the popular classes, but also musically, to recover Latin American folklore. Atahualpa was key in all this, even before Violeta. Atahualpa's music was well-known in Chile. Later, in the university, I encountered the PC, MIR, many revolutionaries and student leaders—some reappeared dead later. All this politicized me. . . . In 1968 we began getting interested in the PC because of the university reform. The response of the PC was much more concrete than MIR's. MIR's position was, reform no, revolution yes! You had to dedicate yourself only to the revolution, which seemed abstract, even absurd.[14]

Carrasco carried out political work alongside the musical development of Quilapayún. He participated in meetings and assemblies, in *trabajos voluntarios*, and helped to organize student demonstrations. He further explained the role of La Jota, saying that it "had a more moderate political approach, it was within the Chilean context. The organization believed in political change but through the democratic system. It was the party closest to

Allende, even more so than the Partido Socialista, Allende's party. We used all forms of struggle but within the democratic system. The PC also had many great artists affiliated with it. Neruda, the whole artistic world was linked to the PC."[15]

Not all the musicians of *la Nueva Canción* were members of La Jota. Mario Salazar, for example, was a long-time member of the Socialist Party through his family. Salazar explained his path to music and the significance of New Song:

> I first came to music playing jazz as a teenager. I played the drums. Finally my mother was about to throw me into the street because of all the noise. As compensation she gave me a guitar. That way I discovered Violeta Parra, Atahualpa.... [T]his was in 1965. That year I moved from Temuco to Santiago to study sociology at the University of Chile.... I met an anthropology student named Julio Numhauser, and we began to work together.... At one party we sang together; we both knew a lot of songs and thought our voices blended well, and we decided to sing together. He had left Quilapayún by then. We wanted to have a different sound, different music, not Andean music like Inti-Illimani or Quilapayún. We tried different styles, tropical rhythms.... We sang some contingent songs about political events; others were more poetic. We sang some very beautiful songs. "Los Colihues," for example, was very popular. People sang it at demonstrations and political events in the 1960s. *Un colihue* is a shoot of bamboo that, when linked together, bend but don't break. We learned about how the Mapuche use it to make weapons, and we were inspired by the discourse of a Mapuche leader to write the song.... We sang a lot in the *poblaciones*, among the campesinos and the poor who were involved in seizing lands (*tomas*). We worked with popular forces and were linked to forces of the Left, La Jota, the Socialist Party, [and] MAPU.[16]

Salazar went on to describe the first speech by Allende after his election, on the Alameda, the main boulevard of Santiago. Some 600,000 to a million people were gathering there in front of La Moneda Palace. Los Amerindios had been invited to sing. "All the people knew our songs," Salazar marveled. "We had to wait at the end of each song because there was such a multitude coming from the Central Station singing that the last verses were delayed."[17]

La Nueva Canción was important to all sectors of the leftist movements of the era. Carlos Zarricueta, who was with MIR at the time, explained that the music and the cultural movement had a strong impact on all young people:

The songs interpreted well what was going on in Chile. . . . The music was strongly linked to the PC. We were very critical of the PC and the UP politically—for example, we condemned the interventions by the Soviet Union, and the PC didn't—but as individuals, we identified with *la Nueva Canción*. The music had social content. It was lyrical; it was high-quality music. . . . The PC was hegemonic in the artistic movement in Chile. MIR people went to the *peñas*, too. . . . The music was very important in politicizing people. It opened new spaces for people to be heard, and the lyrics had social and political content. There were even responses to specific events and realities of the day. It inspired people and mobilized them.[18]

His comments again underlined the political power of music and its capacity to energize and mobilize people.

Another former member of MIR, Héctor Salgado, was a teenager during the Allende government. He was a committed Allendista and was deeply involved in the new music. He said:

La Nueva Canción was not created to play a role. It was very organic. We happened to have Violeta Parra, an amazing woman who was ahead of her time in everything. She became great because her work was unique—her performances, her *arpilleras*, her music. The same with Víctor Jara. And because of Allende, even before he was elected, the whole Left was involved in collective efforts, creating things, getting together and talking, organizing things at the grassroots level. And that is really powerful: when you're able to connect people at the grassroots level and people believe in what they're doing. . . . There was this kind of explosion in Chile in the 1960s: there was very high quality in art, and the music was Chilean."[19]

Salgado was detained after the coup and sent to a prison camp. He was sixteen and accused of being a subversive. After his release, he was expelled from Chile, and he went to the United States. There he got involved with La Peña in Berkeley, which had been opened by Chilean exiles in 1975, and played in the New Song musical group Grupo Raíz. There was also a MIR-affiliated group in France named Karaxú, led by Patricio Manns in its first years. "Our group made three records," Salgado said. "Grupo Raíz went to international festivals. *La Nueva Canción* was becoming global. We started an organization in the United States with Pete Seeger, Jackson Browne, and others around 1984 to link the musicians together." Like those involved in the other parties of the Left, Salgado pointed to the deep interconnections between the counterhegemonic movements of the time and the New Song movement.

Songs as Political Tools?

Mark Mattern has argued that music is a political instrument that should be wielded by musicians to achieve certain ends.[20] Mattern finds Gramsci's analysis of culture overly confrontational and calls for "conciliatory" musical approaches that build bridges between antagonistic social sectors. Music, he argues, does not have to be "confrontational"; at times people should "use music" to achieve political ends by choosing "deliberative" or "pragmatic" musical strategies instead. By "deliberative," Mattern means that people can "use popular music to debate their mutual identity and commitments," and by pragmatic, he means they can "use popular music to organize for collaborative problem-solving."[21] Musicians should use their music not only to protest, he argues, but also to achieve compromise.

Mattern's approach, however, strikes me as overly instrumentalist, missing the complexities and mysteries surrounding the creation of art. His underlying assumptions—that musicians plan their music in such calculated ways, as "strategic choices," and that musical creation can or should be initiated, directed, and "used" to achieve specific political ends, such as collaborative problem solving—seems to misunderstand the creative process and the magic of music. John Street is closer to the mark when he writes that we need to ask "not how music is an instrument of political action, but how it *is* political action."[22] When asked about Mattern's thesis, many musicians told me that music cannot be objectified or dissected in this way; music comes from the human soul, like poetry—from deep passions, concerns, and dreams that poets and musicians try to express artistically. That is, the art of music cannot be reduced to a rational tool, as Mattern implies. It is born through a process of discovery and the search to articulate profound emotions. The expressive quality of the music and the poetry is what matters, as well as the electricity and emotional connection with the audience.

Regarding the idea of music as a tool, Joan Jara quoted her husband as saying, "I function with my heart, not my head. Something touches me inside, and it begins to flourish there until it manages to find a way out."[23] That observation captures the profoundly original, personal, and reflective nature of creating poetry and music. That is, the creation of art is a process of connecting with oneself and with others in powerful, subconscious and emotional ways—Roy's concept of "precommunicative" again comes to mind—as well as conscious and cerebral ways. Joan Jara also noted, "People sometimes talk about the New Chilean Song Movement as though it was a homogenous cultural phenomenon which functioned on the basis of preconceived ideas directed toward definite goals. As far as I could see, it wasn't like that at all. . . . It was essentially a movement of discovery and exploration. . . . Only one thing united everyone, and that was a desire to be part of a revolutionary process and with their work help to develop a new culture."[24]

I asked a number of musicians to comment on the thesis that their music was, or should be, created for specific political ends or determined objectives. They said that this view of the artistic process, of the genesis of song, was misinformed. They argued that music, and art, come from the heart and soul and that music of quality cannot be strategically planned to achieve certain objectives. If such a process were used, they claimed, the songs would be not art but advertisements or propaganda. While the young musicians of *la Nueva Canción* sang against injustice and for liberty as part of their passionate commitment to the struggle for social change,[25] this is quite distinct from the idea of writing songs to achieve specific functional ends. Horacio Salinas of Inti Histórico commented:

> I think generally that art, music—particularly in Latin America, which is a continent that is very, very interesting musically—have always been the product of the life of society, but not an instrument that you can use, I don't believe, for determined ends or to support determined causes. Art has always played a role in human history, a role to make itself part of the discovery of reality and what is behind that reality. Furthermore, the stance of art is essentially critical, from the perspective of the life of the people, the difficulties and afflictions of the people. I think this is very important.[26]

Jorge Coulon, a founding member of Inti-Illimani, rejected the notion of music as part of a political agenda, calling it "very reductionist, reducing the music to propaganda. You can't use the music. Music is a language, which expresses your own identity." He continued:

> We were musicians because we liked the music. Moreover, we were in love with, fascinated with, the discovery of Andean music. We began to discover this enormous wealth of music, of rhythm, of sound. It was unknown, and this was our fascination. We had the luck, in terms of political work, that the PC and the Left had an old tradition of relationships with artists. Neruda was a communist; almost all Chile's intellectuals were of the Left. . . . So there was no relation of utility, let's say. Rather, it was a relation of respect. Nobody ever said to Neruda, "OK—write a poem for the party." And no one ever said to us, "Do this for us." There was great respect, and we were part of this musical tradition.[27]

Seves also noted that La Jota never interfered in the artistic process or gave orders to produce songs. The music was born of obsessions and passions, he explained. It was part of being young and inquisitive, and it was not directed from above:

> *La Nueva Canción* was born spontaneously. It's not at all true that it was a party obligation or resulted from a party order. That's wrong. There were cultural and artistic motivations. It was not organized by the state or any party. The music had to do with the climate of the times: openness, freedom, generosity, fun. It was about the music, about being young, because young people liked to dance. What existed or was born then was in the air. Its roots were spontaneous. . . . In these years, if a group of young people wanted to, they would form a musical or dance group. If La Jota convoked an activity, they would go, but it wasn't required. The original motivation was from being young, from the pleasure of the music. All the institutions were opening up. . . . *La Nueva Canción* helped to create a new identity in Chile. When people went to the *peñas* or heard the music in public places, it was stimulating, knowing it was your music, knowing the country better, feeling validated by discovering the Chilean roots in new songs, something that was ours.[28]

Venegas emphasized the importance of conveying, and awakening, emotion with the music, from the 1960s to the present day. The main objective of Quilapayún, he said, was to have its music impart and provoke emotion within the audience, to reach people's hearts. "We've also developed a form of staging that is a bit different from that of other groups, such as Inti-Illimani," he added. "It's a form of presenting ourselves that's more integral, incorporating elements from the theater to determine our positions on the stage, the way we appear, the black ponchos—all of this is from the days of Víctor [Jara], who taught us a lot in terms of presenting a striking panorama on-stage." He added that the concerts had an intellectual element. The group tried to make people think by asking provocative questions in skits they presented between songs. Finally, Venegas noted that the music unified people and created a sense of community.

A key element, he added, was the communication Quilapayún cultivated with the audience. "We always try to establish *un hilo de plata*. That is very characteristic of Quilapayún, again from the days with Víctor," Venegas said. *Hilo de plata* refers to a silver thread of connection, a special or spiritual bond, a form of energy between the musicians and the public. "It's an image that means that from the moment we appear on the stage, we need to capture the attention of the people and never allow that bond to be lost," Venegas continued. "Everything is planned: changing the instruments after a song, determining who should speak to the audience, whether we need to move to another microphone. All of this was influenced a great deal by Víctor, to present a smooth transition on stage. . . . What interests us is making the audience feel that they are participants. . . . This implies that we don't feel separated from what people feel during the concerts. We are interested in their reactions. We look for people to talk to after concerts. We mix with the public, sign CDs, and so on, and we talk to people about what they liked in the concert. It's nice for us."[29] This last point evokes the idea of the music creating a social relationship between the musicians and the public.

Canciones Contingentes

The *canciones contingentes* (contingent or pamphlet songs) were a subcategory of songs written specifically to respond to current political events. These songs fit most clearly within Mattern's perspective of songs written for a purpose. Especially after Allende's election, as right-wing forces were gathering strength, carrying out strikes and street violence, some musicians rapidly wrote and released many such topical songs to counteract the Right. Often, the lyrics were sarcastic, satiric, and direct; sometimes they were polemical, and the *canciones contingentes* provoked debates within the movement regarding the balance between art and militancy. In one interview, Horacio Salinas addressed the issue when he pointed to "the difficulty in making social justice compatible with song, linking it to appropriate art."[30] Quilapayún strongly believed that there was a need for such songs to respond to urgent situations, to inform people or call them to action. Sergio Ortega was part of the PC's Commission of Culture (Eduardo Carrasco, among other New Song artists, was in La Jota's Cultural Commission), and there were collective discussions about songs that were needed to make a political point.[31] Quilapayún and Ortega were probably the most prolific sources of contingent songs, although many others, including Víctor Jara and Tiempo Nuevo, sang some.

How were such songs different from songs with social and political consciousness, a key characteristic of *la Nueva Canción*? Eduardo Carrasco offered a useful definition: "The difference between political songs and contingent songs is that the latter are composed like jingles, like publicity announcements, more like commercials or propaganda. . . . They are born as a response by the artist to an urgent situation, to denounce something that has occurred. They're created expressly to play a political role."[32] These songs were designed to make a point, not to be poetic or lasting works of art. "We were very aware that these songs weren't at the level of 'La Cantata'—not at all," said Carrasco. "There was a discussion within the movement. . . . But songs like 'La Batea' were tremendously popular, even on the radio, and these songs played a political role. Some people complained about low artistic quality. But there were different options. Everyone did what he or she wanted to without imposing on anyone else. . . . Quilapayún created both forms of music."[33]

Venegas stressed the need for contingent songs in certain situations. If a musician or a group produced only such songs, it might be a problem, he said, but that was not the case with Quilapayún. Contingent songs were just part of Quilapayún's large body of work, which included an extensive repertoire of powerful, poetic songs, as well as sophisticated and haunting instrumentals. Including some such songs in a group's repertoire was important and valuable in the moment, he said. "'Las Ollitas' [The Little Pots], for example, was a way of awakening consciousness in people. You could say there was a political goal. At times, we sang songs to support Allende. Why not?"[34] Written by Sergio Ortega. "Las Ollitas" mocked upper-class women who banged casserole pots to protest against the Allende government—and allowed people to laugh openly at the rich, perhaps for the first time in Chile:

> The right wing has two little pots
> One little, one pretty big
> The little one was just bought
> That one is used only for pounding.

The song mentioned the right-wing group Patria y Libertad (Fatherland and Liberty) and its links to the March of the Pots in another stanza:

> The right has two little pots
> One little, one pretty big
> The little one was just sent over
> By a little errand boy from Patria y Libertad.

Ricardo Valenzuela, former director of DICAP, noted that "these songs had an enormous mobilizing role. They caused a debate, yes. These were 'pamphlet songs' rather than artistic songs. They were instruments of struggle. The music and the lyrics transmitted a political orientation. . . . No one planned this, it was not an order by anyone; it came from collective discussions and from the social and political conditions."[35]

Another contingent song by Quilapayún was entitled "La Merluza." The song encouraged people to eat merluza, a fish that was abundant in Chile, instead of more expensive beef. This was a timely suggestion during the days of the U.S. economic blockade and the strikes by truck owners that stalled the distribution of food in the country. In fact, Quilapayún composed a contingent song to denounce the truck owners' strike, as well. A number of contingent songs became very popular. They were catchy tunes well known to, and sung by, all sectors of the public. Carrasco noted that "even the right-wingers sang 'La Batea' [The Washing Tub]," a witty song with Cuban musical roots that denounced and satirized the Right and Patria y Libertad.[36] During demonstrations and political events, crowds of young people shouted for Quilapayún to sing "La Batea."

Inti-Illimani, among others, did not sing *canciones contingentes*, feeling it was not their style and that *la Nueva Canción* would reach more people by creating lasting works of beauty.[37] They did not want to do "agit-prop" (agitation and propaganda) with their music. Salinas commented, "To us, it was more political to sing Latin American music, which has inherent political and social content. . . . We as a group were never partisans of bringing to our music very politicized lyrics. . . . We never wanted to use song in political battles that way."[38] In one interview in 1972, the group stated: "The future [of New Song] depends on the musical quality and the artistic transcendence that it achieves. . . . A pamphlet that is sung (and badly sung) doesn't help anything, but rather causes damage, by giving arguments to the reactionaries to attack revolutionary artists."[39] Inti-Illimani wrote a pair of articles about the issue, maintaining that a beautiful, poetic song was more faithful to the movement:

> With which creative people could the Right respond to *Cantata Santa María de Iquique*? . . . The matter is clear: they can assassinate a general [General Schneider was killed in 1970], [and] they can try to paralyze a country with their fascist sabotage, but they never will be capable of organizing a mass movement that struggles for its ideals with the strength and the mystique of the popular movement. . . . Art lowered for the masses has been largely overcome and is clearly the worst of paternalism. The solution is not "to make music for the masses" but for the masses to make music themselves. . . . We should work so that the great popular sectors have access to cultural resources.[40]

In short, there were differences and debates within the movement on these songs. But it is important to keep the issue in perspective. The debate was fairly short-lived and did not assume major importance during the exuberant years of the UP, when everything was discussed, criticized, and analyzed as part of the democratic spirit of the time. Nor did it become a conflict: all the musicians and groups followed their own paths, and the music scene flourished.[41] *Canciones contingentes* were accepted as a normal part of street demonstrations, if not part of the lasting contribution of the artists. Later, during the years of exile, as the musicians analyzed the past, the debate became more heated.[42]

Emblematic Songs

The music of *la Nueva Canción* showed that beautiful art and poetry and profound political and social content were not mutually exclusive. The political-poetic resonance of the music of *la Nueva Canción* demonstrated that artistic depth, emotional power, and social consciousness could be combined to produce a tremendous and lasting impact. It is possible to present only a few of the thousands of noteworthy songs and instrumentals of *la Nueva Canción* here. The most memorable reflected social or political passion, communicated profound emotion and commitment, and/or visualized a new future.

Violeta Parra created numerous powerful songs. After years of collecting authentic Chilean folk music, she began to compose her own music and poetry in the late 1950s. One of her songs with social content was "Arriba Quemando el Sol" (Above the Sun Is Burning), in which she laments the miserable conditions of people living in the nitrate region:

> *The rows of huts*
> *face to face, yes sir!*
> *The rows of women*
> *in front of the only basin*
> *each one with her pail*
> *and her face of affliction.*
> *And above the sun is burning.*

The song expressed deep sorrow and indignation at the conditions Parra witnessed and the indifference and injustice of the law and the authorities.

Víctor Jara was one of the most prolific and inspired song-makers of *la Nueva Canción*. Quilapayún and Inti-Illimani sang versions of many of his songs, adding complex harmonies and new instrumental arrangements. (Two striking examples are Quilapayún's version of "El Alma Llena de Banderas" [Soul Filled with Flags] and Inti-Illimani's version of "Luchín.") Jara's "Preguntas por Puerto Montt" (Questions about Puerto Montt; 1969) was a key example of a political song whose artistic excellence elevated it far above a contingent song. "Preguntas por Puerto Montt" recounted how landless families who had been camping on a lot for five days were attacked without warning by Grupo Móvil, the Carabineros' riot control and countersubversive team. The unit had been created and trained to repress student demonstrations and workers' strikes. The Carabineros were financed and trained by the United States, beginning in the early 1960s, as part of the expanding counterinsurgency programs in the hemisphere.[43] (Allende dissolved Grupo Móvil when he became president.) Ten peasants died, including a baby, and sixty more were wounded. The song denounced the massacre:

Very well, I'm going to ask
for you, for you, for him;
for you who were left alone
And he who died without knowing . . .
Ah, he will be most disgraced
He who ordered the shooting
Knowing how to avoid
A massacre so vile
Puerto Montt, oh, Puerto Montt.

In another stanza, Jara specifically named the minister of the interior as responsible for the killing and made an impassioned call for accountability:

You must respond
Mr. Pérez Zujovic,
Why a defenseless people
was answered with guns
Señor Pérez, your conscience
Was buried in a coffin
And your hands will not be cleaned
By all the rains of the South.

Edmundo Pérez Zujovic was Eduardo Frei's minister of the interior and a Christian Democrat, as we have seen. While it is not completely clear whether he authorized the massacre, he did give the order to clear the land. Known for his repressive policies, Pérez Zujovic was an unpopular figure in Chile.[44]

"Preguntas por Puerto Montt" captured the wave of outrage that swept Chile after the massacre. The song probably boosted the legitimacy of the Left in the 1970 presidential elections and further tarnished the reputation of the government and the Christian Democrat Party.[45] Jara first sang the song several days after the massacre in a huge demonstration in Santiago, called by university students to protest the repression. Speakers and artists condemned the crime, and relatives of the victims spoke to the crowd. When Jara sang the song for the first time, a roar of anger and pain arose from the thousands of people in the crowd. Joan Jara notes that the song took on a life of its own: Víctor Jara was asked to sing it wherever he went.[46] "Preguntas por Puerto Montt" enraged the Right and contributed to its particular hatred of Víctor Jara. Some Chileans I spoke with thought that the song had, in effect, signed his death warrant. Joan Jara described violent incidents that occurred after the assassination of Pérez Zujovic. During one concert at a school in which Jara sang the song, conservative students, who had been shouting and heckling the singer, began throwing stones. Later Jara learned that one of Pérez Zujovic's sons had been there.[47]

Jara's "Plegaria a un Labrador" (Prayer to a Farmer) was a beautiful and passionate song that embodied the spirit of hope and struggle of the 1960s. The song won first prize at the First Festival of New Song in 1969. During the festival, Quilapayún accompanied Jara with vocals and music. The song spoke of the power and creativity of the humble rural workers of Chile:

> *Arise and behold the mountain*
> *From whence come the wind, the sun and the water*
> *You who drive the course of rivers*
> *You who sow the flight of your soul*

At the song's end, Jara clearly alluded to the Lord's Prayer when he called on people to unite:

> *Arise and behold your hands*
> *Outstretch them to your brother, in order to grow*
> *Together we will go, united by blood*
> *Now and at the hour of our death, amen.*

Jara's song "Luchín," a moving tribute to a small boy who lived in a *población*, is also a classic. In it, Jara cried out for a better life for all of the children who endured the wretched conditions of the shantytowns:

> *Yes, there are children like Luchín*
> *Who eat earth and worms.*
> *Let's open all the cages*
> *So they can fly like birds.*

Jara composed the music for another poignant song, "Herminda de la Victoria," for a child of the *poblaciones*, coauthored with Alejandro Sieveking. The song told of a baby girl killed by a Carabinero bullet during a *toma* by a landless community:

> *Herminda of La Victoria*
> *Was born surrounded by mud.*
> *She grew like a butterfly*
> *On land that was seized by the people.*

Luis Advis's masterpiece *Cantata Santa María de Iquique*, the ensemble of songs telling the story of the massacre of miners and their families in the North of Chile in 1907, involved close collaboration with Quilapayún. "We invented our own *cantata*, with a national theme," said Eduardo Carrasco. "*Cantatas* existed in Europe, and most people there knew what they were. In Chile, no. So we reinvented a *cantata* within the Chilean context. We wanted to integrate symphonic elements and create a popular opera.... Then Chileans understood what a *cantata* was."[48]

The *Cantata Santa María de Iquique* had a dramatic effect in Chile. The unique music and arrangements, the blending of classical and popular forms, the narrative telling a forgotten story—all of these elements were new and impressive. Chileans were shocked by the history of the massacre. It had been omitted from the history books and forgotten. "This was part of history that we didn't know about, that very few people knew about, because the official story doesn't include such things," Berrú said. "The official story is written by the powerful, who hide many things. *La Nueva Canción* charged itself with relating this history, telling little-known historical episodes that were considered shameful or embarrassing by those who governed. I am sure that this work, which came out before the election, was very important in Allende's victory. I, at least, think this, because many people were moved by hearing it."[49] The final song of the *Cantata Santa María de Iquique* warned Chileans that such episodes did not belong only to the past:

> You who have just heard
> The history that has been told.
> Don't continue sitting there
> Thinking that it's in the past.
> It's not enough, just the memory,
> The song
> will not suffice.
> It's not enough to regret,
> Let's look at reality.
> Perhaps tomorrow or the next day
> Or perhaps a little later
> The history that you've heard
> Will again occur.
> Chile is a country so long
> A thousand things may happen
> If we don't prepare ourselves
> Resolved to struggle.

Sergio Ortega wrote songs that became anthems of *la Nueva Canción* and the UP government. One, "Venceremos" (We Will Win), with lyrics by Claudio Iturra, was a rousing marching song full optimism and hope:

Peasants, soldiers, miners,
The woman of the homeland, as well,
Students, workers, white-collar and blue,
We will do our duty.
We'll sow the land with glory.
Socialist will be our future.
All together we will make history
To comply, to comply, to comply!

Víctor Jara wrote alternative words for the presidential campaign of 1970, directly calling for the election of Allende. "Venceremos" became the campaign song of the UP.

Patricio Manns composed a haunting song in 1970, "No Cierres los Ojos" (Don't Close Your Eyes), warning of impending conflicts with powerful right-wing enemies. Manns wrote the song after Allende's election, when all of Chile seemed to be celebrating. There was a mass triumphal mood, but he felt a sense of premonition.[50] This song interweaves words of homage to the nobility of the working classes of Chile with a call to be vigilant:

They come from the mountain ranges
From the pampa, from the steppe,
From the forests, from the islands.
From the plains or the sea
They are of copper, they are of iron
They are of wool, they are of oak,
They are of sand, they are of snow
They are of stone, they are of salt
They are men of my country. . . .

Take care of your power
Go and be vigilant
Don't close your eyes, don't wake up
Like yesterday.

The song warned Chileans not to take the political change of government for granted: "Go out to combat, the victory is distant." Manns perceived danger years before the coup.

Another emblematic song, "La Exiliada del Sur" (The Exile from the South), featured lyrics taken from the *décimas* of Violeta Parra, with music by Patricio Manns. Manns released the song as a solo version on his album *Patricio Manns* in 1971. While the song was sung by Manns alone, the album was a key example of the collaboration within the cultural movement in Chile and the musical conversation among classical, folk, and rock genres. The album included participation by the Symphonic Orchestra of Chile, Inti-Illimani, and the rock group Los Blops.[51] Shortly afterward, Inti-Illimani released its own version of the song, adding rich harmonies and complex multi-instrumental arrangements. The song contains some of Violeta Parra's classic themes, with its poetry about the tragedies of Chile and her references to leaving parts of herself scattered throughout the country:

> *I left an eye in Los Lagos*
> *By casual carelessness.*
> *The other I left in Parral*
> *In a drinking bar.*
> *I remember as a child*
> *My soul saw such havoc.*
> *Miseries and treacheries*
> *knot my thoughts.*
> *Between the water and the wind*
> *I lose myself in the distance.*

Inti-Illimani's version became hugely popular in Chile, one of the group's most beloved pieces and an archetypal song of *la Nueva Canción chilena*.

Canto para una Semilla (Song for a Seed), the *cantata* written by Luis Advis in 1972 and performed by Isabel Parra and Inti-Illimani, was another classic example of the blending of popular poetry (biographical *décimas* by Violeta Parra), instruments and techniques from *la Nueva Canción*, and elements of opera and symphonic music. Like *Cantata Santa María de Iquique*, *Canto para una Semilla* was a hybrid of classical European musical forms and Latin American influences. Advis was searching for a way not only to put to music the verses of Violeta Parra but to project "her creative personality in various aspects of the reality in which she lived, as well as the symbol that she represents for our times, conflicts, and hopes."[52] The *cantata*, with Parra's verses, developed central themes: "the family," "childhood," "love," "commitment," "denunciation," "hope," "death," "epilogue," and "final song." The piece combined classical orchestra instruments with Inti-Illimani's voices and instruments and Parra's vocals, interspersed with spoken verses by a female narrator.

Perhaps the most famous song of *la Nueva Canción* internationally is "El Pueblo Unido Jamás Será Vencido" (The People United Will Never Be Defeated). Like "Venceremos," it is a spirited marching song, with a shouted chorus that was original and novel in 1973:

On your feet, sing
For we are going to triumph
Flags of unity are now advancing
And you will come marching next to me
And thus you will see your song and your flag flourish
The light of a red dawn
Announces now the life to come

Ortega, who worked with Quilapayún to write the lyrics, apparently was inspired by hearing the shout on the streets of Santiago during a demonstration.[53] "El Pueblo Unido Jamás Será Vencido," which symbolized the hopes and dreams of the UP period, has been translated into numerous languages. For years after the coup it represented resistance to the dictatorship and was sung at demonstrations and at solidarity events worldwide. Even today, forty years later, audiences demand the song at Quilapayún and Inti-Illimani concerts and still rise to their feet, fists upraised, to sing along.

In sum, the testimony of many of the musicians demonstrated that the culture of *la Nueva Canción* was intimately tied to the lived experience, political ideals, and mass movements for social change that characterized the era. In Roy's terms, social relationships were embodied in the music. New Song exemplified an alternative worldview in the Gramscian sense, with its lyrics and its vision of a future of social justice, and became a key democratizing force. As an organic expression of the counterhegemonic political movements of the era, this cultural movement played a central role in opening new spaces for the voices of the excluded, recovering the previously invisible histories of popular struggles, mobilizing and uniting people with a common vision, and constructing a new channel to express demands "from below."

Out of the movement came thousands of original songs and instrumental pieces, deeply penetrating the consciousness of millions of Chileans and crystallizing the movement for social change. While virtually all of the musicians sang politically conscious songs, some dedicated efforts to composing *canciones contingentes* to make an urgent statement or move people to action. These songs, which most closely resembled Mattern's category of "confrontational" songs, were not universally accepted in the movement. In the next chapter, I delve deeper into the political and musical contributions of *la Nueva Canción*.

6

Musical and Political Contributions of *la Nueva Canción*

L*a Nueva Canción* produced a revolution in music, literally transforming the culture of Chile—just as the popular movements of the time were creating a peaceful political revolution. Chile was undergoing a process of democratization pushed "from below" that reconfigured the political and cultural spheres. The popular movements were counterhegemonic in that they challenged and burst through old, ossified structures that had impeded the full participation of large sectors of society. For the first time, masses of the humble people of Chile were becoming protagonists, demanding their basic rights and participating in a new people's culture. "I always mention the same names because they were Víctor's closest associates and also, perhaps, the most visible heads of the song movement," Joan Jara observed, but "there were now hundreds of other groups all over the country. They had sprung up in universities, in factories, in schools, in community centers. Víctor was constantly being invited to act as a judge in workers' song festivals where new composers presented their work."[1] Chile was a creative cauldron in the 1960s, particularly in Santiago. How important was collaboration among the musicians? What was their creative process? How did they compose their songs? Was song writing a collective or individual effort? How did the musicians see their role at the time? Did the music reflect social change—or actively contribute to it? What were the most important musical innovations, and political contributions, of *la Nueva Canción*?

In an evocative analysis, R. Keith Sawyer argues that creativity is enhanced through collective interaction and that it is a social process.[2] He recognizes that there are bursts of creativity in certain historical moments, such as in Florence during the Renaissance. It was not the case that a number of geniuses were suddenly born in Florence. Rather, that explosion of creativity was part of a complex political, economic, and social conjuncture, as well as collaboration and learning among the artists and intellectuals. In effect, Sawyer shows that one must go beyond analyses of the individual and study overarching structural factors. In the case of Florence, Sawyer points to such elements as the political and economic power of the city, the existing systems of apprenticeships and patronage, and cultural values of the community.[3] Artists were mentored and developed as apprentices; artistic individuals did not appear out of nowhere.

Similarly, *la Nueva Canción* was born in the context of major structural changes in the world and in Chile. As new social and political sectors "from below" emerged, making political demands and becoming key actors in Chilean society, the music arose in conjunction with these counterhegemonic movements. "Art is stamped by the culture and time period," Sawyer points out, "Creativity is social in its production and recognition."[4] In Chile, the new embrace of Chilean and Latin American folklore was profoundly linked to the emergent sense of Latin American identity, social concerns, national pride, and pan-American solidarity that was as political as it was cultural. The music of *la Nueva Canción* recognized, valued, and reinterpreted Latin American folk traditions and instruments, bringing a new, socially and politically conscious form of folk-based music to a mass public for the first time.

Steven Johnson analyzes the crucial role of what he calls peer networks in creativity and innovation.[5] Not only do the state and the market create value, he argues, but decentralized groups of people working together innovate by building on one another's work in close surroundings. Often that collaboration is not motivated by commercial reward. Johnson contends that such loose peer networks have laid the foundation for much academic and scientific research, including the scientific revolution during the Enlightenment and, more recently, the development of the Internet. His insights help to explain the extraordinary creativity of the New Song movement. The musicians were in close touch with one another; they were engaged in "musical conversations"; and they experimented with new musical forms during this period, producing many innovations. Moreover, there were new forms of collaboration among various artists working in different fields, including musicians, dancers, and playwrights. As José Seves wrote, "The interdisciplinary collaborations among theater, folk music, classical music are expressed by new works and unprecedented changes in Chilean art in these years. Víctor [Jara] brought the musical language of the campesino to the works of theater he directed. . . . Luis Advis set to music various dramatic works by playwright 'Nené' Aguirre."[6] *La Nueva Canción*'s musicians worked closely with the graphic artists and designers Vicente and Antonio Larrea and Luis Albornoz, who created a design and print shop and worked with the musicians to create innovative album covers and posters. The Ramona Parra Brigade also worked with these designers, and with La Jota, to paint murals throughout the cities with political messages.

In a related argument about collaboration, Jon Gertner shows that the scientific innovations created in Bell Labs were the product of associations among chemists, metallurgists, and others who built on one another's work and linked together the advances being made. As Walter Isaacson comments, sustained innovations "do not occur in an iconic garage or the workshop of an ingenious inventor. They occur when people of diverse talents and mindsets and expertise are brought together, preferably in close physical proximity where they can have frequent meetings and serendipitous encounters."[7] The work of these analysts provides an interesting challenge to those who exalt individualism and perceive innovation as the product of one ingenious person, somehow removed from a social setting.

Collaboration in the New Song Movement

In Santiago in the 1960s and early 1970s, a great deal of collaboration and interchange was taking place among the musicians of *la Nueva Canción*. Moreover, they were surrounded, and inspired, by the tumultuous political events and mass movements of the era. The vast majority of the artists were in Santiago and deeply involved in political as well as cultural activities; the world of *la Nueva Canción* was fairly small in that sense. The musicians knew one another, and many were members of La Jota. They shared perspectives of the importance of Latin American music and a new, revolutionary culture; of political militancy and social consciousness; and of commitment to progressive social change. The collaboration among the musicians had to do with the spirit of collectivity, noncompetition, anti-individualism, and political commitment of the artists to the social movement. "Some 90 percent of the artists were militants of the PC [Partido Comunista (Communist Party)], of the Left," commented Horacio Durán. "There was an identity there."[8]

There were artistic exchanges and a rich cooperation between groups and soloists. At La Peña de los Parra, beginning in 1965, Víctor Jara, Rolando Alarcón, Patricio Manns, Ángel Parra, and Isabel Parra played regularly and worked together—each with an identifiable style—and formed close musical and social bonds. They invited many artists and musicians of *la Nueva Canción* to perform there. La Peña became a key cultural center for *la Nueva Canción*, a gathering place where people could meet friends and hear the new music, as I have shown. During the week, classes were offered for the community to learn guitar and other instruments, art, and music composition, as well as political education, and during the weekend the place was full of people, including intellectuals, students, and artists.[9] As *peñas* appeared across the country, parallel networks of social communication, participation, and collaboration appeared with them, creating an alternative to the restricted commercial networks controlled by the music and entertainment industries.

Víctor Jara was the musical director of Quilapayún from 1966 to 1969, and they played and sang together often in performances and on records. Jara also worked closely with Inti-Illimani, first counseling the group about staging, lighting, and other insights gained from his theater work, and later singing together in different venues.[10] Inti-Illimani collaborated extensively with Patricio Manns. Horacio Salinas and Manns wrote dozens of songs together over many years.[11] There were exchanges and relationships between classically trained composers and musicians and the poets and artists of *la Nueva Canción*. These relationships resulted in a new blending of classical and popular music, as we have seen, including popular *cantatas*.

New Song's poetic lyrics were deeply influenced by Latin America's great poets, in another form of collaboration. In fact, one can trace a line from Chile's outstanding poets—Gabriela Mistral, Nicanor Parra, Pablo Neruda, and others—to the musicians of *la Nueva Canción*. Mistral, who won Latin America's first Nobel Prize in Literature in 1945, had inspired Neruda. He visited her as a youth to show her his early poetry.[12] Neruda and Violeta Parra knew each other in the 1950s; Parra sang at Neruda's house in 1953.[13] Nicanor Parra, Chile's "anti-poet," served as a mentor to his sister Violeta, bringing her to Santiago to study and encouraging her to pursue her songwriting and her singing.[14] Víctor Jara met Violeta Parra in 1957, when she was becoming known for her musical investigations in Chile's countryside. Jara was inspired by Parra, especially her research on Chilean folklore. Like her, Jara had collected songs in the countryside that were being forgotten, and had investigated the roots of Chilean music.[15] Both came from rural backgrounds and humble beginnings. Parra became a mentor to Jara, inviting him to her house to eat, comparing styles and techniques; she encouraged him to pursue his singing and guitar playing.[16] Parra also encouraged him as a composer.

Around the same time in the 1950s, Jara became involved with the folk group Cuncumén. After Jara joined, Cuncumén gradually left behind the "typical" costumes of the *huasos* and peasant girls. Jara introduced real campesino dress, mannerisms, and songs into Cuncumén's repertoire.[17] "That came from Víctor, and it was absolutely new," said Seves. "It was spontaneous. Víctor introduced the authentic language, the music, the clothing of the campesinos. He came from that world."[18] Jara was hugely influenced by Neruda, especially his ground-breaking work *Canto General* of 1950.[19] Jara composed music for Poem 15 of Neruda's early book of poetry, *Veinte poemas de amor y una canción desesperada* (Twenty Love Poems and a Song of Despair; 1924). "Ya Parte el Galgo Terrible" (The Terrible Hound Is Leaving), sung by both Víctor Jara and Inti-Illimani, combined music by Sergio Ortega and poetry by Neruda, and "Aquí Me Quedo" (Here I Stay), with verses by Neruda, was put to music and sung by Jara and by Inti-Illimani. Sergio Ortega wrote music for other poems by Neruda (such as "La Patria Prisionera" [The Imprisoned Homeland], sung by Inti-Illimani). Ángel Parra worked directly with Neruda, releasing one album titled *Ángel Parra Canta a Pablo Neruda* (Ángel Parra Sings to Pablo Neruda); on another, released in 1966 and titled *Arte de Pájaros* (Art of Birds), Neruda recited poems and Ángel Parra sang.

The musicians of *la Nueva Canción* incorporated and set to music the poetry of other great Latin American literary figures, part of the revolution that elevated popular music to new heights. Horacio Salinas of Inti-Illimani put to music poems by Gabriela Mistral ("La Pajita" [The Little Straw]), Cuba's national poet Nicolás Guillén ("Mulata," "Cándido Portinari," "Mi Chiquita"), and the Venezuelan poet Aquiles Nazoa ("Mi Papá y Mi Mamá"). Seves used a poem by Aquiles Nazoa to compose the song "Polo Doliente." Eduardo Carrasco of Quilapayún commented on the significance of the poetry of *la Nueva Canción*: "This sort of poetic elaboration hadn't been present before in popular music. It began with Violeta, with Víctor, with Manns. Violeta was the mother of *la Nueva Canción*, and also part of it. . . . Neruda was a big influence. We musicians wanted to continue in his path."[20] The result of this blending of classical music, folk-based music, and epic poetry was some of the most brilliant music Chile has ever produced.

There were many other crosscurrents among the musicians and poets of the time. Eduardo Carrasco and Horacio Salinas collaborated on the 1974 song "El Rojo, Gota a Gota, Irá Creciendo." Patricio Manns and Silvia Urbina (married at the time) released an album together in 1968, *El Folklore No Ha Muerto* (Folklore Has Not Died). Ángel Parra had a close relationship with Atahualpa Yupanqui, the legendary Argentine folksinger, and Atahualpa became his mentor; Atahualpa was a major poetic and musical influence on him (as was Violeta).[21] Ángel Parra composed Quilapayún's first songs. All of these historical connections speak to the Chilean and pan-American identity of *la Nueva Canción* and the profound impact that the renowned poets of Chile and other Latin American countries had on the young musicians of the 1960s. These cross-cutting relationships were characteristic of the New Song movement, and the collaboration stimulated new musical forms.

Collaboration between Graphic Artists and *la Nueva Canción*

The new music of the 1960s was accompanied by a wave of graphic art that decorated album covers, posters, and walls throughout the cities. Influenced by Cuban poster art and by U.S. popular and psychedelic art, the graphic artists and muralists of Chile in these years were a key part of the explosion of innovative and popular cultural forms. Muralists painted the urban walls of Chile with original designs and frescos daily during Salvador Allende's campaign for president.

The graphic art that adorned the albums of DICAP's New Song artists was vitally important. Vicente Larrea; his brother, Antonio; and their partner, Luis Albornoz (who specialized in photography), spearheaded this pioneering effort. Their revolutionary art had a large impact on the broader cultural scene in Chile, as well. The team designed some one hundred album covers from the late 1960s to 1973. Their posters and album covers redefined the genre in Chile, essentially creating a new art form. Before, most album covers had featured a photograph of the artists. But this small group of designers revolutionized the field, using bright colors, drawings, and modernist images while also incorporating social and political messages in the artwork.[22] Vicente Larrea was influenced by the modernist popular art of Ben Shahn, Herb Lubalin, and Saul Bass of the United States; Saul Bass had worked on graphic designs for the U.S. film *West Side Story* and other movies.[23] There was a noticeable "hippie" influence in their work, as well, which appealed to, and reflected, the youth culture of the 1960s. Antonio Larrea pointed to other influences, such as Mexican muralists. One of his professors, Pedro Lobos, had studied Mexican muralist art.[24]

Vicente Larrea explained that when a cover was needed for the 1967 album *Canciones folklóricas de América* (Quilapayún with Víctor Jara), he and his team were asked to design one.[25] Carlos Quezada of Quilapayún was a fellow art student and friend of the Larrea brothers.[26] At the time, Vicente Larrea was studying interior design and drawing. Rather than opting for a traditional cover, they designed a bucolic, colorful drawing with jungle plants and exotic birds to symbolize the folklore of Latin America. This album cover broke with tradition in Chile and sent a new sort of social and political message. The team—specifically, Antonio Larrea—designed the cover for Quilapayún's 1968 album *Por Vietnam*, the first record issued by JotaJota. The cover featured a photograph taken from a Chinese magazine of a Vietnamese militant raising his rifle in the air. Antonio Larrea worked with the image, reproducing it with different resolutions, contrasts, and sizes, then superimposed one upon the other. The Larreas began to do all of JotaJota's designs.[27]

The spirit of experimentation and creative risk taking was clear in one unconventional album design for Víctor Jara. Antonio Larrea used a photo of Jara to make a design connecting two inverted shots of the musician's profile. The effect was to show Jara with two connected heads looking in opposite directions.[28] The back of the cover for the 1969 album *Pongo en Tus Manos Abiertas* featured this shot.

These graphics had a strong cultural impact in Chile. "We never realized the importance of our work for Chile, how our graphics would mark Chile, until later," Vicente Larrea said. "We didn't gather together all our material until years later. . . . The younger generations, our children and grandchildren, now claim this art as their own. . . . In those years we worked just to make a contribution. There wasn't much pay, but it was part of working for a utopia in those years."[29] Vicente Larrea was involved in the university reform movement in the late 1960s. He and his brother both pointed to the impact of the changing social climate, the atmosphere of freedom and openness to new ideas in design, as a key factor that shaped their art. Their design work was the product of experimentation, of breaking boundaries and exploring different styles, part of the atmosphere of the 1960s, Antonio Larrea said. "People ask if there was political direction. But no—there was a mixture of styles, a search for new things, much creativity. There were many sources for our art. We were always searching. . . . Our work was to create, to be creative; it was the spirit of collective creativity. . . . It affected all the artists and musicians."[30] Like the musicians, the graphic designers were searching for new artistic directions.

During these exuberant years Vicente Larrea and his teammates worked around the clock to produce posters for the struggle for university reform, for musicians and concerts, for the *trabajos voluntarios* (voluntary work projects), and for political events. "We had musicians in the house all the time," Vicente Larrea explained. "Someone would come and say they needed a poster or a brochure, and we would sketch one and print it rapidly. . . . We were busy printing twelve hours a day. . . . We wanted to develop our own art, our own folklore."[31] The art made a strong contribution to Chilean identity in those years and to the burst of cultural innovation, Larrea added.

Antonio Larrea pointed to the cross-fertilization among artists and an environment of creative freedom that was collective, not individual. "There was always communication with the musicians," he said. "The musicians would give us the idea of the album, the songs on the record, and we would create designs or photographs. We would look for how to symbolize key concepts. It was very collective. There was an atmosphere of equality and respect."[32] This small design enterprise played a significant role in the emerging culture of the 1960s and in the success of DICAP. The team produced dozens of posters and album covers at a rapid pace and captured the essence of the era. The artwork for album covers and posters was revolutionizing, with intricate and colorful pictures, original ideas, and avant-garde images that represented the spirit of the youth culture, as well as the committed radical politics of Chile. "The music and the graphic art gave a strong sense of identity to Chileans," said Vicente Larrea. "This was consequential because we weren't copying anyone else's style. Our art represented Chile and *el pueblo*, the people of Chile. People identified with the art because it was *chileno*. There was a pride in ourselves. Young Chileans identified with the artists."[33]

The Ramona Parra Brigade also had an enormous influence on Chilean culture in the 1960s and early 1970s. Created by a resolution at the Sixth Congress of La Jota in 1968,[34] the brigade used public walls to communicate with masses of people, mobilize them, and bring new images of social change to Chilean society. The other parties of the Unidad Popular (UP) created their own teams of muralists, as well. The murals by the Ramona Parra Brigade were particularly ubiquitous in Chile. They were also influenced by modern forms of pop art, Cuban and Mexican muralists, and art of the U.S. counterculture. The renowned artist Roberto Matta collaborated with the brigade on some of its murals. The Larreas had a working relationship with the brigade, helping its artists with designs for their murals and sometimes visiting the La Jota offices to work with brigade members. But again, the movement was organized by the artists, not imposed by any party, Vicente Larrea said. "This was not coming from the PC. People were creative, and the party lent support through its organization, through DICAP, through organizing shows, and so on. But it was a movement from the bottom up."[35]

The Ramona Parra Brigade painted walls in public plazas and in urban neighborhoods to display bold and colorful designs with political messages. Its art was another aspect of the explosion of popular culture in those years. "Like the art of primitive Christians, the urban murals were made of symbols and letters. The dove, the hand, the spike, the star, all are like the language of a new faith that for a long time was realized in the clandestinity of the night,"[36] wrote one author. In 1969, as the UP formed and Allende's campaign began, the muralists joined the effort to elect Allende. The brigade painted the Larreas' artwork from the cover of Inti-Illimani's *Canto al Programa* on walls throughout Chile.[37] With their visual impact and their interconnections with the music and the politics of the time, the muralists were another example of the collaboration of the period that resulted in public artistic innovations. They popularized political messages of Allende's campaign, thus playing a key role as political and social communicators. One of the founders and artists of the brigade, Alejandro "Mono" González, wrote, "One cannot separate art from the human habitat: the cave artists and their sustenance, the primitive Christians and their symbols. Art is a social phenomenon, and therefore the artist is linked to society just as art is linked to religion or to politics. This is reflected especially in the art of the mural or recorded art—it is a social expression."[38]

This fusion of graphic art and *la Nueva Canción* demonstrated that collaboration had a powerful and innovative cultural impact in Chile. The art and the music developed together, each drawing from the currents of freedom and creativity that marked the country in those years. Essentially, whole new fields of art and music were created.

The Creative Process of the Musicians

In some musical groups, the musical direction was in the hands of one person, who took charge of arrangements, harmonies, and instrumental parts,[39] but there was also participation from all the musicians in new songs. There seemed to be a different approach in the groups Quilapayún and Inti-Illimani. In Inti-Illimani, Horacio Salinas and José Seves collaborated on the composition of a number of songs, but both said that it was difficult for more than two people to compose a song together. In contrast, in Quilapayún "there is a lot of participation; it's a collective effort," said Ricardo Venegas. "Some songs, like 'Malembe,' came out of jam sessions! But we send all our raw material to Eduardo [Carrasco], the musical director. . . . The process of creating a song is magical."[40]

Not all musicians of *la Nueva Canción* worked the same way. While some created songs through a collective process, others found that songs and poetry came to them as individuals, unbidden. Others said that rather than waiting for inspiration, they had to dedicate time to elaborate and develop the music. Here I relate responses from some of the prominent songwriters of *la Nueva Canción* in terms of their creative processes.

Horacio Salinas, a prolific creator of music (he does not write lyrics), said that composing songs was "work like any other. You have to dedicate yourself." When asked how he wrote music—whether it arrived through inspiration or hard work—he responded:

> It's not so much inspiration. One always has a disposition—an ability, too—to create what one creates. This ability is always present. What happens is that sometimes there must be time and space allotted for one to be able to do such things. In such times, one is 100 percent dedicated and concentrated, in a much fuller way. . . . But this question of inspiration. . . . It doesn't exist. What does exist is a necessity, almost biological, to create, to take a leap, to decompress, to look at things and deliberate. . . . In this process there is sometimes a moment when one finds something more interesting [and] others

less so, perhaps. Then there is work to do afterward—a period of observation, of letting things settle, which on some occasions means you have to leave something aside, because it isn't very interesting.

When asked whether the process of creating new songs was a collective process within the group, Salinas said: "It's relatively collective, but some people don't give many opinions. . . . Do you know what a *camello* is? It's a horse painted by a committee! It's a picture painted by many hands. . . . Things are consensual, but there is a matrix idea, an idea that makes everything coherent." When asked whether other members of the group contributed parts with their own instruments, he responded, "Yes, . . . but under direction. . . . The directing is very important, because without it you end up with a *camello*: things are produced that aren't coherent."[41]

Seves agreed. "For us, the collective process does not exist," he said. "Two can write a song, like [John] Lennon and [Paul] McCartney. When I compose songs, I show them to Loro [Horacio Salinas], and he'll tell me to pay attention to one thing or another. When I was listening to a lot of Afro-Peruvian music, I began 'Samba Landó,' and Loro suggested a flute, a way to accompany the melody. The two of us worked on the song together."[42] When asked how he created songs, he said:

> For me, composing a song is the result of obsessions, of an idea haunting me. Sometimes the motivation of the lyrics will inspire the music. One can imagine a certain state of mind that the music can represent. . . . I have a song, "Cantantes Invisibles," that was born when I was listening to a lot of Puerto Rican music. Puerto Rican music is different from Cuban *son*. It has some Afro-Cuban elements, but Puerto Rican music is different. I love this music, and I realized that some of the songs reflect problems—immigration problems, identity problems—but at the same time, the music is danceable, happy. It still makes a social critique. It gave me the idea for "Cantantes Invisibles," a song dedicated to the people who sing on the streets, in buses, but remain invisible in the media. And this song of mine had no play on the radio! . . . Sometimes the music comes first, and sometimes the lyrics come first. With the song "Colibrí," I found the music as I was playing around on the guitar. I wrote the words as *décimas*, ten verses. The song is linked to my father, of looking for shipwrecked people when they're let out of prison. I found the music first in this case. . . . It was the opposite with "Cándidos." The inspiration for that song was the book *Autumn of the Patriarch*, by Gabriel García Márquez.[43] The book is written in rhythmic prose that I liked very much. It was a long process to compose this song.

I saved material over a long period. I noticed his use of words and how the cadence changed. I started forming stanzas from them. . . . I noticed in the book that when there were words with accents on the first syllable, a tragedy was about to happen. Various popular songs also use these sorts of words to make sarcastic comments. Moreover, the book is based on the lives of Latin American tyrants. Whenever there are popular uprisings and ensuing repression, there are more words with accents on the first syllable. I looked for such words to put in my song. This song involved a lot of work to develop.

Patricio Manns related a different sort of creative process. For him, the music and the lyrics often arose together, whole and complete. "A song could emerge in a bus or in another environment. It arrives, it presents itself. I don't exert any effort," he said. "It germinates within oneself, the song appears."[44] Manns offered his views on why there were so many musical innovations at the time. "It was a special period," he said. "There were many original composers: poetry was flourishing in ways that have never come again. There were new songs every week, with so much creativity; every night people produced more music." In exile, Manns continued to work with Inti-Illimani to collaborate on new songs, but the process took place long distance, often by telephone. Manns was living in France, and Inti-Illimani was living in Italy. Salinas would sing or play music over the phone, and Manns would compose lyrics to the song, he commented. But the distances imposed by exile took a toll on the process of collaboration. "In Chile, it was easier to work with other people," Jorge Coulon said in an interview in 1980. "To work with other people, such as Patricio Manns, we have to go to Paris . . . and Paris isn't very close. It isn't easy to put together a poet and a musician and create songs. We've had to begin writing some lyrics—some good, some bad."[45] Coulon's comment made clear that the collaboration that was possible in Santiago had stimulated musical creativity through the blending of talents and ideas.

Carrasco wrote about the process of collaboration that took place when Víctor Jara became the musical director of Quilapayún:

He was a soloist, and what he had done with Cuncumén or other groups hadn't required him to deploy his musical talents. For him, [our collaboration was] an enriching experience, made up of small discoveries, new melodies that emerged every day, and new ideas for songs that responded to our necessities as a group. It's interesting to point out that many of the songs Víctor created in this period were not for soloists, like his previous songs. They included choruses, responses, more complex instrumentalization. For that reason, it is not an exaggeration to say that there were mutual influences in this period and intense poetic and musical collaboration.[46]

Jara brought a sense of discipline to the young musicians of Quilapayún, who had not been too serious before. He also imparted his knowledge of theater, developing a stage presence for Quilapayún that reflected a seriousness and gravity that matched their songs. But Jara never imposed himself, Venegas said. "Our process has always been very collective, participatory. Víctor never gave orders. He proposed things, but he was always very respectful of all of the musicians. That attitude of respect stayed with Quilapayún."[47] Carrasco agreed: "Víctor was the director we needed. He wasn't the type to impose an idea that he had in his head and that he wanted to realize with others who were his tools. Rather, he was a collaborator who participated in a common project and who oriented things in the sense of their own natural evolution. He was like a force that pushed the seed to develop into the tree that it had to be. . . . It was truly an experience of collective work in which every one of the participants expanded his own creative potential."[48]

Carrasco also related the developing ways of composing songs collectively within the group:

> During the preparations for our album *Basta*, we had an interesting experience: because we were short a song to end the LP, we resolved during a rehearsal to put ourselves to work and try to make a song as a common project. We took a poem by Nicolás Guillén and began to put it to music. The beginning of a melody occurred to one person; another invented a response; another arranged the rhythm; and thus, in a true rapture of collective inspiration, the song "La Muralla" was born, one of the few songs of this period that we still sing. Afterward, we kept using this method, and we've been able to see that collective composition of songs is possible. It's true that this supposes a certain discipline in the common work, but this exercise demonstrated that, with a good system, many things can be addressed that, by definition, seem impossible. Creative expression is eminently individual, but song—a genre in which there are more or less established forms—can lend itself to collective work.[49]

Ángel Parra, a soloist, had another perspective on the creative process in this period:

> There was a lot of collaboration. But I don't think it was a source of creativity. For example, Víctor would make records and ask me to play the *guitarrón*, but he came with the song prepared. Or Rolando

[Alarcón] would ask me to play the *quena* on one of his songs. Each person had his own personal style. No one sounded the same as anyone else. But there was a great sense of accompaniment, of friendship, of solidarity. We worked together every weekend at La Peña, and we played guitar together—with Víctor, for example. On . . . Mondays, Víctor would be there playing guitar with Isabel. It was beautiful. Without envy, without concerns. When they contracted me to be on the radio, I invited everyone—everyone! I would say, "Yes, I'll come. But you have to invite the others." . . . Between Quilapayún and Inti-Illimani there was more collaboration, perhaps; also with Víctor with "Los Siete Estados" [The Seven States]. Maybe with others.[50]

Parra also commented, "Rolando helped with 'El Oratorio,' just as I played the *quena* and Isabel played the *charango* in 'Si Somos Americanos.' We helped each other. There was an interchange of knowledge and experience without any claims, without wanting to make these records 'duets,' which appeared later in the music industry. And we did it without charging a peso. It was something very lovely and perhaps unique. What we lived in those years was extraordinary."[51] This sort of collaboration among the artists was widespread and created an environment of collective learning and sharing that was conducive to creativity.

Ángel Parra was home-schooled by his mother and, like many other young musicians of the 1960s, never learned to read music. "I use my brain," he said, with humor. "I write the music and the lyrics at the same time. Luckily, there are tape recorders if I need one. . . . I work alone. I'll sing a new song once, twice, rearrange things, sing it again, and the song remains. I use formulas that are simple and straightforward. I like the message to be simple and direct, clear. The challenge is to be direct, poetic, and profound."

Musical Contributions of *la Nueva Canción*

La Nueva Canción transformed the culture of Chile, as we have seen. The musicians pointed to a number of innovations and creative breakthroughs that occurred during the 1960s and early 1970s, some of which have been discussed in this book. José Seves, for example, stressed the new cross-fertilization between classical music and popular music, the fusion of the two, as a key innovation of *la Nueva Canción*. Eduardo Carrasco concurred: "The *cantatas* were an important example of this innovation. They incorporated the participation of classical musicians and their resources to develop new musical forms—from symphonies, for example: counterpoint, complex harmonies, and classical instruments."[52] Horacio Salinas described such fusion this way: "Violeta was the first to do this. 'Volver a los 17' used a Venezuelan *cuatro*, which became a typical characteristic of New Song, and the song had classical elements. . . . The roots of New Song were in folklore, and we created new departures. One foot was in Latin American folk, and the other was in creativity, invention, a certain intellectual claim, more complex forms from the classical world of music."[53] The previous hierarchical structure of Chile's musical culture dissolved as classical and popular elements were combined.

Quilapayún had another innovative musical project in mind: to create a popular opera in the Chilean context. The group's members perceived a certain logic, branching from *Cantata Santa María de Iquique* to the development of new musical forms, said Carrasco.[54] In Europe, for example, there had been an evolution from religious musical forms to narratives and instrumental development, culminating in arias and operas. The members of Quilapayún recognized that in Chilean popular music there were also expressions of tragic histories and romances in folklore. There was a tradition of poetic historical narratives, myths about huge earthquakes or shipwrecks. The aim of Quilapayún was to build from this tradition and to create a popular opera. The group was working with Pablo Neruda and groups of young people but was never able to complete the project because of the coup.

The musicians also pointed to the importance of the new musical—and political—identity that emerged with New Song as a key contribution. "Andean music became massively known for the first time," Seves said, "and *la Nueva Canción* helped to create a new identity in other senses: knowing the music was ours, it was Chilean, although the music was born of Latin American folklore from many countries."[55] He identified the Mexican *guitarrón*, the Colombian *tiple*, and the Peruvian *cajón* as instruments brought into Chilean music by Inti-Illimani. Carrasco also highlighted the new musical identity that emerged in Chile in the 1960s. "It was important that new elements were incorporated that weren't considered part of our national music before—Andean music, for example. Today, Andean music is considered Chilean, as is the use of the *quena* and the *charango*. There was a redefinition of Chilean identity." Beyond instilling a sense of continental solidarity in Chileans, *la Nueva Canción* integrated parts of the country—the North and the South, which had not been considered fully "Chilean" before—and marginalized social classes into the music, expanding the sense of Chilean identity.

Interestingly, some of the musicians of *la Nueva Canción* were open to incorporating U.S.- and European-influenced rock-and-roll, despite the fierce dedication to realizing Latin American identity. Seves explained that the Beatles' harmonies and vocal choruses made a large impression on young Chilean musicians in the 1960s and were adapted by some singers.[56] The rock historian Fabio Salas also highlighted the major influence of the Beatles in contributing to the spirit of rebellion in the 1960s.[57] Most groups and solo-ists of la Nueva Canción were dedicated to acoustic instruments. But Víctor Jara and Ángel Parra incorporated elements of rock such as electric gui-tars in some of their songs. Both recorded songs with the Chilean band Los Blops, which drew inspiration from the Beatles, among other rock groups. Los Blops participated in Víctor Jara's album El Derecho de Vivir en Paz (The Right to Live in Peace; 1971) and with Ángel Parra on Canciones de Patria Nueva/Corazón de Bandido (Songs of the New Homeland/Heart of a Bandit; 1971).[58] "Víctor was interested in the lyrics they had," said Joan Jara. "He believed that folk music was alive, living, and dynamic—it wasn't just music from the past."[59] Los Blops recorded albums with both DICAP and the La Peña de los Parra labels. Illapu incorporated an electric bass guitar. In short, another innovation of la Nueva Canción was the blending of elements of rock and folk by some musicians.

Yet another musical innovation of la Nueva Canción, along with the incorporation of new instruments, was its development of instrumental music, which was not present in earlier Chilean musical traditions. In tra-ditional Chilean folk music, one or two guitars and perhaps an accordion were typically used. Not only did the New Song musicians greatly enrich the variety of instruments in their music. They also developed instrumen-tal interludes, or complete songs, that were almost orchestra-like, moving instrumentalization from a secondary to a primary role. "In particular, in Chile, instrumental music began to be developed, along with a new way to sing in choruses," Horacio Durán said. The lack of instrumental music "probably had to do with the scarcity that we had in Chile of indigenous instruments. We incorporated the indigenous instruments of Bolivia, Peru, Ecuador, and the North of Chile [and] produced a new kind of multi-instru-mental music. Quilapayún began this revolution. For us it was a great con-tribution."[60] The music of Inti-Illimani is celebrated for its intricate musical rhythms, structures, and tempos, as well as the interweaving of numerous string and wind instruments. The song "Polo Doliente," for example, fea-tures a change of key and tempo and a multifaceted instrumental dialogue among guitar, tiple, cuatro venezolano, and harp in a complex interchange and counterpoint.

Perhaps the most important innovation was New Song's synthesis of tra-ditional rhythms and melodies of folk music with modern, original, complex elements. Rodrigo Torres noted in his 1980 work that the music combined tradition and renovation.[61] Using traditional folk music as a base, the song-writers created imaginative new compositions that brought in discordant notes and harmonies, multiple and unusual chord progressions, modern chords such as minor and diminished sevenths and ninths, and new ways to play the guitar and other instruments. Their politically aware and committed lyrics were profoundly different from earlier forms of folk music, as was their consciousness of Latin American and international connections. In addition, the song lyrics were poetic as well as politically and socially conscious. The lyrics, by the songwriters themselves or from classical Latin American poets, elevated the music to new heights by combining social conscience with sublime poetic structures and meanings.

Quilapayún initiated another departure in the 1970s that can be seen as both musical and political. The musicians decided to form new Quilapayún groups, in effect reproducing the original group, to draw in new people, including high school students and women, and get away from the idea of "stars." The various groups could perform in different parts of the country at the same time, thus responding to multiple requests for the very popular group to perform throughout Chile. Carrasco said:

> This was a mix of several ideas. In Latin America and elsewhere, an artist must invent and reinvent—especially, reinvent ideas that may be from elsewhere but can be reconfigured in the Chilean context. We did this with the *cantata*. . . . It was also the root of the idea of forming new Quilapayún groups. We had four groups of young people, about fifty persons. We taught them our repertoire, and they began to develop their own. We were involved in this project when the coup came. But several of the musicians stayed with Quilapayún: Hugo Lagos, Ricardo Venegas, "Huaso" Carrasco, and Juan Valladares, who later sang in Ortiga.[62]

This initiative was also a key example of collaboration. The older members of Quilapayún were training and mentoring younger musicians, some of whom went on to become important artists in Chile during the traumatic period of dictatorship.

Ricardo Venegas discussed his incorporation into one of Quilapayún's "clone" groups. Venegas had been greatly influenced by the Beatles and taught himself to play the guitar by listening to their songs. "In 1972, a good friend who played the *quena* showed me an ad in *El Siglo*," he said. "Quilapayún was searching for musicians. We decided to apply. . . . I ended up staying with the group. I thought it was important to do it, not only to play music, but also to help send a message to others about our commitment, our heart. I left my studies. There was a cost later, but I'm not sorry. . . . Quilapayún diversified; there were five or six groups at the same time. I remember our group played in Punto Arenas. . . . It was a way to de-personalize the group, and people accepted it. It was the mystique of Quilapayún."[63]

Juan Valladares further explained the significance of the multiple Quilapayúns:

I joined Quilapayún with a group of teenagers. I was only fifteen. We saw an ad in the magazine *Ramona,* which was published by La Jota, that called for interested young people to audition for a project of Quilapayún. We couldn't believe the ad! It was like a dream.

Quilapayún was already very well known and popular. It was central in *la Nueva Canción chilena* and in the political process of the Unidad Popular. . . . They already had a history. They presented a lot of concerts at schools, to the youth. . . . We listened to their records and to those of Inti-Illimani and Ángel and Isabel Parra. . . . This was in 1971. We presented ourselves at the audition—various friends and I, adolescents. . . . There were two groups. One was made up of teenagers, and one was made up of women. That made an impression! The groups at that time were either all women or all men. There weren't many mixed groups. . . . So we formed two new groups, similar to the central group of Quilapayún. . . .We called them "the Old Men." That was their nickname. They were twenty-four or twenty-five![64]

Valladares explained that each of the "Old Men" was in charge of one of the new groups. "Willy Oddó was in charge of our group," he said. "We called him Uncle Willy. . . . He taught us the repertoire, including *Cantata Santa María* . . . , and this meant that we could perform when Quilapayún was on tour in Europe or the United States. We could play during the voluntary work projects, in factories, in the North or South, accompanying a senator or congressperson during campaigns of the UP." Valladares said that Quilapayún drew on the experience of an agit-prop group in East Germany that used its music to send topical messages. Other musicians in *la Nueva Canción* teased his group, calling its members "Quilapayuncitos" (little Quilapayúns). All of the Quilapayún groups had a similar sound and stage presence, thus multiplying the impact of the group throughout Chile. "They were our idols!" said Valladares.

Political Contributions of *la Nueva Canción*

La Nueva Canción played a crucial political role, as well as a key musical role, in Chile and in the world. First, New Song embodied an alternative worldview and the possibility of a new future of social justice. The music told forgotten histories, serving as a vehicle for historical memory. The music had a combative quality, a new militancy and political conviction, that empowered and mobilized people. The "hymns" of the movement, such as "Venceremos" and "El Pueblo Unido," brought crowds to their feet to sing and chant with the musicians. The musicians were organic intellectuals in the Gramscian sense, with their critique of existing political injustices and power structures. Moreover, the musicians articulated a future of social equality that stirred working-class, peasant, student, and intellectual sectors of Chilean society and inspired their hopes and dreams. Thomas Turino has analyzed the ways in which the arts provide us with a glimpse of what might be. "Musical experiences foreground the crucial interplay between the Possible and the Actual," he writes. Human beings need "the Possible"—hopes, dreams, aspirations—in life, and the arts can "awaken us from habitual routines. . . . The arts are a realm where the impossible or nonexistent or the ideal is imagined and made possible."[65] In this sense, *la Nueva Canción* communicated the dream of a better society and a better world and helped make them possible.

A second central way that New Song made a political impact was in its power to raise political consciousness. It was a politicizing and educating force: people learned from the songs, and people began to develop a new sense of political life and a new sense of identity. Eduardo Carrasco discussed the reciprocal relationship between reflecting social change and helping to create it. "It's not one or the other," he said. "The music was an expression of change: political, economic, social, and cultural change. *La Nueva Canción* was one of the manifestations of this global change in society. At the same time, the music had consequences in terms of consciousness within society. There was a certain active element. The songs presented certain problems, called attention to them. Both of these aspects intertwined."[66] Patricio Manns also wrote about the power of song to raise consciousness and mobilize people:

> Because of their words (the text), songs are a definitive and unique form of communication born of language and surpassing poetry, precisely because they harness music and text in the same yoke. This is why songs play such a major social role. . . . A song is written for many people and its mobilizing power is such (there is no defense against a good song) that here and now, just as in the past and in the future, it is, was, and will be a multidirectional weapon of enormous constructive power. . . . In our age liberators and minstrels are the first to be assassinated. . . . Let us understand clearly that we will be asked to spill our blood for a hundred years for the right to sing for a day.[67]

A third political impact of the music was to give voice to the voiceless. The music became an important democratizing force in this sense by making the excluded and marginalized visible, telling their stories, and awakening others to their demands for social change. The music created awareness of the lack of justice in society and the difficulties faced by marginalized groups. Víctor Jara's album *La Población* of 1972, as I have analyzed, spoke movingly of the hardships of the shantytown dwellers and brought them to a larger audience. This is one example among many.

A fourth contribution was the music's power to convoke people and unify them in a common struggle. "There were huge numbers of people on the Left before the coup," noted Fabio Salas. "*La Nueva Canción* had an enormous impact on the country, convoking many thousands of people, and not only from the Left."[68] In the 1960s, *la Nueva Canción* articulated the passions and demands of the rising social movements. With the beginning of Allende's presidential campaign in 1969, the music attracted people to pro–Unidad Popular events and communicated the possibility of electing a popular government. Every political rally and speech had a cultural component, and the musicians opened the events. "Musicians did draw people to political acts," said José Seves, "but there was a reciprocal effect. It was prestigious for the unions and others organizing events to include the music and for artists to participate, but it was also prestigious for us to be part of these popular political events."[69] The large gatherings instilled new social relationships among people in the crowd, in Roy's sense. There was a new awareness that the problems people faced were not individual at all but widely shared; they were not the result of personal inadequacies but of structural inequities. To realize this was a deeply politicizing experience. During the UP government, the musicians continued to sing of Chile's realities and also sang in support of the government, using the power of song to communicate with large publics. The contingent songs were a new means of social and political communication and a response to rapidly changing events, although they were not universally accepted, as I have shown.

A fifth political impact of *la Nueva Canción* was its function as an innovative means of popular social communication. The songs spread counterhegemonic ideas and messages directly to masses of people through concerts and gatherings, large and small, throughout Chile and elsewhere, bypassing the conservative media. Indeed, the New Song concerts may have reached more people than newspapers or television, which were not accessible to many people in the Chilean countryside. In this sense, the music carried out social functions: it informed people, empowered people, transmitted new ideas. This does not mean that the songs were pamphlets, although some were designed to be exactly that. As many musicians argued, taking the music of Latin America, the music of Chile, to masses of people was politically important in and of itself. The music helped to create a new sense of pride in Latin American identity. Moreover, the poetic-political songs of *la Nueva Canción* told histories in moving ways that were mobilizing and illuminating politically but simultaneously were works of art. In 1970, Inti-Illimani produced *Canto al Programa* (Song to the Program) to popularize Allende's program when it was essentially blocked by the conservative media. Ángel Parra released *Canciones de la Patria Nueva* (Songs of the New Homeland) in 1972. Patricio Manns and Ángel Parra both wrote songs that warned about impending dangers from the political Right. As semiofficial representatives of Chile's new UP government, the musicians of *la Nueva Canción* communicated the hopes and aspirations of Chileans to the world when they traveled abroad, inspiring an enormous solidary movement with Chile.

A sixth political impact of the music was that it contributed to democratizing the culture of Chile. The artists felt that their role was not only to perform but also to stimulate masses of people to participate in cultural activities; to develop their creativity in tandem with others; to participate in music, dance, and theater; and to link art to their own lives and experiences. "Culture for All" was one of Allende's Forty Measures. While Allende's goals were implemented only partially, the late 1960s and early 1970s saw a massive wave of creativity from "below" in Chile. Ordinary people began to learn to play the guitar and sing, to join theater and dance groups, and to participate in creating a popular culture. Víctor Jara commented on this phenomenon:

> Today *la Nueva Canción* is basically the language of the people, of the youth in Chile. . . . There are new composers among the workers, in factories, in the copper mines and the coal mines who organize their own festivals and compose their own songs. The songs speak of their work and their experiences. They never had this opportunity before, and the festivals are something extraordinary. There are composers no one had ever heard before, not even their own *compañeros*. In these festivals they appear with songs that are noteworthy, impressive. And we in *la Nueva Canción* are happy because now the music is everywhere. It belongs to everyone.[70]

During these years in Chile, there was also a huge expansion of popular theater and dance and massive distribution of inexpensive books and newspapers among large sectors of society, reflecting pent-up demand for cultural development, as well as the new, socially conscious role of the artists.

A final political (as well as musical) contribution of *la Nueva Canción* was that it formed a permanent part of Chile's cultural patrimony and heritage and was a source of strength and solidarity for Chileans both before and after the coup. Max Berrú spoke of returning to Chile in 1988 after Inti-Illimani's fifteen-year exile. Augusto Pinochet and the dictatorship were still in power, but the musicians had recently learned that the regime had lifted the ban on their return. At the airport, some five thousand people were waiting to greet them. They boarded a bus and went to a park, where thousands more Chileans had gathered spontaneously to hear them sing. Inti-Illimani improvised a concert. Berrú said:

> What made such an impact on me was that the people knew all the lyrics and sang along with us, including the most recent songs we'd done. What this said to me, and to my comrades, was that somehow they had heard the tapes, copied them clandestinely and passed them around to others. This was something so enormous, so important, that we'd entered the heart and soul of the people. It had fortified them to keep on struggling. How many people have stopped me to say, "Thank you for this song." One woman came to me and told me that "Dolencias" [Afflictions] was the most beautiful for her because when she was tortured she thought of the song and could bear it. Imagine that something like this could happen—the result of work that was ethically correct.[71]

As Gitano Rodríguez wrote, "*La Nueva Canción* has been an element of identity for thousands of Latin Americans, born in exile or not. In any place in the world where there is a group of Chileans, they will be singing the songs of *la Nueva Canción*."[72]

Canto al Programa

An interesting example of a political contribution by *la Nueva Canción* that emerged from a request from the PC was the genesis of the album *Canto al Programa* by Inti-Illimani. Sergio Ortega of the PC's Commission of Culture asked the classical musician Luis Advis and Inti-Illimani to collaborate on a musical interpretation, with interspersed narration, of Allende's Forty Measures, and the artists agreed with the idea. "Quilapayún was out of the country, and it was urgent to do *Canto al Programa*," Berrú recalled. "We felt it was important to do it. . . . Allende's program was not being diffused adequately because the private media attacked Allende constantly and tried to make people think a coup was necessary. The media was owned mainly by the right wing. . . . Most of the radio stations were against Allende."[73] *Canto al Programa* was a way to counter the strident misrepresentations—or the silence—of the mass media regarding Allende and take his program directly to the people. The media—radio, television, and newspapers—was a major instrument of the Right to undermine the UP and spread fear and panic in the public. "It fell to us, as the group Inti-Illimani, to interpret the Forty Measures of Allende's Unidad Popular program in eleven songs that featured the lyrics of the popular poet Julio Rojas," Berrú added. "He wrote the text, and Sergio Ortega—a great musician also—and Luis Advis composed the music. In one month, they taught us the repertoire, and we recorded it. It was a way of letting ordinary citizens understand what the UP was proposing."[74]

Horacio Durán noted that "this was the only time we did a work at the request of the commission," but that there was no imposition; "We agreed with the idea."[75] "The commission promoted culture in the PC," said Horacio Salinas. "The commission asked us to prepare *Canto al Programa* as a way to promote Allende's program, as well as our music."[76] Cecilia Coll, former head of the Cultural Commission in La Jota (which was separate from the PC's commission), explained that La Jota saw cultural activities as a way to attract young people to political and social movements and to raise political consciousness, a policy that dated back to Recabarren.[77]

Berrú, like the other original members of Inti-Illimani, reiterated that the group normally did not sing contingent, or pamphlet, songs: "Little by little we began entering the song of denunciation. But it wasn't our departure; ours was strictly musical. . . . Over the years, we began doing songs that made denunciations, through our contact with Víctor, Patricio Manns, the activism in La Jota. All of this began opening more paths toward songs with social militancy that was more direct. But we always guarded the aesthetic. About that we were intransigent. The only album we did that could be considered *panfletario* was *Canto al Programa*, . . . but we always put the aesthetics first."[78] Many of the songs on that album (e.g., "Vals de la Educación para Todos" [Waltz of Education for All]) transcended slogans and jingles, however, and were quite beautiful, and several captured the imagination of the public. "Venceremos" and "Canción del Poder Popular" (Song of Popular Power) became UP hymns. "Once we presented *Canto al Programa* in Lota," Berrú said. "The narrator wasn't an actor but one of the miners. It was so moving. He spoke with such force. . . . Everything we did, in the end, was part of the political struggle. But our contribution was to communicate through music, to communicate the reality of Chile."[79]

Apparently, Luis Advis felt pressured by the PC to prepare *Canto al Programa* quickly.[80] Advis, as noted earlier, was not a member of the PC, although he worked closely with the musicians associated with La Jota. Sergio Ortega, the brilliant and prolific composer who co-wrote *Canto al Programa* with Advis, was a strong personality who was dedicated to using his art for a political purpose. "I define the music I have written for the past ten or fifteen years as music for the transition from capitalist society to socialist society," he said in 1978, "music that . . . intends to influence the correlation of forces, to change them in favor of the people."[81] Ortega defended and promoted the use of forceful lyrics and militant *canciones contingentes*, and at times this caused resistance from some of the musicians. Jorge Coulon, for example, wrote about an amusing incident in which Ortega's original words

to "Venceremos" were so virulent that members of Inti-Illimani called on
PC leaders to join the discussion and tone them down.[82] Ortega continued to
work with both Quilapayún and Inti-Illimani in the years of exile after 1973.

The Musicians as Leaders

Many of the musicians, caught up in the tumult of the period, did not perceive themselves as cultural or political leaders. For example, Ángel Parra
said, "Our music reflected social change, nothing more. We accompanied
the popular movement with music, with joy. But song can't do more than
that." When told that his attitude seemed modest, that the musicians were
able to convoke and unify thousands of people, and that *la Nueva Canción*
represented the struggles and aspirations of millions, he replied:

> I think we have to maintain a modest attitude, above all because we
> were a people defeated by a national army. . . . There is no reason to
> claim that we created change, constructed this or that. Some do, but
> I don't. I have a critical attitude. . . . It's true that we had the power to
> draw many people. That's why we were invited to events! But in the
> 1960s, everything was very "artisanal," without direction or orga-
> nization. At some events there were no microphones! Many times,
> things were thrown together. . . . If we did have some sort of leader-
> ship role, we weren't conscious of it.[83]

Seves made a similar comment. When asked whether he thought *la
Nueva Canción* was part of a counterhegemonic movement in Chile in the
1960s, he answered that "we were not very conscious" of this role being
played by the musical movement. "Ours was not a struggle to be dominant
or hegemonic but to be heard, for our musical language, the culture of those
we considered to be *el pueblo*, to be heard. We had to break the monopoly,
create space for other music," he said. Seves pointed out the importance of
forerunners such as Margot Loyola, who had created folklore groups even
before Cuncumén to educate Chileans about their heritage and their culture. "In 1978, we in Inti-Illimani discovered Nicomedes Santa Cruz of Peru
when we were exploring Afro-Peruvian music. Then we found that Margot
Loyola had already interviewed him in 1952. There is also a photo of her
dancing with Elías Lafferte, who, with Recabarren, was a founder of the PC.
It's always the same: there is a social nucleus that unites folk music with the
people, with popular parties and labor unions."[84] Seves was making a link
between the culture of the people represented in folklore and organizations
of the working classes in Chile.

I asked Horacio Salinas about his views of the cultural struggle in the

1960s. "In this sense the PC was important," he said. "The PC was success-ful in its relation to the artists, because the struggle of the time was to put popular traditions, the world of Latin American popular culture, in the place it deserved. It was a struggle to recognize the identity of Latin America. And there was resistance. Look at the case of Violeta [Parra]. She is the great-est artist this country has produced, and yet we, the Chileans, have little appreciation for her, because in this society there is still a sense of rejection of popular culture, for culture that reflects the life of the people."[85] His com-ment again illustrated the counterhegemonic nature of New Song.

Certainly, the elites and the armed forces regarded the musicians and popular artists as dangerous "internal enemies" with leadership power. The violent repression of the artistic movement and the artists themselves dem-onstrated that. Moreover, as Fernando Reyes Matta points out, "In spite of its meager and wholly insufficient presence in the dominant mass media systems, [the music] manages to become widely known and rapidly dissemi-nated from country to country."[86] That observation again speaks to the social and political power of New Song. Without much commercial airplay or pro-motion by the capitalist music industry, *la Nueva Canción* became a cultural phenomenon of tremendous force because of its ability to touch hearts and souls and to embody the dreams and aspirations of masses of people.

The Interaction of the Musicians with the Popular Classes

When asked about the political influence of *la Nueva Canción*, Max Berrú talked about the impact of Inti-Illimani's travels on its members themselves. He emphasized that he and the other musicians were privileged to be able to travel throughout the country singing for the workers and others during the Allende years:

> When we were contracted by the UTE, we traveled as a group to all the provincial capitals where the university had a branch, and there we would sing. . . . We as professionals—I was an engineer, and the other *compañeros* were studying other careers—also gave classes to train people. So they used us in both ways, but more in singing. We traveled all over Chile. . . . In Iquique, we practiced singing *Canto para una Semilla*, the *cantata* by Luis Advis with verses by Violeta Parra. . . . To create that work, we went to one of the first popular seaside resorts, created by Allende for the workers and their families, close to Iquique. The campesinos would come from the South to the North to get to know the place during their vacations. The miners also went there to take a break. It was on a beach called Huayquique. The military took over the resort; now it belongs to them. . . . We were

there for a month. Every day we went to Luis Advis's house to practice. . . . We had the satisfaction and pleasure to get to know so many
working people, miners and workers from the South. Groups of fifty
people would come for a week. We would sing for them, then sing to
wish them farewell, then sing to welcome the next group. Because we
were there for a month, we sang to four different groups that came.
This was a beautiful experience for us. For example, an old man and
his family came who had never seen the sea. They lived far from it,
in the *salitreras* [nitrate regions]. It impressed us.[87]

Seves referred to the same experience:

We would often support candidates from La Jota with our music—
for example in the campaigns for congressional deputies. We played
at workplaces, at construction sites on lunch breaks, even on street
corners. This was an important support for the candidates, because
art lends a certain prestige to an event. The people received it well. . . .
In 1972, when we were working on *Canto para una Semilla*, we visited Luis Advis and his family in Iquique. This album was born from
his idea to make a *cantata* for Violeta. The UP government had built
a resort by the sea for workers, so unionists from the CUT [Central
Única de Trabajadores de Chile] and others could relax there. They
gave us rooms, and we practiced with Advis. During our free time,
we spent time with the miners and other workers. They would drive
us to union halls and other places. . . . Many of them were killed after
the coup.[88]

Seves related another story about how impressed he was by the ordinary
Chileans he met while travelling with the UTE's *escuela de temporada* (seasonal school) in the South.[89] This history reflected the spirit of the people of
Aysén, who lived far from the Chile's central zone but who were ready for
social and political change:

In Puerto Aysén, I had a very special experience. I met a person—
unfortunately, I don't remember her name. A woman came, perhaps
fifty years old, looking for me after the last class that I taught, at
about ten o'clock in the evening. She was a campesina woman with
certain working-class features. She told me that she had five adopted
children. "I have two girls who are from a Mapuche family who live
with me," she said. "They are sixteen and eighteen years old. I want to
help them, because they are very shy, very introverted, and I thought
that you might be able to help them by teaching them guitar."

The woman told Seves that she composed songs and played guitar. Intrigued, Seves said he would teach the girls to play the guitar and wanted the woman to teach him her campesina ways of playing and techniques she knew. She agreed. At her house, she showed him two books full of songs she had composed. He recounted:

> She also had a poem that she showed me. At the end of the poem were sketches with colored pencils: figures, flowers, children's faces. Everything around the poem was adorned with drawings. One of the things she wrote was about the nationalization of copper. She said, "Although I'm a Christian Democrat, I embrace this, because finally Chile is for the Chileans." . . . This woman was really another Violeta Parra. She also made handicrafts. . . . I never saw her again. . . . For me, [this experience] meant to encounter something essentially of the people, rich, educated, cultured, interesting.

La Nueva Canción wrote a new page in the political and cultural history of Chile. The movement enriched the lives of the musicians and artists, as well as the lives of hundreds of thousands of ordinary Chileans, who began to dream. The New Song movement was a product of the social and political movements of the time and collaboration among the artists, which was unselfish and profound. The creative explosion was linked to the deepening democratization of society.

That the movement had a deep political impact was made clear in 1973 when the bloody coup was carried out by the armed forces, with secret backing from Washington. I review the coup and its immediate aftermath in Chapter 7.

7

The Coup and Its Aftermath

On September 11, 1973, the armed forces launched a coordinated military coup. Salvador Allende recently had told his aides, including General Augusto Pinochet, that he would announce a plebiscite on September 11 to ask the Chilean people whether they supported his presidency.[1] Clearly the military feared that the vote would go in his favor. As the coup began, Allende went to the government palace with his closest advisers and swore he would not surrender. The trade union leaders told all workers to go to their workplaces to prepare to defend them. Allende broadcast a final, stirring speech in which he addressed the workers, women, and youth of Chile. Soon afterward, military planes bombed the few remaining pro-Allende radio stations. After several hours, military aircraft bombed La Moneda Palace, setting it aflame. Allende died inside. His death has been ruled a suicide.

This chapter presents a schematic summary of the coup and its immediate aftermath, especially regarding the musicians of *la Nueva Canción*. The period after the coup—the long "third phase" of the New Song movement, when many of the musicians were in exile—deserves a book-length study of its own. Here I review the devastation wrought by the military regime on Chilean society in the name of freedom. The political parties of the Left offered contrasting evaluations and explanations for the coup, which gradually became public. They ranged from condemnations of U.S. imperialism to self-criticism to critiques of Allende as too reformist.[2]

The military detained thousands of supporters and officials of the Unidad Popular (UP), who had done nothing illegal but were now enemies of the state. Others were "disappeared," tortured, and murdered. A climate of terror pervaded the country. Political parties were outlawed or dissolved. The regime's Decree Law 77 of October 1973 banning the parties was a manifesto on the evils of class struggle and the military's intention to extirpate Marxism from Chile.[3] A curfew was instituted; Congress was closed; and censorship of the press was imposed. Martial music filled the airwaves. The regime tortured thousands of people in stadiums and secret prisons; there was no due process, and the rule of law was suspended. Chilean society fell into the grip of state violence and terror. According to official government investigations carried out in the years since the coup, some three thousand Chileans "disappeared," and some forty thousand were tortured under Pinochet's bloody regime, which endured until 1990.[4] Many more died and tens of thousands were exiled.

The Coup of September 11

The regime tried to project an image of itself as a renovating force that would cleanse the country of socialist ideas and programs and introduce national greatness. In practice, the anticommunist and messianic ideology of the military, rooted in national security doctrine, destroyed decades of social advances in Chile and used terror to control society. The military dictatorship imposed what became known as "*el apagón cultural*" (the cultural blackout). In October 1973, a month after the coup, Pinochet gave a self-legitimizing and fiercely anticommunist speech in which he said, "Education must form in young people the grand values of the nation, without seeking any form of indoctrination or political consciousness-raising, since that endangers the sacred respect for the internal liberty of each human being." In other speeches, Pinochet made clear that he considered the UP a communist infiltration of Chilean society and considered all of the artists dangerous communists.[5] Pinochet proclaimed that he would restore Western, Christian civilization to Chile. The fifteenth decree of the dictatorship closed all newspapers except *El Mercurio* and *La Tercera* (part of the *Mercurio* empire).[6]

"All the welfare functions of government, businesses, careers, or organizations were considered subversive, and banned," said Patricia Díaz Inostroza, formerly of Grupo Abril. "The years 1974 to 1976 were terrible. There was an imposed silence. . . . People burned their records of *la Nueva Canción* and records by DICAP. People were in terror of being found with them, [a]lthough no one could find an actual decree explicitly banning them. . . . Gradually people began getting together in clandestine groups, playing the banned music; little by little, resistance appeared."[7]

The murder of Víctor Jara was one of the earliest and most infamous crimes committed by the military junta. Jara was detained at the Universidad

Técnica del Estado (State Technical University; UTE) in Santiago, along with hundreds of other professors and students, immediately after the coup.[8] Allende had been scheduled to give a speech there on September 11. Jara and thousands of others were taken to the Chile Stadium. There he was viciously tortured and his hands were broken.[9] According to recent testimony, Jara was finally shot in the head, and his body was machine-gunned. The autopsy showed forty-four bullet wounds. Max Berrú said:

> For me, one of the hardest blows was his death. . . . I found out when Inti-Illimani was in Italy on a tour. . . . [I]t was the death that was most painful for me. I began having a recurrent dream about him. He would arrive in a sort of cloud, a funnel cloud. He was in the center, and he was coming to a rehearsal with us in Santiago. He'd be there, talking to us, but suddenly this cyclone would come and take him away. I had that dream hundreds of times. For sixteen years, I kept having this dream. Finally, I was worried and saw a psychologist, and she said, "Don't worry. You had a good friendship with him. It's understandable. You loved him. When you return to Chile, it will pass." And it was true. After I returned to Chile, I never had the dream again.[10]

There were few advances in the case in Chile until 2012. The family and the Víctor Jara Foundation, backed by supporters from Chile and abroad, never stopped pushing for justice, and a new judge finally ordered the arrest of eight military officers that year. For the first time on camera, a former conscript testified that one of the officers had shot the brutally tortured Jara at point-blank range in a "game" of Russian roulette with another officer. Many of the suspects had served at Tejas Verdes, an army base that was a notorious center of military plotting and subversion against the Allende government. The base was directed by Colonel Manuel Contreras, a colonel who became chief of the newly created National Intelligence Directorate (Dirección de Inteligencia Nacional; DINA): the Gestapo-like secret intelligence organization that carried out the vast majority of disappearances in Chile and specialized in torture.[11] The CIA station chief in Chile helped organize DINA in 1973–1974, contacting Brazilian military and police officers to train DINA operatives in "unconventional" tactics.[12] Tejas Verdes became the site of one of the regime's clandestine concentration camps, where political prisoners were secretly held and brutally tortured. Contreras soon became a key commander of the multinational covert intelligence network known as Operation Condor. Condor was a cross-border system to "disappear," torture, and assassinate exiled political opponents. It was set up in the early 1970s by the military intelligence apparatuses of six military states—Argentina, Bolivia, Brazil, Chile, Paraguay, and Uruguay—also supported by the CIA.[13]

In the days immediately after the coup, the worker-organized factories and militant shantytowns were bombed and overrun by military tanks. There was some scattered armed resistance by people trying to defend the government—at the Indumet factory and the La Legua shantytown, for example—but the military rapidly overpowered them.[14] The *poblaciones* were militarized and occupied and under constant surveillance by military helicopters. The military renamed them to erase names such as Violeta Parra, Recabarren, and Havana. "The Awakening of Maipú" was named "General Baquedano," for example, and "Nueva Habana" (New Havana) was renamed "New Dawn." A main street in the Providencia neighborhood was renamed "September 11" in honor of the coup. This was part of the junta's strategic plan to erase the heritage of the UP. The "cleansing" of the city included whitewashing murals and changing the names of streets and parks.[15] It was a campaign that, ironically, echoed Gramsci's insight that names of streets and urban spaces were part of the hegemonic-counterhegemonic struggle.

Soldiers and militants from Patria y Libertad (Fatherland and Liberty) burned books in the streets. Pinochet created a commando of officers—including many who soon became key torturers in secret detention centers and commanders in Operation Condor—to eliminate opposition figures throughout Chile. The squadron, which became known as the Caravan of Death, traveled by helicopter from the North to the South of Chile to extrajudicially execute people who had been detained. Many of those murdered were former UP officials, and some were constitutionalist military officers.[16] Chileans were so accustomed to legal norms and constitutional practices that many victims of the Caravan of Death had voluntarily turned themselves in when they were summoned. Soon the regime and the nascent DINA began creating hundreds of secret torture centers to hold "disappeared" people.[17] Before the coup, the CIA had prepared arrest lists and lists of key locations for the military to take over during the coup. The CIA also worked with the junta to improve its image after the coup, funding media outlets to paint the regime in a positive light and build public support. The CIA also paid the travel expenses of junta spokesmen.[18]

High-ranking figures in the UP—including Miguel Lawner of the PC, who directed the Urban Improvement Corporation; José Tohá of the PS, a former defense minister and interior minister; Enrique Kirberg of the PC, the rector of UTE; Defense Minister Orlando Letelier of the PS; Sergio Bitar of the Izquierda Cristiana (Christian Left), a former mining minister; Senator Luis Corvalán, secretary-general of the PC; and Senator Hugo Miranda of the Radical Party; among many others—were detained and sent to Dawson Island, a remote navy base, where they were subjected to savage interrogations. Tohá was moved among different detention centers and viciously tortured. His health deteriorated rapidly. He died in 1974, and the regime declared his death a suicide. A reexamination of his body in 2012 found that third parties had been involved and that his death was a homicide.[19]

Pablo Neruda also died in the first days after the coup. His house had been raided and was finally destroyed by a military commando.[20] He was taken by ambulance from his house in Isla Negra to Clinic Santa María in Santiago. Mexico had offered him asylum, and he was planning to leave in a matter of hours. But he died after being given an injection by a member of the clinic's medical staff.[21] For years, his death was attributed to cancer. In 2011, however, Neruda's former driver and confidante went public with his conviction that the poet had been poisoned at the clinic. Neruda's body was exhumed in 2013; as of this writing, the investigation is still under way.[22] Despite the military terror in Chile, Neruda's funeral procession on September 25, 1973, convoked thousands of people in mourning. They accompanied his coffin to the cemetery and shouted "Compañero Pablo Neruda—presente! Compañero Salvador Allende—presente! Compañero Víctor Jara—presente!"[23] It was the first massive act of resistance to the military regime. Joan Jara escaped from Chile with her two daughters shortly thereafter, with assistance from the British Embassy.

In October, Cardinal Raúl Silva Henríquez called together the Christian churches and the Jewish community to form the Comité de Cooperación para la Paz en Chile (Committee of Cooperation for Peace in Chile) to oppose human rights abuses, investigate disappearances, and protect people persecuted by the dictatorship. In December 1975, Pinochet closed the committee; Cardinal Silva responded by creating the Vicaría de la Solidaridad, a similar institution that became crucial in the defense and protection of people targeted by the regime.[24]

Popular Culture Targeted

The Pinochet dictatorship moved to crush the counterhegemonic movements, including the cultural movement, and forcibly impose the hegemonic culture from an earlier era: an imaginary Chile, a land of European descendants with the values of the landowning *patrón*. Indigenous people, campesinos, and the working classes were erased. The regime replaced the vibrant symbols of the Allende period with militarized cultural icons. "The regime turned back the clock to a country that never really existed," said Rodrigo Torres.[25] "There was repression of ideas, images, sounds, voices." The regime ransacked the offices of DICAP, destroying the masters of the music. Military squadrons invaded the offices of the Ramona Parra Brigade and MAPU headquarters in Santiago.[26] The regime acted to eradicate UP ideology and culture from society and replace it with a new, militarized worldview. Luis Hernán Errázuriz has shown how the regime's "symbolic violence" deeply traumatized Chileans and established domination through terror: carrying out forced haircuts of men, whitewashing murals, outlawing red and black colors, requiring military-style parades and swearing-ins of school-age students, establishing a cult of the gulag and militarized patriotism, and so on. The aim of the regime was totalitarian, he writes: to force people to deny their convictions and "change the mentality of people" through terror.[27] Men with beards were forcibly shaved, and women were required to wear skirts rather than pants. The *golpistas* were particularly enraged by the changing role of women and their political activism during the 1960s and 1970s, and sexual torture was a prominent feature of the secret detention centers.[28]

Quilapayún and Inti-Illimani, who were in Europe at the time of the coup, escaped direct repression, but their enforced exile devastated them, and many others, including the Parras, Osvaldo "Gitano" Rodríguez, and Patricio Manns. The military dictatorship banned the two groups from returning to Chile for the next fifteen years. "Our tour turned into a solidarity mission," said José Seves. "We sang in many, many different acts. Some were demonstrations in the streets, almost spontaneous. Many times we divided up: three would go to one demonstration, and the other three would go to a different one. We'd say a few words, in Spanish, thanking people for their solidarity. And later, the tour continued to the Netherlands, Sweden, Germany."[29] Inti-Illimani was welcomed by church groups, social and political organizations, and peace activists throughout Europe. "After a few days, we began to get more news and grasp the magnitude of what had happened," Seves continued. "In the Netherlands, we saw the first images of Santiago. Bodies were floating in the River Mapocho. La Moneda Palace was bombed. We were in shock. . . . There was total repression. We wondered what had happened to so many *compañeros* of La Jota. We learned of many deaths, many detained in concentration camps. . . . Little by little we got involved in trying to save people, help them enter clandestinity, help them escape or survive in Chile. There was a lot of fear, a lot of risk."

Berrú spoke of learning about the coup in Europe:

The demonstrations of solidarity were spontaneous. For example, on the night of [September] 11, we had programmed a concert in a working-class neighborhood in Rome, and the *compañeros* said they'd understand if we wanted to cancel. We thought about it and decided not to. We decided that as of that moment, we were going to work to regain democracy. That concert transformed itself into a demonstration. The next day, all of the parties in Italy—even the right-wing ones—organized a demonstration in the streets. We went as a group to sing. The DC [Christian Democrat Party], PC, PS, all of the parties participated. It was a huge and multitudinous protest. It needed no publicity because hundreds of thousands of people came. We began, from the first day, to work with the solidarity groups. . . . In the end, we did play a very important role because there were thousands of acts of solidarity all over the world in which we could take part, and it was incredible for us.[30]

In Santiago, Isabel Parra, Patricio Manns, and Patricio Castillo found refuge at the Venezuelan Embassy and later left the country. Gitano Rodríguez went to the Argentine Embassy and then left for exile. Payo Grondona escaped to exile in Argentina. Héctor Pavez went into exile, as well. He died in Paris. Sergio Ortega found refuge at the French Embassy and then left for exile in that country. Tito Fernández was detained and tortured but freed. He stayed in Chile but had to abandon his repertoire of songs. Luis Advis stayed in Chile but stopped composing music.[31] Luis Enrique "Kiko" Elgueta, a singer from Lonquimay and a member of MAPU, disappeared in Buenos Aires[32]—indicating a Condor operation. Jaime Esponda, the former student organizer of the DC who left to join MAPU, recalled that the military regime had told him to present himself. He was tortured twice, once for two weeks at the Navy War College. The torturers asked him where the hidden arms and where the key leaders were. He knew nothing about this.[33] After he was released—in part because a Catholic priest intervened— he began to work with the church's Vicaría de Solidaridad human rights group. "*La Nueva Canción* never disappeared," Esponda said. "All of the records were prohibited, but people had clandestine parties and meetings. They were a type of therapy. We laughed, and we sang songs of Quilapayún, Pato Manns, Rolando Alarcón, Víctor Jara. . . . [T]hey helped us survive."[34]

Ángel Parra was detained in his house and then taken to the National Stadium, which was being used as a massive detention and torture center. "At first they confused me with another person," Parra said. "But all the prisoners applauded when they saw me! I'll never forget that. They were thinking, 'This is our singer. He's here with us.' I was with my public!"[35] Parra was sent to Chacabuco, a prison camp in a desolate region in the North. Incredibly, prisoners at Chacabuco managed to construct rudimentary instruments and play music to maintain their spirits and optimism. The Vicaría de Solidaridad managed to have some guitars brought in, as well. The detainees rapidly organized themselves, setting up classes in language, music, and art. They began to present performances every Sunday, with music, comedy, poetry, and theater, and even the military guards attended these "shows." Ernesto Parra of Los Curacas, also detained in Chacabuco, recalled that detainees made *quenas* from plastic tubes.[36] The detainees began playing music composed by Ángel Parra (no relation to Ernesto Parra) and formed groups to play together. "The music helped us survive," Ernesto Parra explained. "We survived with our classes, with our music. . . . We sang 'white songs'—they seemed innocuous but had hidden messages. Ángel wrote one piece that was religious, speaking of Christ, the Bible—but it carried a message that denounced torture. . . . Chacabuco became a mini-city. We created a library, a store, a newspaper, shows on Sundays, Sunday Masses, an old folks' center. We were well-organized." Ángel Parra wrote music for a Mass that described the situation of a suffering prisoner and how he was killed. Because it had a religious theme, the military guards allowed it to proceed.[37] Luis Alvarado of the PS was also detained in Chacabuco. "It was exactly like a German Stalag," he remembered. "There were nine hundred people there. Most of us survived; four or five disappeared. The Vicaría de Solidaridad had a list of the detainees so the armed forces could not disappear them."[38]

The regime imposed strict censorship throughout the country. Television and radio broadcast military marches and hymns. The military prohibited all art and music related to *la Nueva Canción*, which was considered "communist music" or "un-Chilean music." Only "bad Chileans" would listen to such music, and they were treated as subversives.[39] Owning an album of *la Nueva Canción* risked detention and torture. Mariela Ferreira of Cuncumén, who was detained in her own house, recalled, "One of the Carabineros told me, after seeing my albums by Víctor, Inti-Illimani, and Quilapayún, 'We're going to kill all of you communists.' . . . It frightened the Right to realize the power of music. . . . The mix of political lyrics and sound was important, but even more, the music was a key element of the social movements, the historical moment, the marches, the hopes of millions. The music transmitted that."[40] Singing *Cantata Santa María* was now a crime.[41] Some musicians were called to a meeting in which a regime functionary said that from then on, the indigenous instruments of *la Nueva Canción* were banned. Miguel Davagnino remembered, "Colonel Pedro Ewing said in this meeting, with Héctor Pavez and others, that never again would Chileans hear *quenas*, *zampoñas*, and other Marxist instruments."[42] The regime named Benjamín Mackenna of Los Huasos Quincheros to assist the military with cultural policies and then appointed him to the government's Secretariat of Cultural Relations.[43] Los Huasos Quincheros represented the military regime at the inaugural act of the 1974 World Cup in Germany and later serenaded Henry Kissinger with traditional *cuecas* and *tonadas* when he visited Chile.

Although DICAP was raided and the masters and records were destroyed, copies of some of them were stored in DICAP's offices in Europe and elsewhere, so not all were lost. The IRT label was also raided, and much material was burned. The regime created blacklists in radio and television

to exclude anyone associated with the Left and decreed that a specific version of the *cueca* was now the official dance of Chile. Schools were required
to teach it in all physical education classes, and the dance was mandated in
championships and festivals. Today many Chileans recall "the *cueca* of the
military coup" with irony and distaste.[44] *Huasos* were reintroduced as the
symbol of Chile's national identity, and sports such as soccer and boxing
were used to build a nationalist spirit.[45] The military closed dozens of radio
stations and publications and four Santiago newspapers, and two more went
out of business shortly after the coup. The remaining four were conservative
and pro-coup. In 1979, one scholar analyzed five ways in which the regime
controlled the press: closure and suspension of media, seizure and destruction of printed matter, expulsions of foreign correspondents, state ownership
of some media units, and propaganda activity. On the radio, the great majority of the music was foreign once again, and many of the leading Chilean
artists and composers fled the country if they could.[46] The state withdrew
support for the arts, considering culture a market commodity and part of
the private sphere. Similarly, an elitist concept of culture as selective and
exclusive, mainly reserved for the educated upper classes, again predomi-
nated; European arts and traditions were exalted, and popular culture was
denigrated. These ideas were consistent with the regime's neoliberal economic model.[47] A discretionary tax of 22 percent was created that could be
applied to theaters and concerts if the regime decided their offerings were
not "cultural events," pricing such events beyond the reach of many ordinary
people.[48]

Immediately after the coup, the notorious Operation Condor began to
coalesce. In 1974, the as yet unnamed repressive system claimed its first
high-profile victim: the Chilean constitutionalist General Carlos Prats and
his wife, Sofia Cuthbert, were assassinated in Buenos Aires, where they had
been living a quiet exile, in a powerful car bombing. In 1975, Condor targeted a leader of the Chilean Christian Democrat Party, Bernardo Leighton,
and his wife, Ana Fresno, who were in exile in Rome. The couple was severely
wounded but survived. In 1976, Orlando Letelier, who was exiled after his
release from Dawson Island, was assassinated with a young colleague, Ronni
Moffitt, in a car bombing on the streets of Washington, DC. The U.S. expa-
triate Michael Townley, a DINA and Condor operative, was involved in all of
these crimes. Condor also hunted down, tortured, and killed many activists,
unionists, and other political opponents in exile.

Universities were raided by the military; "subversive" books and articles
were destroyed; and entire majors (such as "Instructor of Folklore") were
outlawed.[49] Military officers took over administration of the university campuses. Regional branches of the public universities (the University of Chile

and the UTE) were closed. The dictatorship outlawed the Student Federation of Chile (Federación Estudiantil de Chile; FECH) and forced up to twenty thousand students and staff out of the universities.[50] Assisted by the so-called Chicago Boys, disciples of the free-market theorist Milton Friedman, the regime imposed a radical free-market economic program characterized by privatizations, wage controls, reduced duties on imports, the abolition of tariffs and taxes, and an open door for foreign investment. Chile's social welfare state was dismantled, and over time an entrepreneurial class emerged. Unions were repressed. By 1975, real wages and per capita social spending had plummeted to 63 percent of their 1970 levels. Some forty-three thousand people were dismissed from public service, and unemployment reached 18.7 percent.[51] Malnutrition and disease increased, and social problems, such as domestic violence, began to rise. New laws decimated protections for workers, benefits, and minimum wages. The gap between the wealthy—and the wealthy saw their fortunes vastly improved during the regime—and the poor dramatically widened. One government study showed in 1975 that 21 percent of the population lived in "extreme poverty."[52] The public health care, social security, and educational systems were privatized. The regime worked to establish a culture of consumerism, individualism, profitmaking, and political apathy. The combination of brutal repression and economic restructuring brought drastic change to Chile, reversing decades of social gains by and for the working classes. Many national businesses collapsed under the onslaught of cheap goods and foreign investment from abroad.[53] One business owner compared the Chicago Boys to religious fanatics.[54] Conservative and neoliberal economists heralded Chile as a model of neoliberal economics and capitalist development. But by the 1980s, Chile had one of the highest levels of wage inequality in the world.[55]

On June 20, 1975, Pinochet declared, "There will be no elections in Chile during my lifetime or in the lifetime of my successor."[56] In its Constitution of 1980, the regime put into place controls and "guardian structures" aimed at consolidating the militarized model and preventing any leftist or popular government in the future. Article 8, for example, declared, "Any action by an individual or group intended to propagate doctrines attempting against the family, or which advocate violence or a concept of society, the State or the juridical order of a totalitarian character or based on class warfare, is illegal and contrary to the institutional code of the Republic." Before Pinochet stepped down in 1990, he imposed a "binominal system" of federal elections, which ensured the Right would receive a disproportionate percentage of the vote. An extensive review of Pinochet's policies and mandates is beyond the scope of this study. But the dictatorship abruptly altered Chile's historical path in political, economic, and cultural dimensions.

Signs of Resistance

Despite the iron grip of the military, incipient signs of resistance began to appear. The human rights organization Group of Relatives of the Detained and Disappeared (Agrupación de Familiares de Detenidos Desaparecidos; AFDD) formed in 1975. Just as the military regime was decreeing the official *cueca*, the Conjunto Folklórico of the AFDD invented the *cueca sola*. In contrast to the traditional *cueca*—a dance in which a man and a woman interact as partners in a flirtatious and playful way—the *cueca sola* featured a woman dancing alone, symbolizing physical loss, absence, and pain. The *cueca sola* became a strong symbol of resistance to the horrors of the dictatorship, expressing the pain of thousands of families.[57]

Although New Song was banned, people listened to the music surreptitiously in their homes. "The music became a legend; it was necessary to hear it and preserve it," said Ricardo Venegas, a member of Quilapayún who had remained in Chile.[58] As audiocassettes became increasingly widespread in the 1970s, people exchanged tapes of New Song music among themselves, and people who traveled abroad returned with new cassettes that were copied and distributed through subterranean networks. In 1974, the classical musician Jaime Soto León, the former musical director of DICAP, formed a new group named Barroco Andino and invited Venegas, among others, to participate. "Many of the members were formerly with the Quilapayún 'clones,'" Venegas explained. "Other groups such as Ortiga began to appear, recapturing the sounds of *la Nueva Canción,* transmitting a message, and continuing the tradition. It showed that New Song had not died."[59] To defy the dictatorship's ban on indigenous instruments, Barroco Andino performed the classical instrumental music of Bach, Vivaldi, and Beethoven, among others, using *quenas, charangos*, and *zampoñas*. At first, Barroco Andino played only in churches, where the group was protected by the figure of Cardinal Silva Henríquez. But gradually the musicians played elsewhere. Barroco Andino recorded its first album in 1974. The record included classical pieces along with a version of "Ojos Azules" (Blue Eyes; a traditional Andean song associated with New Song) and the Paul McCartney song "Eleanor Rigby."[60] Like Venegas, other members of Barroco Andino went on to join Quilapayún (Patricio Wang and Fernando Carrasco) and Inti-Illimani (Renato Freyggang) in exile. The appearance of Barroco Andino was extremely important in terms of pushing open a public space for the music, evoking *la Nueva Canción* and reconnecting former Allende supporters with one another and with a sense of community, resistance, and hope.

Gradually other groups and soloists began to appear, including Ortiga, Santiago del Nuevo Extremo, Schwenke y Nilo, Sol y Lluvia, Eduardo Peralta, and Isabel Aldunante. Ricardo García, who had coined the name

Nueva Canción, also christened this musical trend, naming it *Canto Nuevo* in 1976. The name—which in Spanish has the same approximate meaning as *Nueva Canción*—captured the roots and continuity of the music with New Song. But the lyrics of *Canto Nuevo* were symbolic, coded, and metaphorical in the heavy atmosphere of repression. Some of the artists avoided political meanings completely and sang love songs. Overall, *Canto Nuevo* was more than a cultural movement; a network emerged, semi-clandestinely, relinking people from the social movements and enabling a strategy to connect with old comrades and take some action denouncing disappearances, feeding hungry children, organizing acts of solidarity, and reconstructing old movements.[61] Many of these networks had the protection of the Catholic Church and Cardinal Silva Henríquez.

New *peñas* began to appear, as well. The singer Nano Acevedo opened the *peña* Doña Javiera in 1975 and invited numerous *Canto Nuevo* musicians and poets to perform.[62] The DINA and the Carabineros were always there, infiltrating the audience; detaining, harassing, and following people; and periodically shutting down the *peña*. There was sabotage, and small bombs exploded periodically. Acevedo himself was detained more than twenty times and questioned by the notorious DINA (and Condor) officer Marcelo Moren Brito. But the Peña Doña Javiera became a treasured place of solidarity and liberated space for opponents of the regime, an outpost of music and freedom surrounded by the suffocating repression of the dictatorship.

Other courageous individuals worked to keep the music alive. In 1975, Miguel Davagnino created a new radio show, "Nuestro Canto" (Our Song), on Radio Chilena. He gradually began to play indigenous and *Canto Nuevo* music, at some risk. He played the album by Barroco Andino and considered that an important breakthrough. "This record allowed us to cross the rigid border the dictatorship had erected to block the poets and musicians," he said. "People began to call, and one woman was crying, saying she thought she'd never hear such music again."[63] Davagnino began to play music by Silvio Rodríguez from Cuba, but the regime reacted by shutting down his show a number of times. But the show was never permanently closed because it was protected by the Catholic Church. In 1976, Ricardo García organized a festival of folk music. Some eight thousand people went to the Caupolicán Theater. The regime required every person to show his or her identification to enter, and the musicians were required to submit their songs for approval in advance.[64] García was somewhat protected by his fame but was blacklisted and unable to work. But in 1976, he established a small record company with Carlos Necochea, a former member of Los Curacas, called Alerce (a hardwood tree of the Chilean island Chiloé). Alerce, operating from a small and poorly equipped basement space, recorded *Canto Nuevo* singers, allowing them to receive a small income from sales, and reissued some New

Song music. Only the Catholic Church's radio channel played the music. From the outset, the label was not a commercial enterprise. Instead, it was a means to regroup the artists, preserve the links with and memory of *la Nueva Canción,* and reactivate social and cultural networks. Garcia's daughter, Viviana Larrea, who took over the company after her father's death, said:

> Just as DICAP was a parallel means of distributing music during earlier years, Alerce became a parallel network. Alerce, with the musicians and social organizations, created distribution networks and a series of circuits through which the artists could communicate with the public, semi-clandestinely. . . . It was very modest, of course, and we were always under surveillance by the intelligence agencies. . . . We had some materials from DICAP, and my father had links with the musicians in exile. . . . Alerce was fundamental. It opened new spaces. We produced records, and more than that, we provided a meeting space for the artists, we worked closely with them.[65]

During the dictatorship Alerce had no support from the PC or La Jota, which were under heavy state repression. The label functioned with the collaboration of the artists, and records were sold hand to hand, almost underground.

The human rights lawyer Roberto Garretón observed that periods of repression in Chile corresponded to different presidential terms in the United States.[66] The worst stage of state violence was between 1973 and 1976, he pointed out, when Richard Nixon and Henry Kissinger, and then Gerald Ford, were in office. After Jimmy Carter was elected president in 1976, there was a noticeable change in Chile: the first opposition magazine appeared; repression of the music, indigenous instruments, and *peñas* lessened; and the curfew was relaxed. Some prisoners being held at DINA's clandestine torture centers Villa Grimaldi and Cuatro Alamos were released. In 1977, when Carter's term began, DINA was replaced by the Central Nacional de Informaciones. The U.S. government began investigating the 1976 assassination of Letelier and Moffitt in Washington, DC, as the Carter administration began implementing its program to promote human rights and distance Washington from military dictatorships in Latin America and elsewhere.

"New spaces opened up in 1977," the *Canto Nuevo* singer Patricia Díaz said. "The movement began to regroup little by little. People began singing songs by Jara, by Parra again. There was more folk music. Ricardo García began organizing meetings and recitals."[67] Díaz's group, Grupo Abril, played at semi-clandestine *peñas*, as well. However, the political police continued to enter to interrogate the singers, inspect their lyrics, and prohibit certain songs. The Catholic Church and the Vicaría de Solidaridad provided protection for the artists and for many other people, but the regime continued to arbitrarily revoke permissions for festivals or forbid the production of certain forms of music.[68]

It would be seventeen years before the Pinochet regime left government, only to assume a guardian role and indirect political tutelage during the first civilian governments in Chile that began in 1990. An in-depth analysis of the dictatorship period is beyond the scope of this book. My aim has been to offer a brief overview of the traumatic political, economic, social, and cultural changes imposed on Chileans in the first years after 1973. I now turn to my concluding analysis of the significance of *la Nueva Canción* in Chile.

8

Conclusion

This book has shown that the New Song movement was rooted in popular musical traditions in Chile and Latin America that were passed down through the generations. In Chile, these traditions were rediscovered through the efforts of folklore researchers such as Violeta Parra, Margot Loyola, Gabriela Pizarro, and Héctor Pavez, among others. *La Nueva Canción* was based in folklore, but the young musicians created new departures and invented new musical, instrumental, and poetic forms that revolutionized the musical culture of Chile and became known worldwide.

The New Song movement was an organic part of the broader popular movements of the time and played a key role in the democratization movement "from below" to transform Chilean state and society. As Víctor Jara said in 1973, "It was song that was born from the necessities of the country, the social movement of Chile. It wasn't song apart from that."[1] After World War II, Chile had entered a period of rapid modernization, urbanization, and capitalist reorganization, resulting in new tensions and severe social disarticulation. Burgeoning social movements began to push to win a political voice and fight for basic rights. Conditions in the mines, the haciendas, and the factories were extremely harsh. The situation in the countryside was particularly abysmal, with nearly feudal relations between owners and peasants. Chile's elitist democracy and its exploitative economic structures were challenged by newly active groups of militant peasants, workers, *pobladores*, and students, working with political parties and social organizations.

The New Song movement captured the struggles and aspirations of these sectors "from below" and the social realities they faced in Chile and Latin America. Mariela Ferreira put it well: "The mix of political lyrics and sound was important, but even more, the music was a key element of the social movements, the historical moment, the marches, the hopes of millions: the music transmitted that."[2] The music crystallized what large sectors of society were thinking and feeling through a popular medium and instilled hope that another future was possible. The musicians were organic intellectuals in Gramsci's sense, communicating through their music a critique of oppressive socioeconomic structures and the possibility of transforming society. Formerly invisible social sectors and marginalized people became protagonists and universal figures in New Song. The artists expressed the deepest emotions and hopes of broad popular sectors and politically committed intellectuals. The music had a transversal quality, as well, crossing borders to communicate with people around the world who had similar dreams of social justice. New Song was a collective language, beloved by people who shared the ideals of the era. The music was deeply embedded in new social relationships, new political aspirations, and new social movements.

The Musicians

The musicians, poets, and artists of *la Nueva Canción* were important catalysts of cultural transformation in Chile. The movement dramatically changed the musical culture of the country and played a key role in changing the political culture, as well, fused with significant social movements and political organizations. As these counterhegemonic forces merged and became stronger, both the political and cultural arenas were significantly democratized. With deeper democratization and more freedom, formerly marginalized sectors involved themselves in cultural expression at a level never before seen in Chile. The result was an explosion of "people's culture" that began in the second half of the 1960s and intensified during the government of the Unidad Popular (UP). In the context of Latin America, the role of the Chilean New Song musicians was particularly important and powerful because they were organically linked to political parties of the Left and popular movements deeply involved in these sociopolitical transformations. The musicians were troubadours of the growing counterhegemonies in Chile. New Song was not a movement that sought to dominate; rather, it sought to express the invisible and suppressed music, values, and culture of majority populations of the region. The songs of *la Nueva Canción* created consciousness, questioned existing relations of power, and expressed the dream of a better future. The musical movement helped to attract masses of people to the cause of social change; it helped to create, build, sustain, and mobilize communities of activists and militants.

The social, political, and cultural movements of the 1960s in Chile arose during a time of systemic and state-level change, the result of political and technological shifts, as shown in this book. From a historical structural perspective, human agency interacted with fluctuating structural conditions as people moved to seize new political openings to push political and social demands. Gramsci noted that new cultural movements arose during periods of social and political change. He argued that the working classes needed their own organic intellectuals to challenge the hegemony of the dominant culture, which reflected the interests of the powerful and instilled the message that the status quo was normal, inevitable, and unchangeable. The cultural hegemony of the elites was a crucial pillar of class domination, contended Gramsci, because it limited what masses of people considered possible. The New Song musicians, I have argued, defied the "rationality" of Chile's hegemonic system—as did other political actors such as political parties and social organizations—and large numbers of Chileans began to dream that equality and social justice were attainable. The New Song movement popularized democratic and socialist ideas that began to erode significantly the cultural and political hegemony of Chile's long-standing elites. The artists were agents of cultural change who helped to create a new people's culture and a new sense of Chilean identity. As Edward J. McCaughan has noted, in a similar argument, "Art associated with social movements helped to constitute, not simply reflect, the dramatic social and political changes. . . . The social power of activist artists emanates from their ability to provoke movement constituents and other publics to see, think, imagine, and even feel in meaningful new ways."[3] There was a major cultural change in Chile, and the musicians and artists played a central role in convoking and stimulating it. *La Nueva Canción* represented the new norms and values of the era and a deep social consciousness. Indeed, the armed forces believed this, as the 1973 dictatorship moved to eradicate all traces of the movement and the cultural symbols of the UP.

The research undertaken for this book indicates that culture is not static; rather, it can be shaped by social and political forces. Culture does not simply reflect the current situation, the winners and losers, dominant and dominated. It also contains the seeds of change and can enter a state of flux that can be influenced by human action and by institutions. Certainly, Gramsci held this view. New Song was a unique form of political communication that expressed the yearning for progressive social change. In this sense, *la Nueva Canción* played a key role in popularizing and diffusing an alternative worldview in the Gramscian sense, a sense of fresh possibilities. The movement moved masses of people to visualize alternative possibilities and act to achieve them, highlighting the role of human agency in reshaping political structures. The New Song musicians' singing—their performances on street corners, at festivals and political rallies, at campaign stops, before gatherings of unions and students: all of these musical events became part of the political mobilization of the era in Chile. The musicians helped to *create* political and cultural change. Some Chileans believed that "Preguntas por Puerto Montt" and *Cantata Santa María de Iquique*, with their anguished political messages and denunciations, helped turn the 1970 election to Allende.

This book has also shown that another part of the explanation for the burst of creativity in Chile in this epoch was the proximity and close associations among the musicians of *la Nueva Canción* and the classical musicians; the poets and the artists; and the musical, political, and artistic interchanges among them, as well as their close connections to the larger world of the popular movements and political parties. The musicians were not isolated individuals; they were enmeshed in a social and political setting that fostered passion and creativity.

The Role of Institutions

In 1980, Rodrigo Torres wrote that Chile traditionally had been impoverished by the extreme "elitization" of culture due to "the marginalization of vast sectors of the population and cultural agents, which lacked the resources necessary either to access or to generate cultural works."[4] He pointed to other key factors: the concentration and centralization of cultural production and the extreme commercialization of cultural works, which posed enormous limitations to the creativity of ordinary Chileans. All of this is what began to change in the 1960s as culture was democratized. New Song, accompanied by new graphic artworks in public spaces, dance and theater companies, opportunities for people to read and to learn music and art, caught fire in Chile and spread throughout the population, spurring the creativity of ordinary people. All of these changes intensified during the government of the UP, when control of the state shifted from the elites to a coalition committed to Chile's popular majorities. One of Allende's campaign slogans was that culture would be for everyone, not just the few.

The role of state institutions such as the University of Chile and the National Library had been important historically in creating an infrastructure for training in the arts and for diffusing cultural works to the public. Beginning with the Frente Popular (Popular Front) in the 1930s, the state and the university had financed the formation of national ballet and theater troupes, symphonic orchestras, university choruses, and other entities. During the Allende period, other key institutions—other universities, the Central Única de Trabajadores de Chile, CUT), and organizations built by the artists and political parties—were fundamental in the development of a "people's culture" that was not dependent on market forces or class status.

The New Song movement was a product of musical experimentation and many influences, national and international, political and artistic, which this book has tried to capture in all their complexity. While the movement had important support from institutions such as La Jota, the universities, and the Allende government, the movement was not created or directed by any of them. Clearly the Communist Party (Partido Comunista; PC) and La Jota, with their deep roots in the cultural world of Chile, provided an environment that fostered and cultivated the New Song movement. But the New Song movement did not belong to any political party; its roots were deep and diverse, emerging from the cultural history of Chile, the social movements, and the international and national contexts. The musicians and artists, amid these complex influences, were independent and autonomous, and they created a musical revolution. While many of the New Song musicians joined La Jota, many did so after they already had begun playing music. The relationship was a reciprocal collaboration between the revolutionary youth organization and the artistic movement. Miguel Davagnino, the radio personality, observed that the PC and La Jota noticed the burgeoning movement and offered to assist with infrastructure, not the other way around.[5] Similarly, Horacio Salinas noted that the power of the cultural phenomenon of *la Nueva Canción* took everyone by surprise, including the PC. "There was little reflection then," Salinas said. "There wasn't time, everything was hectic. Just recently we're beginning to understand more about what happened and why."[6] Max Berrú commented that "there was an environment of interest and incentive [for New Song] within La Jota. But the decision to form musical groups was personal; La Jota didn't decide to form *Nueva Canción* groups."[7] Eduardo Carrasco noted, "The movement of *la Nueva Canción* was spontaneous. The PC had an important role, but the movement didn't arise from the PC; it came from the social movement. It had to do with many factors: Chile Ríe y Canta, the agrarian reform, the progressive sectors of the Christian Democrats and other parties, and the PC as well. There were propitious conditions for the emergence of New Song. The party did well in terms of coordinating with the movement, orienting it, contributing to it. But the party didn't direct the movement. . . . Many people interested in the music had nothing to do with the political parties."[8]

The artists themselves, in conjunction with students, unionists, municipalities, and peasant organizations, created the first informal structures to diffuse the new music: the *peñas*. A key component of the growing movements for social change, particularly *la Nueva Canción*, was this ingenuity in circumventing the machinery of the dominant culture—elite control of radio and television stations, ownership of theaters and performance venues, all of which provided the tools for political control and censorship—through the creative powers of people and the support of key organizations.

We have seen that few spaces were open in the 1960s for the young artists, especially for their more political songs, in the music industry. The New Song movement broke the grip of the hegemonic culture in at least five ways: (1) through the spontaneous creation of *peñas* throughout the country; (2) through the formation of DICAP, the record label organized by the artists and La Jota, which brought *la Nueva Canción* recordings to tens of thousands of Chileans; (3) through the efforts of key individuals such as Ricardo García, Camilo Fernández, René Largo Farías, Rubén Nouzeilles, and Miguel Davagnino, who worked in the music industry or mainstream media but were impressed by the new wave of music and provided opportunities for the artists; (4) through the organization of New Song festivals and tours, bringing greater recognition to the artists and the movement; and (5) through university support, especially from, the State Technical University (Universidad Técnica del Estado; UTE), for key groups and soloists by providing salaries to them, helping to organize engagements, and giving access to university campuses all over the country. After Allende was elected, the government also organized cultural events featuring New Song artists, although those events were not a major priority of Allende's administration, given the difficult situation it faced with its efforts to nationalize key industries and move Chile toward constitutional socialism. The movement might well have been truncated, confronted by a wall of indifference or rejection by the dominant media and elite groups, without the resources and institutions of the *peñas*, the universities, the state media, and the PC and, to a lesser extent, the UP government, which allowed the New Song movement to expand and reach new audiences throughout the country and the world.

The *Peñas*

After Ángel and Isabel Parra founded la Peña de los Parra in 1965, students at universities and in popular organizations quickly followed with their own *peñas* across Chile. *Peñas* appeared in schools, community centers, working-class neighborhoods, small municipalities, and union locals, moving beyond intellectual circles and into the popular sectors. The *peñas* were the first innovation from the grassroots that allowed the movement to surmount the blockages of the mass media. They attracted people intrigued by the new musical and political currents and cemented a sense of unity and solidarity, combining political commitment with musical experimentation and discovery. Many of the soloists and groups of *la Nueva Canción* became known through the parallel system of the *peñas*.

DICAP

The creation of JotaJota, renamed DICAP, was the second crucial parallel mechanism allowing the New Song movement to bypass the restrictions of the music industry. Clearly, the resources and connections of the PC and La Jota were important here. Through its links with the CUT, DICAP distributed thousands of albums, reaching unionized workers with the new music. The networks that existed among union and peasant organizations and the PC made them a potent counterhegemonic force. Roberto Márquez of Illapu commented, "The role of the PC was very important. It had a clear cultural project. One of the most important vehicles to reach the masses was song. DICAP allowed many musicians to be heard. An alternative vision was multiplied. . . . Songs register in people's minds and hearts, and this has a multiplying effect. Songs can be an important instrument of mobilization."[9] DICAP became a key counterhegemonic institution. Davagnino noted, "DICAP and the Organización Nacional de Espectáculos, which organized concerts, offered opportunities to the new groups. DICAP was much more than a record label. It promoted artistic quality, Chile's cultural patrimony, noncommercial music."[10] DICAP was a channel for politically conscious and noncommercial music to reach masses of people.

Key Figures in the Music Business

Important figures in the music industry (named above) were the first to open access to artists such as Violeta Parra in the 1950s, as we have seen. Ricardo García organized key music festivals to promote New Song and actually named the musical current. Commercial labels such as EMI-Odeon produced albums by Víctor Jara, Quilapayún, Inti-Illimani, and other New Song musicians in the 1960s, especially their less overtly political work. The importance of the commercial labels for the distribution of the music should not be underestimated. Through the commercial labels, the music of Patricio Manns, Rolando Alarcón, Ángel Parra, and others was made available to a mass audience for the first time. The explosion of *la Nueva Canción* was complex; it would be oversimplifying to credit only DICAP for the success of the movement.

Festivals and Tours

The musicians participated in tours that were organized by the artists themselves, by the UTE's extension program, by the Organización Nacional de Espectáculos, and, later, by the UP government. The movement's links with the unions, sometimes facilitated by the PC, as well as with the universities and the world of arts were key to the circulation of the music. The artists also were deeply involved in electoral campaigns for UP candidates, the PC, and the broader Left, and the PC's global connections provided political and professional opportunities to the artists. "There was an effort [by La Jota] to make sure the artists had audiences because the movement was so new," Salinas explained. "There was a cultural policy, but not imposed: it was part of the life of the party. . . . Militancy was something natural in the world of intellectuals and artists. . . . The PC had the intelligence to invest energy in the Commission of Culture to provide spaces for the creativity of the artists and create infrastructure to facilitate their work."[11] The domestic and international networks and the organizational infrastructure of the PC and La Jota—built over a period of decades—were certainly significant for spreading New Song and the new "people's culture." The PC had been a strong presence within Chile's cultural world since the early twentieth century. It would be difficult to separate the PC and La Jota from the success and political influence of *la Nueva Canción*, although it must be remembered that other parties of the Left, such as the Socialist Party, the Revolutionary Left Movement (Movimiento de Izquierda Revolucionaria; MIR), and the Unitary Movement for Popular Action (Movimiento de Acción Popular Unitario; MAPU) also participated in New Song and were important, and musicians were members of other parties, as well as La Jota. Tours were organized by other political parties, by René Largo Farías, and by the Allende government itself. The Catholic University, as a result of the university reform, also took a key role in sponsoring the Festivals of New Song.

University Support

The UTE was especially crucial for the development of culture during the Allende years. As a result of the university reform, the UTE was deeply involved in development projects throughout Chile, opening its courses to working-class people, launching a national campaign to end illiteracy, offering practical courses in agriculture and forestry at its branches throughout Chile, and offering courses in folklore. The UTE's initiative to contract twelve music groups, soloists, and orchestras, including Inti-Illimani, Quilapayún, and Cuncumén, was a major support for cultural expansion. "What before had been the result of individual effort, improvisation, chance and sheer will-power, now came to be based on much more solid structures and organizations," wrote Joan Jara.[12] Eduardo Kirberg, rector of the UTE, and Cecilia Coll, the head of its extension program, played key roles in promoting the music via university structures and provided a modest income that freed the musicians to develop their music.

The New Song movement, as part of the counterhegemonic movement of the 1960s and early 1970s, challenged the rigid hierarchies of social class in Chile. It began to reshape long-entrenched structures of power—until the coup. The musicians and poets contributed to the deepening of democracy in Chile in those years. Masses of people embraced the music even though it was largely shunned by the music industry and commercial mass media. The artists were organic intellectuals in Gramsci's sense of honoring the lives and struggles of ordinary people, communicating their hopes and aspirations, denouncing unjust power relations and the stark conditions of the vast majority, and challenging the hegemonic system. Some, such as Violeta Parra and Víctor Jara, carried out fieldwork and research in the countryside and in the *poblaciones*, and all were social communicators committed to the cause of social justice. Through the medium of popular music, the artists helped to build a powerful counterhegemonic movement in Chile that succeeded in changing the culture and politics of Chile, if only for a time.

Mario Salazar of Amerindios explained the significance of New Song in the cultural-political transformation of Chile in these years: "*La Nueva Canción* is song that reflects the reality of those from below. Those without land, those who work the land. It is a vindication of their right to dream, to the possibility of creating something new. . . . What terrified the Right was that *la Nueva Canción* began to create a new common understanding, a new reality, when humble workers who used to keep their eyes on the floor began to look at the boss directly, eye to eye, and call him '*compañero*' instead of 'sir.'"[13] Salazar's observation demonstrated that *la Nueva Canción* contributed to changing political awareness in society in Gramscian terms, creating a "new common sense" and fostering more egalitarian social relationships in the popular consciousness.

During the three years of the UP government, the music and the musicians entered a new stage of development. The music was identified with the government and its social and political ideals, and there were new opportunities for the music to be heard. Although the government lacked the resources to provide much support, the New Song musicians played at events and acts of the UP, traveled as unofficial cultural representatives, and enjoyed new access in venues that previously were closed. "We performed in government acts voluntarily, without pay," said Salinas.[14] "We were honored to do it." *La Nueva Canción* bonded people in ways conducive to social action. The music united people of the Left, and people beyond the Left, and empowered them. The collaboration among the musicians and artists produced a cauldron of creativity in Chile during this epoch; there was a new environment of freedom and risk taking, experimentation and creativity, and unfolding political horizons that engendered new art forms.

Today, New Song is part of the cultural patrimony of Chile. The songs evoke and symbolize a historical period and are embedded in the historical memory of Chileans (as well as non-Chileans). But the music is far more than a relic of the past. Many of the original musicians have continued to create, develop, and grow in new directions, producing an abundance of musical departures and significant work up to this time. Many continue to record albums and perform at large concerts, where they are welcomed as beloved figures. Younger musicians have drawn inspiration from the movement and many consider themselves descendants of *la Nueva Canción*. The dictatorship of Augusto Pinochet was unable to erase *la Nueva Canción* from the hearts and minds of the people of Chile. Tens of thousands of students— young people not yet born in the 1970s—sang the UP anthem "El Pueblo Unido" during massive marches to demand high-quality and free public education in 2011. The music is alive still because it continues to express through its stirring and beautiful music the solidarity and determination of social movements and continues to evoke dreams of a different future. Perhaps most important, it conveys a profound commitment to the lives of *el pueblo*, the vast number of people who still experience social injustice. The New Song movement, through the magic of music and its capacity to move people both emotionally and politically, has brought enormous politi- cal power to counterhegemonic movements fighting for progressive social change.

Notes

CHAPTER 1

1. Banco Central de Chile, "Chile Social and Economic Indicators 1960–2000" (Santiago: Banco Central, 2002), 910–911, 930. For a stark look at conditions in Chile, see also Cathy Lisa Schneider, *Shantytown Protest in Pinochet's Chile* (Philadelphia: Temple University Press, 1995).

2. Peter Winn, *Weavers of Revolution: The Yarur Workers and Chile's Road to Socialism* (New York: Oxford University Press, 1986), 35, 43, chap. 2.

3. Lois Hecht Oppenheim, *Politics in Chile: Democracy, Authoritarianism, and the Search for Development,* 2d ed. (Boulder, CO: Westview, 1999), 9.

4. U.S. Senate, *Covert Action in Chile, 1963–1973*, Staff Report of the Select Committee to Study Governmental Operations with Respect to Intelligence Activities (Church Commission Report), December 18, 1975, 33–34.

5. He was referring to Violeta Parra and Víctor Jara specifically, but the insight applies to all of the New Song composers: Rodrigo Torres, *Perfil de la creación musical en La Nueva Canción chilena desde sus orígenes hasta 1973* (Santiago: CENECA, 1980), 37. Early articles on New Song in English include Albrecht Moreno, "Violeta Parra and 'la Nueva Canción Chilena,'" *Studies in Latin American Popular Culture* 5 (1986): 108–126; Nancy Morris, "Canto Porque es Necesario Cantar: The New Song Movement in Chile, 1973–1983," *Latin American Research Review* 21, no. 2 (1986): 117–136.

6. José Seves to the author, e-mail communication, January 22, 2014. The original Inti-Illimani separated. Since 2004, there have been two Inti groups, one of which is Inti-Illimani Histórico.

7. For theories of the globalization of culture and "cultural hybridity" in studies of culture and communication, see Marwan Kraidy, *Hybridity* (Philadelphia: Temple University Press, 2005); John Tomlinson, *Globalization and Culture* (Chicago: University of Chicago Press, 1999).

8. Ángel Parra, interview with the author, January 24, 2013, Santiago.

9. Ricardo Venegas, interview with the author, February 1, 2013, Santiago.

10. Seves e-mail (January 22, 2014).

11. Horacio Durán, interview with the author, July 31, 2012, Santiago.

12. For an insightful analysis, see Tomás Moulian and Isabel Torres D., "¿Continuidad o cambio en la linea política del Partido Comunista de Chile?" in *Estudio multidisciplinario: El partido comunista en Chile*, ed. Augusto Varas (Santiago: Ediciones CESOC-FLACSO, 1988).

13. See, e.g., Greg Walz-Chojnacki, "Canto al huaso, canto al pueblo: La música y el discurso político de la identidad chilena durante los años sesenta y la Unidad Popular," ISP Collection, Paper 505, 2004.

14. For overviews of Chilean music, see Luis Advis and Juan Pablo González Rodríguez, eds., *Clásicos de la música popular chilena: 1900–1960*, 3d ed. (Santiago: Sociedad Chilena del Derecho de Autor, 2009), 19–21; Álvaro Godoy and Juan Pablo González Rodríguez, eds., *Música popular chilena: 20 años, 1970–1990* (Santiago: Departamento de Programas Culturales de la División de Cultura del Ministerio de Educación, 1997), 13–14; Juan Pablo González, Oscar Ohlsen, and Claudio Rolle, *Historia social de la música popular en Chile, 1950–1970* (Santiago: Ediciones Universidad Católica de Chile, 2009); Marisol García, *Canción valiente 1960–1989: Tres décadas de canto social y político en Chile* (Santiago: Ediciones B Chile, 2013).

15. José Seves, interview with the author, August 11, 2011, Santiago; Parra interview (January 24, 2013).

16. Thomas Turino, *Music as Social Life: The Politics of Participation* (Chicago: University of Chicago Press, 2008), 105.

17. Ibid., 18, 34–35, 38, 40–41, 184–185. See also Fernando E. Rios, "Bolivian Nationalism, French Exoticism, and the Rise of an Andean Folkloric-Popular Music Tradition," paper presented at the 31st International Congress of the Latin American Studies Association, May 30–June 1, 2013, Washington, DC.

18. Venegas interview (February 1, 2013).

19. Turino, *Music as Social Life*, 155–157.

20. The former member Silvia Urbina related that the members of Cuncumén decided on the name in a session with Miguel Lawner, a friend and communist militant, in 1957. He read from a Mapudungun dictionary, and they all chose "Cuncumén" as the name: Silvia Urbina, interview with the author, January 30, 2013, Santiago.

21. R. Keith Sawyer, *Explaining Creativity: The Science of Human Innovation* (New York: Oxford University Press, 2006), 25.

22. Eduardo Carrasco, interview with the author, August 9, 2011, Santiago.

23. Carlos Contreras, *Nueva Ola* singer, and Juan Castro, radio executive, interviews by the author, August 5, 2013, Santiago.

24. Joan Jara, *Víctor: An Unfinished Song* (London: Jonathan Cape, 1983), 190. For the scores and words of all Jara's songs, see Claudio Acevedo, Rodolfo Norambuena, José Seves, Rodrigo Torres, and Mauricio Valdebenito, *Víctor Jara: Obra musical completa*, 2d ed. (Santiago: Fundación Víctor Jara, 1999).

25. Seves interview (August 11, 2011).

26. Recent books on Violeta Parra include Jorge Montealegre Iturra, *Violeta Parra* (Santiago: Editorial USACH, 2011); Karen Kerschen, *Violeta Parra: By the Whim of the Wind* (Albuquerque: ABQ Press, 2010); Mónica Echeverría *Yo, Violeta* (Santiago: Random House, 2010); Eduardo Parra Sandoval, *Mi hermana Violeta Parra: Su vida y obra en décimas* (Santiago: Lom Ediciones, 1998).

27. Max Berrú, interview with the author, June 14, 2011, Santiago.

28. Horacio Salinas, interview with the author, July 26, 2011, Santiago.

29. Horacio Durán, Inti-Illimani Histórico, interview with the author, June 13, 2011, Santiago.

30. Jorge Coulon, *La sonrisa de Víctor Jara* (Santiago: Editorial USACH, 2009), 62. In contrast, the Argentines who founded *el Nuevo Cancionero* wrote a manifesto expressing their convictions regarding popular song in 1963.

31. John Street, *Music and Politics* (Cambridge: Polity, 2012), 96.

32. Nelly Richard, "Lo político en el arte: arte, política e instituciones," paper, Arcis University, Santiago, n.d., http://hemisphericinstitute.org/hemi/es/e-misferica-62/richard.

33. Jara, *Víctor*, 77; Coulon, *La sonrisa de Víctor Jara*, 37.

34. Osvaldo "Gitano" Rodríguez, *Cantores que reflexionan* (Madrid: Ediciones LAR, 1984), 196–197.

35. Seves interview (August 11, 2011); see also José Seves, "Travesía: Puentes musicales," entry dated December 7, 2006, joseves.blogspot.com.

36. This was one of Gramsci's questions, as well: see David Forgacs and Geoffrey Nowell-Smith, eds., *Gramsci: Selections from Cultural Writings* (Cambridge, MA: Harvard University Press, 1991), 87.

37. Antonio Gramsci, "Art and Culture," in ibid., 98.

38. Antonio Gramsci, "Popular Literature," in ibid., 378.

39. Durán interview (July 31, 2012); Parra interview (January 24, 2013). Jorge Coulon of Inti-Illimani said, "I don't think the musicians change anything, but when there is a change, the music accompanies that change." Damaso González, "Inti-Illimani 45 años de lucha y música," *El Diario/La Prensa* (New York), October 4, 2012.

40. Street, *Music and Politics*, 99.

41. John Street, "'Fight the Power': The Politics of Music and the Music of Politics," *Government and Opposition*, 2003, 130.

42. Antonio Larrea, interview with the author, August 16, 2012, Santiago.

43. Ernesto Parra, interview with the author, August 23, 2012, Santiago; Mario Salazar, interview with the author, August 23, 2012, Santiago.

44. Salinas interview (July 26, 2011).

45. José Seves, interview with the author, June 26, 2012, Santiago.

46. Juan Carvajal, former artistic director, DICAP, interview with the author, August 15, 2012, Santiago; Ricardo Valenzuela, former general director, DICAP, August 21, 2012, Santiago. See also Gustavo Miranda Meza, "Cuando la cultura se escribe con la guitarra. El sello DICAP y la política de las Juventudes Comunistas, Chile 1968–1973," presentation at El Primer Congreso Chileno de Estudios en la Música Popular, June 2011, Santiago.

47. Venegas interview (February 1, 2013).

48. Some of the recent English-language books on music and politics and social life are Courtney Brown, *Politics in Music: Music and Political Transformation from Beethoven to Hip-Hop* (Atlanta: Farsight, 2008); David King Dunaway and Molly Beer, *Singing Out: An Oral History of America's Folk Music Revivals* (New York: Oxford University Press, 2010); Daniel Fischlin and Ajay Heble, eds., *Rebel Musics: Human Rights, Resistant Sounds, and the Politics of Music Making* (Montreal: Black Rose, 2003); Nancy Love, *Musical Democracy* (Albany: State University of New York Press, 2006); Robin D. Moore, *Music and Revolution: Cultural Change in Socialist Cuba* (Berkeley: University of California Press, 2006); William G. Roy, *Reds, Whites, and Blues: Social Movements, Folk Music, and Race in the United States* (Princeton, NJ: Princeton University Press, 2010);

Sawyer, *Explaining Creativity*; Turino, *Music as Social Life*; Eric Zolov, *Refried Elvis: The Rise of the Mexican Counterculture* (Berkeley: University of California Press, 1999).

49. See, e.g., Antonio Gramsci, *The Prison Notebooks* (New York: International Publishers, 1971); Theodor W. Adorno, *Introduction to the Sociology of Music*, trans. E. B. Ashton (New York: Continuum, 1989).

50. See, e.g., Kate Crehan, *Gramsci, Culture and Anthropology* (Berkeley: University of California Press, 2002); Forgacs and Nowell-Smith, *Gramsci*; Adam David Morton, *Unravelling Gramsci: Hegemony and Passive Revolution in the Global Political Economy* (London: Pluto, 2007). I thank Kate Crehan for a useful conversation about Gramsci on May 12, 2013, in New York City.

51. Antonio Gramsci, "The Intellectuals," in *Selections from the Prison Notebooks of Antonio Gramsci*, ed. Quentin Hoare and Geoffrey Nowell-Smith (London: ElecBook, 1971), 145.

52. Antonio Gramsci, "State and Civil Society," in Morton, *Unravelling Gramsci*, 120.

53. Crehan, *Gramsci, Culture and Anthropology*, 172.

54. Antonio Gramsci, "The Question of the Language and the Italian Intellectual Classes," in Forgacs and Nowell-Smith, *Gramsci*, 168.

55. Morton, *Unravelling Gramsci*, 114, 117.

56. Antonio Gramsci, "On Italian History," in Hoare and Nowell-Smith, *Selections from the Prison Notebooks*, 303.

57. Gramsci, quoted in Morton, *Unravelling Gramsci*, 92.

58. Antonio Gramsci, "The Modern Prince," in Hoare and Geoffrey Nowell-Smith, *Selections from the Prison Notebooks*, 444.

59. Antonio Gramsci, "The Study of Philosophy," in ibid., 643.

60. Crehan, *Gramsci, Culture and Anthropology*, 5, 101. See also Antonio Gramsci, quoted in Hoare and Geoffrey Nowell-Smith, *Selections from the Prison Notebooks*, 12.

61. Crehan, *Gramsci, Culture and Anthropology*, 104.

62. Morton, *Unravelling Gramsci*, 78, 97.

63. Gramsci, "The Study of Philosophy," 652.

64. See, e.g., Fernando Henrique Cardoso and Enzo Faletto, *Dependency and Development in Latin America* (Berkeley: University of California Press, 1979); Barrington Moore, *Social Origins of Dictatorship and Democracy: Lord and Peasant in the Making of the Modern World* (Boston: Beacon, 1966); Robert W. Cox, "Social Forces, States, and World Orders: Beyond International Relations Theory," *Millennium* 10, no. 2 (1981): 126–155, reprinted with a postscript in Robert O. Keohane, ed., *Neorealism and Its Critics* (New York: Columbia University Press, 1986). See also Robert W. Cox, *Production, Power, and World Order: Social Forces in the Making of History* (New York: Columbia University Press, 1987); Guillermo O'Donnell, *Bureaucratic Authoritarianism* (Berkeley: University of California Press, 1988); Timothy P. Wickham-Crowley and Susan Eckstein "'There and Back Again': Questioning New-Social-Movement Analysis for Latin American and Reasserting the Powers of Structural Theories," paper presented at the International Congress of the Latin American Studies Association, October 7–10, 2010, Toronto.

65. Franklin D. Roosevelt, "The "Four Freedoms," Address to Congress, January 6, 1941, in *Congressional Record* 87 (1941): pt. 1.

66. Stephen Streeter, *Managing the Counterrevolution: The United States and Guatemala, 1954–1961* (Athens: Ohio University Press, 2000).

67. Paul Drake, "Chile, 1930–58," in *Latin America since 1930: Spanish South America*, ed. Leslie Bethell (Cambridge: Cambridge University Press, 1991). Cambridge Histories Online, Cambridge University Press, October 27, 2012, http://universitypub

lishingonline.org/cambridge/histories/chapter.jsf?bid=CBO9781139055246&cid=CBO9 781139055246A010.

68. Gabriel Salazar, *En el nombre del poder popular constituyente (Chile, Siglo XXI)* (Santiago: Lom Ediciones, 2011).

69. Luis Corvalán Lépez, *Los comunistas y la democracia* (Santiago: Lom Ediciones, 2008), 123–128. The Chilean historian Iván Ljubetic Vargas of the Centro de Extensión e Investigación Luis Emilio Recabarren (CEILER) documents some fifty massacres in the twentieth century in "Masacres perpetradas en Chile en el siglo XX," unpublished list, 2013, in my possession.

CHAPTER 2

1. Lois Hecht Oppenheim, *Politics in Chile: Democracy, Authoritarianism, and the Search for Development*, 2d ed. (Boulder, CO: Westview Press, 1999), 4. For detailed political histories in English, see this book and Brian Loveman, *Chile: The Legacy of Hispanic Capitalism*, 2d ed. (New York: Oxford University Press, 1988). There is a voluminous literature in Spanish and English.

2. Sofía Correa Sutil, *Con las riendas del poder: La derecha chilena en el siglo XX* (Santiago: Debosillo, 2011), 86, 92–93; Rodrigo Baño, "Los sectores populares y la política: Una reflexión socio-histórica," *Política*, no. 43 (Spring 2004): 46. See also Tomás Moulian, *Chile Actual: Anatomía de un mito* (Santiago: Lom Ediciones, 1997).

3. Sergio Bitar, *Chile: Experiment in Democracy* (Philadelphia: Institute for the Study of Human Issues, 1986), 8.

4. Ibid., 9.

5. Joan Jara, interview with the author, June 8, 2011, Santiago. For an insightful explanation of the roots of this class consciousness, see Peter Winn, *Weavers of Revolution: The Yarur Workers and Chile's Road to Socialism* (New York: Oxford University Press, 1986), 84–89.

6. See, e.g., Marcelo Casals Araya, *El alba de una revolución* (Santiago: Lom Ediciones, 2010), 36–38, 57–58.

7. J. Samuel Valenzuela and Arturo Valenzuela, "Chile: The Development, Breakdown, and Recovery of Democracy," in *Latin America: Its Problems and Promise*, 2d ed., ed. Jan Knippers Black (Boulder, CO: Westview, 1991), 491.

8. Loveman, *Chile*, 4.

9. For more detail, see ibid., 370–375; Correa Sutil, *Con las riendas del poder*, 47–48, 54–55.

10. Sergio Grez, *La "cuestion social" en Chile: Ideas y debates precursores, 1804–1902* (Santiago: Dirección de Bibliotecas, Archivo y Museos, Centro de Investigaciones Diego Barros Arana, 1995); Gabriel Salazar, *En el nombre del Poder Popular Constituyente (Chile, Siglo XXI)* (Santiago: Lom Ediciones, 2011).

11. Loveman, *Chile*, 181; Oppenheim, *Politics in Chile*, 10.

12. Osvaldo Rodríguez cites one in *Cantores que reflexionan* (Madrid: Ediciones LAR, 1984), 60. Fernando Barraza cites another in *La nueva canción chilena* (Santiago: Quimantú, 1972), 19.

13. Juan Pablo González, interview with the author, June 25, 2012, Santiago. See also Marisol García, *Canción valiente* (Santiago: Grupo Zeta, 2013), 19–26.

14. Ian Roxborough, Philip J. O'Brien, and Jacqueline Roddick, *Chile: The State and Revolution* (New York: Holmes and Meier, 1977), 1–4.

15. Luis Corvalán Lépez, *Los comunistas y la democracia* (Santiago: Lom Ediciones, 2008), 17.

16. Lessie Jo Frazier gives government figures showing no fewer than 1,000 killed (Lessie Jo Frazier, *Salt in the Sand: Memory, Violence, and the Nation-State in Chile, 1890 to the Present* [Durham, NC: Duke University Press, 2007], 303, n. 7). Iván Ljubetic of the Centro de Extensión e Investigación Luis Emilio Recabarren (CEILER) gives the estimate of "more than 2,000": Iván Ljubetic, "Masacres perpetradas en Chile en el siglo XX," unpublished list in my possession, 2013. Romina A. Green Rioja writes that the figure of 3,600 is accepted by most scholars: Romina A. Green Rioja, "Historiography and Memory: The 1907 Massacre of Nitrate Workers and Their Families at Escuela Santa María in Iquique," http://www.academia.edu/885560/Historiography_and_Memory_the_1907_Massacre_of_Nitrate_Workers_and_their_Families_at_Escuela_Santa_Maria_in_Iquique_Chile.

17. González interview (June 25, 2012).

18. For studies of the anarchist movement, see Sergio Grez, *Los anarquistas y el movimiento obrero: La alborada de la IDEA en Chile, 1893–1915* (Santiago: Lom Ediciones, 2007); Peter DeShazo, *Urban Workers and Labor Unions in Chile, 1902–1927* (Madison: University of Wisconsin Press, 1977). For a study of the Communist and Socialist parties, see, among others, Casals Araya, *El alba de una revolución.*

19. Corvalán Lépez, *Los comunistas y la democracia*, 18. See also Recabarren's founding statement of principles and his program: Luis Emilio Recabarren, "El socialismo: ¿Qué es y cómo se realizará?" *El Despertar de los Trabajadores* (Iquique), October 8–November 21, 1912. This section benefited from a discussion with Alejandro del Rio, Partido Comunista of Chile, July 25, 2012, Santiago.

20. María Alicia Vetter, "The Educational Philosophy of Luis Emilio Recabarren and its influence on the Chilean working class and its class struggle strategies," paper presented at the Adult Education Research Conference, 2006.

21. Corvalán Lépez, *Los comunistas y la democracia*, 19.

22. I am grateful to Iván Ljubetic for sharing this work and his knowledge of Recabarren: Iván Ljubetic, interview with the author, July 4, 2013, Santiago.

23. Cited in Corvalán Lépez, *Los comunistas y la democracia*, 22.

24. José Seves, interview with the author, August 11, 2011, Santiago.

25. Jara interview (June 8, 2011).

26. Joan Jara, interview with the author, August 4, 2011, Santiago.

27. Michael Löwy, ed., *El marxismo en América Latina* (Santiago: Lom Ediciones, 2007), 15–16. See also Luis Emilio Recabarren, "La revolución rusa y los trabajadores chilenos," in Löwy, *El marxismo en América Latina*, 92–104; Jorge Arrate, *Salvador Allende, ¿sueño o proyecto?* (Santiago: Lom Ediciones, 2008), 50–52. Ljubetic argues that the party did not change in terms of its statutes, structure, or organization, and therefore the PC can legitimately trace its roots to 1912.

28. Oppenheim, *Politics in Chile*, 12.

29. Valenzuela and Valenzuela, "Chile."

30. Tomás Moulian, "La vía chilena al socialismo: Itinerario de la crisis de los discursos estratégicos de la Unidad Popular," in *Cuando hicimos historia: La experiencia de la Unidad Popular*, ed. Julio Pinto Vallejos (Santiago: Lom Ediciones, 2005), 42–43; see also Oppenheim, *Politics in Chile*, 14–20, for a detailed discussion of the political parties.

31. Moy de Tohá and Isabel de Letelier, *Allende: Demócrata intransigente* (Santiago: Amerinda Ediciones, 1986), 12.

32. See the Central Unitaria de Trabajadores website, which locates the roots of CUT in these earlier federations, http://www.cutchile.org/Portal/index.php?option=com_content&view=category&layout=blog&id=298&Itemid=54.

33. Olga Ulianova, who researched Soviet archives, found evidence that twenty-five Chileans joined the International Brigades in the Spanish Civil War, although there may have been others in other units: Olga Ulianova "A sesenta años de la Guerra Civil Española: Combatientes chilenos en las brigadas internacionales," *Estudios Avanzados Interactivos* 5, no. 7 (2006): 1–37.

34. Corvalán Lépez, *Los comunistas y la democracia*, 27.

35. Rodríguez, *Cantores que reflexionan*, 54–56.

36. Casals Araya, *El alba de una revolución*, 22.

37. See Loveman, *Chile*, 248, 255, 259.

38. Ibid., 249–250.

39. De Tohá and de Letelier, *Allende*, 12.

40. Tânia da Costa Garcia, "Canción popular, nacionalismo, consumo y política en Chile entre los años 40 y 60," *Revista Música Chilena* 63, no. 212 (2009), http://www.revistamusicalchilena.uchile.cl/index.php/RMCH/article/viewArticle/198/188; Rodrigo Torres, *Perfil de la creación musical en la nueva canción chilena desde sus orígenes hasta 1973* (Santiago: CENECA, 1980), 6–8.

41. Fernando García, interview with the author, August 6, 2012, Santiago.

42. Cited in Torres, *Perfil de la creación musical en la nueva canción chilena desde sus orígenes hasta 1973*, 8.

43. García interview (August 6, 2012).

44. Fernando García, "Lo social en la creación musical chilena de hoy," *Revista Aurora*, no. 11 (May–June 1967): 15, cited in Patricia Díaz Inostroza, *El canto nuevo chileno* (Santiago: Editorial Universidad Bolivariana, Colección Cultura Popular, 2007), 79–80.

45. Jara interview (June 8, 2011).

46. Cathy Schneider, *Shantytown Protest in Pinochet's Chile* (Philadelphia: Temple University Press, 1995), 32–37.

47. Robert H. Holden and Eric Zolov, eds., *Latin America and the United States: A Documentary History* (New York: Oxford University Press, 2000), 179.

48. "Memorandum of Conversation, E. T. Stannard, President, Kennecott Copper Corp., and Spruille Braden, Assistant Secretary of State, among others, at the State Department, Washington, 12 November 1946," in ibid., 180–181.

49. "Memorandum of Conversation, Mario Rodríguez, Chilean Chargé d'Affaires, and Spruille Braden, at the State Department, 12 November 1946," in ibid., 181.

50. "Entrevista a Beto Pastene," http://www.colectivobrp.cl (accessed November 29, 2007). See also http://www.graffiti.org/santiago/brp.html.

51. Corvalán Lépez, *Los comunistas y la democracia*, 30.

52. Adam Feinstein, *Pablo Neruda: A Passion for Life* (London: Bloomsbury, 2008), 199.

53. Frazier, *Salt in the Sand*, 166.

54. Anthony W. Pereira, *Political (In)justice: Authoritarianism and the Rule of Law in Brazil, Chile and Argentina* (Pittsburgh: University of Pittsburgh Press, 2005), 50.

55. Correa Sutil, *Con las riendas del poder*, 170–171.

56. Carlos Huneeus, *La guerra fría chilena: Gabriel González Videla y la ley maldita* (Santiago: Debate, 2009).

57. Loveman, *Chile*, 255, 258–259.

58. U.S. State Department, "United States Overseas Internal Defense Policy," 1962, in J. Patrice McSherry, *Predatory States: Operation Condor and Covert War in Latin America* (Lanham, MD: Rowman and Littlefield, 2005), 25.

59. Alain Rouquié, *The Military and the State in Latin America* (Berkeley: University of California Press, 1987), 133, 242.

60. U.S. Central Intelligence Agency, "CIA Activities in Chile," September 18, 2000, https://www.cia.gov/library/reports/general-reports-1/chile.

61. See McSherry, *Predatory States*; J. Patrice McSherry, "Death Squads as Parallel Forces," *Journal of Third World Studies* 24, no. 1 (Spring 2007): 13–52.

62. Osvaldo Rodríguez, *La nueva canción chilena: Continuidad y reflejo* (Havana: Ediciones Casa de las Américas, 1988), 42–43.

63. A summary and partial transcript of the congress are available online. "Primer Congreso Nacional de poetas y cantores populares de Chile," *Anales de la Universidad de Chile* 113, no. 93, series 4 (1954), http://www.anales.uchile.cl/index.php/ANUC/article/viewArticle/1758/1666.

64. Ignacio Ramos Rodillo, "Políticas del folklore: Representaciones de la tradición y lo popular. Militancia y política cultural en Violeta Parra y Atahualpa Yupanqui," master's thesis, University of Chile, Santiago, 2012, 115, 119.

65. See Ericka Verba, "Violeta Parra, Radio Chilena, and the 'Battle in Defense of the Authentic' during the 1950s in Chile," *Studies in Latin American Popular Culture* 26 (2007): 151–165.

66. Rodrigo Torres, "Cantar la diferencia: Violeta Parra y la canción chilena," *Revista Musical Chilena* 58, no. 201 (January 2004): 3.

67. Ramos Rodillo, "Políticas del folklore," 113, 121.

68. Torres, "Cantar la diferencia," 4.

69. Ángel Parra, interview with the author, January 24, 2013, Santiago.

70. Fernando Rios, "Andean Music, the Left, and Pan-Latin Americanism: The Early History," *Diagonal* 2 (2009), www.cilam.ucr.edu/diagonal/issues/2006/Rios.pdf. See also Juan Pablo González, "The Chilean Way to the Andes: Music, Politics and Otherness," *Diagonal* 2 (2009), http://www.cilam.ucr.edu/diagonal/issues/2006.

71. Horacio Salinas, interview with the author, July 8, 2013, Santiago.

72. Horacio Durán, interview with the author, July 9, 2013, Santiago. González discusses this issue in "The Chilean Way to the Andes."

73. Rodríguez, *La Nueva Canción chilena*, 47–50; Díaz Inostroza, *El canto nuevo chileno*, 58–59.

74. See the analysis in Torres, "Cantar la diferencia," 53–73.

75. Mario Garcés, "Construyendo 'las poblaciones': El movimiento de pobladores durante la Unidad Popular," in Pinto Vallejos, *Cuando hicimos historia*, 57–59. See also Mario Garcés, *Tomando su sitio: El movimiento de pobladores de Santiago, 1957–1970* (Santiago: Lom Ediciones, 2002).

76. For more on Cuncumén, see Carlos Valladares M. and Manuel Vilches P., *Rolando Alarcón: La canción en la noche* (Santiago: Quimantú, 2009).

77. Silvia Urbina, interview with the author, July 12, 2013, Santiago.

78. Jacques Chonchol was a key figure in this sector of the DC. He later led Frei's land reform program: see Mario Amorós, "La iglesia que nace del pueblo: Relevancia histórica del movimiento cristianos por el socialismo," in Pinto Vallejos, *Cuando hicimos historia*, 108. My understanding of the DC was enhanced by conversations with Jorge Montealegre, especially on August 1, 2012, Santiago.

79. Moulian, "La vía chilena al socialismo," 40; de Tohá y de Letelier, *Allende*, 39.

80. De Tohá y de Letelier, *Allende*, 39.

81. Ibid., 52. The numbers are slightly higher for each in Loveman, *Chile*, 264.

82. Bitar, *Chile*, 2.

83. Loveman, *Chile*, 265.

84. Jaime Esponda, interview with the author, August 14, 2012, Santiago.

85. Franck Gaudichaud, "Construyendo 'Poder Popular': El movimiento sindical, la CUT y las luchas obreras en el período de la Unidad Popular," in Pinto Vallejos, *Cuando hicimos historia*, 82.

86. U.S. Senate, *Covert Action in Chile, 1963–1973*, Staff Report of the Select Committee to Study Governmental Operations with Respect to Intelligence Activities (Church Commission Report), December 18, 1975, 11, 16–17.

87. Ibid., 6.

88. The Church Commission Report stated, "The CIA mounted a massive anti-communist propaganda campaign . . . which relied heavily on images of Soviet tanks and Cuban firing squads and was directed especially to women. . . . 'Disinformation' and 'black propaganda'—material which purported to originate from another source, such as the Chilean Communist Party—were used as well. . . . [A] CIA-funded propaganda group produced twenty radio spots per day in Santiago and on 44 provincial stations; twelve-minute news broadcasts five time daily on three Santiago stations and 24 provincial outlets; thousands of cartoons, and much paid press advertising. By the end of June, the group produced 24 daily newscasts in Santiago and the provinces, 26 weekly 'commentary' programs, and distributed 3,000 posters daily. The CIA regards the anti-communist scare campaign as the most effective activity undertaken by the U.S. on behalf of the Christian Democratic candidate": ibid., 17.

89. Margaret Power, "The Engendering of Anticommunism and Fear in Chile's 1964 Presidential Election," *Diplomatic History* 32, no. 5 (November 2008): 931–953.

90. Parra interview (January 24, 2013).

91. Volodia Teitelboim, *Neruda: An Intimate Biography*, trans. Beverly J. DeLong-Tonelli (Austin: University of Texas Press, 1991), 452.

92. Pablo Neruda, *Confieso que he vivido* (Barcelona: Plaza and Janes, 1974), 449.

93. U.S. Senate, "Covert Action in Chile," 18.

94. For an excellent summary, see Ellen Herman, *The Romance of American Psychology: Political Culture in the Age of Experts* (Berkeley: University of California Press, 1995), chap. 6. See also Irving Louis Horowitz, ed., *The Rise and Fall of Project Camelot: Studies in the Relationship between Social Science and Practical Politics* (Cambridge, MA: MIT Press, 1967); Robert A. Nisbet, "Project Camelot: An Autopsy," in *On Intellectuals: Theoretical Studies, Case Studies*, ed. Philip Rieff (Garden City, NY: Doubleday, 1969), 283–313.

95. A SORO memo says that Camelot's "objectives are: First, to devise procedures for assessing the potential for internal war within national societies; Second, to identify with increased degrees of confidence those actions which a government might take to relieve conditions which are assessed as giving rise to a potential for internal war. . . . Within the Army there is especially ready acceptance of the need to improve the general understanding of the processes of social change if the Army is to discharge its responsibilities in the over-all counterinsurgency program of the U.S. Government": Office of the Director, Special Operations Research Office, American University, December 4, 1964, Washington, DC, cited in Horowitz, *The Rise and Fall of Project Camelot*, 47–49.

96. Cited in Horowitz, *The Rise and Fall of Project Camelot*, 47.

97. Herman, *The Romance of American Psychology*, 165.

98. Ángel Parra to the author, e-mail communication, September 5, 2012; Rodrigo Torres, interview with the author, August 19, 2011, Santiago; Karen Kerschen, *Violeta Parra: By the Whim of the Wind* (Albuquerque: ABQ Press, 2010), 174–176.

99. Rodríguez, *Cantores que reflexionan*, 27–28. The lyrics to Atahualpa's "Preguntitas sobre Dios" (1969)—apparently his first recording of the song, although it was written years earlier—are different from Rodríguez's version. I translate Atahualpa's lyrics here.

100. Loveman, *Chile*, 280–281.

101. Oppenheim, *Politics in Chile*, 25.

102. Ibid.

103. Esponda interview (August 14, 2012).

104. Andrés Pascal Allende, *El MIR chileno: Una experiencia revolucionaria* (Rosario, Argentina: Cucaña Ediciones, 2003), 10. For a fascinating set of interviews with members of the PC, MIR, and the PS and their ideological differences, see Colin Henfrey and Bernardo Sorj, *Chilean Voices: Activists Describe Their Experiences of the Popular Unity Period* (Atlantic Highlands, NJ: Humanities Press, 1977). For a more personal view of MIR, see Carmen Castillo Echeverría, *Un día de octubre en Santiago* (Santiago: Lom Ediciones, 1999), originally published in 1980 in French. She was a MIR militant romantically involved with the MIR leader Miguel Enríquez.

105. Mónica Echeverría and Carmen Castillo, *Santiago-Paris: El vuelo de la memoria* (Santiago: Lom Ediciones, 2002), 150.

106. Alejandro Yáñez B., "Allende y la reforma universitaria en la UTE," http://www.generacion80.cl. Yáñez was a student leader representing FRAP.

107. "Declaración del 25 de Mayo, 1961," cited in ibid., 4.

108. Ibid., 8. Yáñez was the FRAP candidate in 1962 and became president of the student organization of UTE.

109. Ibid., 13.

110. Esponda interview (August 14, 2012).

111. See Fernando Castillo Velasco, *Lecciones del tiempo vivido* (Santiago: Catalonia, 2008); Castillo Velasco and Mónica Echeverría, interview with the author, July 17, 2012, Santiago.

112. Rodrigo Torres, interview with the author, July 9, 2011, Santiago.

113. Esponda interview (August 14, 2012).

114. Gustavo Moya Silva, journalist and former leader of FECH Valparaíso, "Testimonio," October 15, 2005, http://testimonioymemoria.blogspot.com/2005/10/testimonio-de-gustavo-moya.html.

115. For more on MAPU, see Esteban Valenzuela Van Treek, "Cristianismo, revolución y renovación en Chile: El Movimiento de Acción Popular Unitaria (MAPU) 1969–1989," Ph.D. thesis, University of Valencia, Spain, 2011.

CHAPTER 3

1. The musicologist and musician Patricia Díaz made this observation as a discussant in J. Patrice McSherry, "Conceptualizando la nueva canción chilena," presentation at Universidad Alberto Hurtado, Santiago, August 2012.

2. Musicians still in Chile began to build a new song movement, called *Canto Nuevo*, a heritage of *la Nueva Canción* and an important source of resistance to the dictatorship: see, e.g., Patricia Díaz Inostroza, *El canto nuevo chileno* (Santiago: Editorial Universidad Bolivariana, Colección Cultura Popular, 2007).

3. Eric Zolov, *Refried Elvis: The Rise of the Mexican Counterculture* (Berkeley: University of California Press, 1999), 238–239. Zolov argues that the U.S. Information Agency's approach was naïve, underestimating the way rock was adapted in counterhegemonic ways in various countries.

4. "A Conversation with Jorge Coulon of Inti Illimani," http://uprisingradio.org/home/2007/07/10/a-conversation-with-jorge-coulon-of-inti-illimani. For more on Inti-Illimani, see Luis Cifuentes Seves, *Fragmentos de un sueño: Inti Illimani y la generación de los 60,* 2d ed., Internet version by Cancioneros.com, 2000, http://www.cancioneros.com/co/3719/2/fragmentos-de-un-sueno. See also Horacio Salinas, *La canción en el sombrero* (Providencia, Chile: Editorial Catalonia, 2013).

5. Raúl Encina T. and Rodrigo Fuenzalida H., *Víctor Jara: Testimonio de un artista* (Santiago: Centro de Recopilaciones y Testimonio, 1988), 22.

6. Víctor Jara, interview on Televisión Panamericana, Peru, July 1973, https://barrocopost.wordpress.com/2013/09/15/concierto-completo-victor-jara-en-peru-17-de-julio-de-1973.

7. Horacio Durán, interview with the author, June 13, 2011, Santiago.

8. Rodrigo Torres, interview with the author, July 30, 2012, Santiago.

9. Quoted in Osvaldo Rodríguez, *Cantores que reflexionan* (Madrid: Ediciones LAR, 1984), 53–54.

10. Nano Acevedo, *Los ojos de la memoria* (Santiago: Cantoral Ediciones, 1995), 50–51; Juan Castro and Carlos Contreras, interview with the author, August 5, 2013, Santiago. For more on *la Nueva Ola,* see Juan Pablo González, Oscar Ohlsen, and Claudio Rolle, *Historia social de la música popular en Chile, 1950–1970* (Santiago: Ediciones Universidad Católica de Chile, 2009), 631–687.

11. César Albornoz, interview with the author, August 10, 2011, Santiago.

12. Mariela Ferreira, interview with the author, June 25, 2012, Santiago.

13. José Seves, interview with the author, July 27, 2011, Santiago. Albornoz made a similar point: Albornoz interview (August 10, 2011). See also Fabio Salas Zúñiga, *La primavera terrestre: Cartografías del rock chileno y la nueva canción chilena* (Santiago: Editorial Cuarto Propio, 2000), 25–32; Memoria Chilena, 2004, http://www.memoriachilena.cl/temas/index.asp?id_ut=lanuevaola.

14. Castro and Contreras interview (August 5, 2013).

15. Ercilia Moreno Chá, "Argentina," in *Garland Handbook of Latin American Music,* 2d ed., ed. Dale A Olsen and Daniel A. Sheehy (New York: Routledge, 2008), 405.

16. For a study of the influence of Yupanqui and Violeta Parra, see Ignacio Ramos Rodillo, "Politicas del folklore: Representaciones de la tradición y lo popular. Militancia y política cultural en Violeta Parra y Atahualpa Yupanqui," master's thesis, University of Chile, Santiago, 2012. For more on *Neofolklore,* see González, Ohlsen, and Rolle, *Historia social de la música popular en Chile,* 337–356.

17. Rodrigo Torres, *Perfil de la creación musical en la nueva canción chilena desde sus orígenes hasta 1973* (Santiago: CENECA, 1980), 21.

18. The New Song musicians José Seves of Inti-Illimani and Ernesto Parra of Los Curacas both mentioned the influence of Raúl Shaw Moreno: Jose Seves, interview with the author, June 18, 2013, Santiago; Ernesto Parra, interview with the author, July 19, 2013, Santiago. See also Salinas, *La canción en el sombrero,* 36, 68–69.

19. José Seves, interview with the author, August 21, 2012, Santiago.

20. Patricio Manns, interview with the author, August 6, 2011, Concón.

21. Miguel Davagnino, interview with the author, July 24, 2013, Santiago. Juan Pablo González has identified Violeta Parra's 1963 album—some of her most political songs, recorded in France (e.g., "La Carta")—as the birth of New Song. However, the album, titled *Canciones Reencontradas en París,* was not released until eight years later (see Juan Pablo González, "La buena salud de la nueva canción chilena," *El Mercurio,* September 1, 2013).

22. Manuel Vilches, interview with the author, July 16, 2012, Santiago. See also Carlos Valladares M. and Manuel Vilches P., *Rolando Alarcón: La canción en la noche* (Santiago: Quimantú, 2009).

23. Vilches interview (July 16, 2012).

24. Alfonso Padilla, interviews with the author, June 15, 2011, July 16, 2012, and January 17, 2014, Santiago.

25. Torres interview (July 30, 2012). For García's account, see Ricardo García, "La nueva canción también vencerá," *Ramona*, date illegible (circa 1971), in my possession.

26. Mariela Ferreira, interview with the author, August 25, 2012, Santiago.

27. Seves interview (August 21, 2012).

28. Max Berrú, interview with the author, July 11, 2012, Santiago.

29. Horacio Salinas, interview with the author, July 8, 2013, Santiago.

30. Roberto Márquez, interview with the author, July 20, 2012, Santiago.

31. Alejandra Lastra and Patricio Manns, e-mail to the author, July 20, 2013.

32. Castro and Contreras interview (August 5, 2013).

33. Vilches interview (July 16, 2012).

34. The song was metaphorical, since there had been no recent wars in Chile: Valladares and Vilches, *Rolando Alarcón*, 73–76; José Pablo López, "1965 La batalla de las refalosas," *Revista Ercilla*, no. 1562 (April 28, 1965), reproduced by Manuel Vilches, June 19, 2009.

35. Cited in López, "1965 La batalla de las refalosas."

36. See Juan Pablo González, "Tradición, identidad y vanguardia en la música chilena de la década de 1960," *Aisthesis*, no. 38 (2005): 200.

37. For analysis of one of his works, see Silvia Herrera Ortega, "Una aproximación a la relación música-política a través de la cantata La Fragua del compositor Sergio Ortega (1938–2003)," presentation at the Seventh Week of Music and Musicology, Universidad Católica Argentina, Buenos Aires, October 20–22, 2010.

38. César Albornoz, "La cultura en la Unidad Popular: Porque esta vez no se trata de cambiar un presidente," in *Cuando hicimos historia: La experiencia de la Unidad Popular*, ed. Julio Pinto Vallejos (Santiago: Lom Ediciones, 2005), 150.

39. Ángel Parra, personal e-mail communication to the author, May 5, 2013.

40. Interview with Manns, in Rodríguez, *Cantores que reflexionan*, 101–102. The album was not released until 1967.

41. Rodríguez, *Cantores que reflexionan*, 82.

42. Interview with Manns, in ibid., 103.

43. José Miguel Varas, "Impromptu de Manns," in *En busca de la música chilena*, ed. José Miguel Varas and Juan Pablo González (Santiago: Cuadernos Bicentenario, 2005); Miguel Davagnino, interview with the author, July 26, 2012, Santiago.

44. Durán interview (June 13, 2011).

45. Claudio Acevedo, Rodolfo Norambuena, José Seves, Rodrigo Torres, and Mauricio Valdebenito, *Víctor Jara: Obra musical completa*, 2d ed. (Santiago: Fundación Víctor Jara, 1999), 12.

46. Mariela Ferreira, interview with the author, August 13, 2012, Santiago.

47. Joan Jara, *Victor: An Unfinished Song* (London: Jonathan Cape, 1983), 84.

48. Jara, interview with Televisión Panamericana.

49. Greg Walz-Chojnacki, "Canto al huaso, canto al pueblo: La música y el discurso político de la identidad chilena durante los años sesenta y la Unidad Popular," Independent Study Project (ISP) Collection, paper 505, 2004, http://digitalcollections.sit.edu/isp_collection/505, 7, 9–11.

50. Acevedo et al., *Víctor Jara*, 35–36; Naín Nómez, "Prologue," in *Víctor Jara: Deja su huella en el viento* (Santiago: Lom Ediciones, 2012), 11–15.

51. Torres, *Perfil de la creación musical en la nueva canción chilena desde sus orígenes hasta 1973*, 5.

52. Salinas interview (July 8, 2013).

53. Acevedo et al., *Víctor Jara*, 50.

54. José Seves, "Víctor Jara en la Peña de los Parra," December 26, 2005, http://jo seves.blogspot.com/2005/12/victor-jara-en-la-peña-de-los-parra.html.

55. René Largo Farías, *La nueva canción chilena* (Mexico City: Casa de Chile, 1977), 17.

56. Seves interview (July 27, 2011). See also Gabriela Bravo Chiappe and Cristian González Farfán, *Ecos del tiempo subterráneo: Las peñas en Santiago durante el régimen militar 1973–1983* (Santiago: Lom Ediciones, 2009), 28–31.

57. Ángel Parra, interview with the author, January 24, 2013, Santiago.

58. Pablo Aguilera, "Las peñas folklóricos: ¿Negocio o difusión?" *Onda*, no. 27 (1972): 25–27.

59. Max Berrú, interview with the author, June 14, 2011, Santiago.

60. Osvaldo Rodríguez, *La nueva canción chilena: Continuidad y reflejo* (Havana: Ediciones Casa de las Américas, 1988), 61; Manns interview (August 6, 2011).

61. Ernesto Parra, interview with the author, August 29, 2012, Santiago.

62. Berrú interview (June 14, 2011).

63. Eduardo Carrasco, interview with the author, August 9, 2011, Santiago. See also Juan Pablo González, "The Chilean Way to the Andes: Music, Politics and Otherness," *Diagonal* 2 (2009), http://www.cilam.ucr.edu/diagonal/issues/2006.

64. Torres, *Perfil de la creación musical en la nueva canción chilena desde sus orígenes hasta 1973*, 41–42.

65. Andrián Pertout, "Inti-Illimani: Chilean Folk Legends," *Mixdown Monthly*, no. 66 (October 6, 1999), http://www.pertout.com/Inti-Illimani.htm.

66. Berrú, Carrasco, Coulon, Durán, Salinas, Seves, and Venegas interviews in 2011, 2012, and 2013.

67. See the official website at http://www.quilapayun.com.

68. Ricardo Valenzuela, interview with the author, August 21, 2012, Santiago. See also Jan Fairley, "La Nueva Canción Latinoamericana," *Bulletin of Latin American Research* 3, no. 2 (1984): 113.

69. Eduardo Carrasco, interview with the author, August 14, 2013, Santiago.

70. Juan Carvajal, interview with the author, August 15, 2012, Santiago. See also Eduardo Carrasco, *Quilapayún: La revolución y las estrellas* (Santiago: Ediciones de Ornitorrinco, 1988), 131.

71. Valenzuela interview (August 21, 2012).

72. Carrasco interview (July 26, 2012).

73. Julio Alegría, Aparcoa, interview with the author, August 19, 2013, Santiago; Cecilia Coll, former head of La Jota's Cultural Commission, interview with the author, August 27, 2013, Santiago.

74. Alegría interview (August 19, 2013); Max Berrú, interview with the author, August 28, 2013, Santiago.

75. Berrú interview (July 11, 2012).

76. Ibid. (June 14, 2011).

77. Valenzuela interview (August 21, 2012).

78. Carrasco interview (August 9, 2011). See also "DICAP: Cuatro años," *Ramona*, 1 (March 27, 1972): 38–39.

79. Valenzuela interview (August 21, 2012).

80. Carvajal interview (August 15, 2012).

81. Valenzuela interview (August 21, 2012).

82. Carrasco interview (August 14, 2013).

83. Claudio Rolle, "La nueva canción chilena: El proyecto cultural popular y la campaña presidencial y gobierno de Salvador Allende," *Pensamiento Crítico*, no. 2 (2002): 2. The Sierra is the mountain range from which the Cuban revolutionaries operated.

84. Joan Jara writes that Víctor Jara was criticized by the PC for writing a song about Che Guevara: Jara, *Víctor*, 114. See also Jorge Coulon, *La sonrisa de Víctor Jara* (Santiago: Editorial USACH, 2009), 43.

85. Carrasco, *Quilapayún*, 130–131.

86. In a speech in 1963, Corvalán said that he publicly disagreed with Nikita Krushchev's dictates regarding the production of artistic works in the Soviet Union and that the Chilean PC never interfered in the work of the artists. He stated in 1967 that all the party asked of the artists was that "they march with the working class" and "support them as best they can in their combats. . . . We appreciate as well the art that simply brings culture in general, love, joy, and beauty to our people": Luis Corvalán, *De lo vivido y lo peleado: Memorias* (Santiago: Lom Ediciones, 1997), 91; Luis Corvalán, *Tres períodos en nuestra línea revolucionaria* (Dresden: Verlag Zeit im Bild, 1982), 24–25. I am grateful to Iván Ljubetic for sharing these sources from his personal library.

87. Carvajal interview (August 15, 2012).

88. Valenzuela interview (August 21, 2012).

89. Fabio Salas Zúñiga, interview with the author, August 12, 2011, Santiago.

90. Salas Zúñiga, *La primavera terrestre*, 80–81.

91. Cathy Cockrell, "Horacio Salinas Performs '60s Music, Chilean-style," *Berkeleyan*, April 27, 2005, http://berkeley.edu/news/berkeleyan/2005/04/27_salinas.shtml.

92. Jorge Coulon, interview with the author, July 7, 2011, Santiago.

93. José Seves, interview with the author, June 26, 2012, Santiago. See also José Seves, "El exiliado del sur: La connección peña de Valdivia y Santiago," 2010, https://es-es.facebook.com/notes/inti-illimani-hist%C3%B3rico-salinas-seves-dur%C3%A1n/el-exiliado-del-sur-la-conecci%C3%B3n-pe%C3%B1a-de-valdivia-y-santiago/334605466580644.

94. Gabriela Bade, "Inti-Illimani," http://www.musicapopular.cl/3.0/index2.php?op=Artista&id=18.

95. Max Berrú, interview with the author, June 15, 2012, Santiago; Seves interview (June 26, 2012); "A Conversation with Horacio Salinas," Center for Latin American Studies, University of California, Berkeley, October 6, 1999. See also https://www.facebook.com/inti.illimani.historico/info.

96. Berrú interview (June 14, 2011).

97. Fairley, "La Nueva Canción Latinoamericana," 107.

98. "Resolución final del encuentro de la canción protesta," in *Latin America and the United States: A Documentary History*, ed. Robert H. Holden and Eric Zolov (New York: Oxford University Press, 2000), 260–261.

99. Horacio Salinas, interview with the author, July 26, 2011, Santiago.

100. Coll interview (August 27, 2013). Leonard Kósichev, *La guitarra y el poncho de Víctor Jara* (Moscow: Editorial Progreso, 1990), 145.

101. Gabriela García, "El rey de la reina," *El Mercurio Revista*, August 2012, 83.

102. Between 1968 and 1973, enrollment at the UTE increased from some 9,000 students to more than 32,000. The number of branches and institutes at the university grew from nine in 1968 to twenty-four in 1973, extending from the North to the South

of Chile. The number of full-time professors increased from 500 in 1968 to 2,551 in 1973. New majors and programs were created, linked to developing the country economically and technically, and the university was opened to workers and their children: see Alejandro Yáñez B., "Allende y la reforma universitaria en la UTE," http://www.generacion80.cl, 14.

103. Carlos Orellana, ed., "Entrevistas sobre la nueva canción," 1978, http://www.quilapayun.com.

104. For García's description, see José Osorio, ed., *Ricardo García: Una obra transcendente* (Santiago: Editorial Pluma y Pincil, 1996), 103.

105. Jara, *Víctor*, 126.

106. Fernando Barraza, *La nueva canción chilena* (Santiago: Quimantú, 1972), 45; Jara, *Víctor*, 128.

107. Miguel Lawner, interview with the author, August 26, 2011, Santiago; Jorge Arrate, *Salvador Allende, ¿sueño o proyecto?* (Santiago: Lom Ediciones, 2008), 53–54.

108. Gabriel García Márquez, "Why Allende Had to Die," *New Statesman*, March 1974, http://www.newstatesman.com/world-affairs/2013/04/why-allende-had-die.

109. The figure for Frei is from Jorge Arrate and Eduardo Rojas, *Memoria de la izquierda chilena 1850—2000* (Santiago: Javier Vergara Editor, 2003), chap. 5, http://www.socialismo-chileno.org/PS/index.php?option=com_content&task=view&id=96&Itemid=50). The second was provided to Olga Ulianova by Sergio Ovalle, regional secretary of the PC's Santiago South district in the 1960s: Olga Ulianova, e-mail to the author, August 26, 2013.

110. See, e.g., Carolina Olmedo Carrasco, "El muralismo comunista en Chile: La exposición retrospectiva de las Brigadas Ramona Parra en el Museo de Arte Contemporáneo de Santiago, 1971," in *1912-2012: El siglo de los comunistas chilenos*, ed. Olga Ulianova, Manuel Loyola, and Rolando Álvarez (Santiago: Instituto de Estudios Avanzados, USACH, 2012), 299–314.

111. The Church Commission later reported that "the most prominent of the rightwing paramilitary groups was Patria y Libertad (Fatherland and Liberty), which formed following Allende's September 4 election, during so-called Track II. The CIA provided Patria y Libertad with $38,000 through a third party during the Track II period, in an effort to create tension and a possible pretext for intervention by the Chilean military": "Hearings before the Senate Committee to Study Governmental Operations with Respect to Intelligence Activities," in U.S. Senate, *Covert Action in Chile, 1963–1973* (Church Commission Report), December 4 and 5, 1975, 31.

112. Ibid., 20.

113. Jorge Montealegre, interview with the author, July 14, 2013, Santiago.

114. Church Commission Report, 22.

115. Ibid., 9, 13.

116. Margaret Power, *Right-Wing Women in Chile: Feminine Power and the Struggle against Allende, 1964-1973* (University Park: Pennsylvania State University Press, 2002), 130–133.

117. Ibid., 133; Davagnino interview (July 26, 2012); Montealegre interview (July 14, 2013); Iván Ljubetic Vargas, "Operación Andalién," Blog Boletín Rojo, October 7, 2012, http://elboletinrojo.blogspot.com/2012/10/operacion-andalien_7.html.

118. Jara, *Víctor*, 140; Valladares and Vilches, *Rolando Alarcón*, 139; González, Ohlsen, and Rolle, *Historia social de la música popular en Chile*, 264–265.

119. Barraza, *La nueva canción chilena*, 45; Acevedo, *Los ojos de la memoria*, 56–57; Rodríguez, *Cantores que reflexionan*, 138.

120. Berrú interview (June 14, 2011). For a video of these events, see Catholic University, "Réquiem de Chile: René Schneider Chereau," 2010, http://www.youtube.com/watch?v=MltoIVkQPMI.

121. See, e.g., Róbinson Rojas, *The Murder of Allende and the End of the Chilean Way to Socialism* (New York: Harper and Row, 1975).

122. For the leaked series of ITT memos, see *Subversion in Chile: A Case Study of U.S. Corporate Intrigue in the Third World* (Nottingham, U.K.: Spokesman Books, 1972), 30, 44–45. For an internal view of the rise of mutinous anticommunist factions of the military, see Carlos Prats, *Memorias (Testimonio de un soldado)* (Santiago: Ediciones Puehuén, 1985).

123. "It will make no difference that Allende is coming to power as the first Communist head of state ever democratically elected. It is foolish to believe he will give democracy another chance in six years. Whatever the trappings, there is unlikely ever to be another truly free election in Chile": ITT internal memo dated October 26, 1970, in *Subversion in Chile*, 84.

124. For the original memos and commentary, see Peter Kornbluh, *Chile and the United States: Declassified Documents Relating to the Military Coup, September 11, 1973*, Electronic Briefing Book no. 8, National Security Archive, George Washington University, http://www.gwu.edu/~nsarchiv/NSAEBB/NSAEBB8/nsaebb8i.htm.

125. "Introduction" and ITT internal memo dated October 25, 1970, in *Subversion in Chile*, 15, 81; Church Commission Report, 13, 23–25; Mónica González, *Chile, la conjura: Los mil y un días del golpe* (Santiago: Ediciones B, Grupo Zeta, 2000), 93.

126. Church Commission Report, 26.

127. "Genesis of Project FUBELT," declassified CIA memorandum for the record, September 16, 1970, www2.gwu.edu/~nsarchiv/NSAEBB/NSAEBB8/docs/doc03.pdf.

128. U.S. Central Intelligence Agency, *CIA Activities in Chile* (Hinchey Report), September 18, 2000, https://www.cia.gov/library/reports/general-reports-1/chile/index.html#5.

129. Church Commission Report, 13.

130. Chief of Station, Santiago, to CIA Headquarters, telex, October 8, 1970, in Hinchey Report.

131. Hinchey Report.

132. "Genesis of Project FUBELT."

133. "Chile Buries Slain General as Martyr," *New York Times*, October 28, 1970.

CHAPTER 4

1. Miguel Lawner, interview with the author, August 26, 2011, Santiago. See also Claudio Rolle, "La nueva canción chilena: El proyecto cultural popular, la campaña presidencial y el gobierno de Salvador Allende," *Pensamiento Crítico*, no. 2 (2002): 2.

2. Ernesto Parra, interview with the author, July 19, 2013, Santiago.

3. Rodrigo Torres, interview with the author, July 30, 2012, Santiago.

4. Thomas Wright has noted that, given the centralized nature of the Chilean system, municipal elections are a good indicator of national trends. The first percentage is cited in U.S. Senate, *Covert Action in Chile, 1963–1973*, Report of the Senate Select Committee to Study Governmental Operations with Respect to Intelligence Activities (Church Commission Report), December 18, 1975, 51; the second, in James Petras and Frank T. Fitzgerald, "Authoritarianism and Democracy in the Transition to Socialism," *Latin American Perspectives* 15 (January 1988): 95.

5. Joan Jara, *Víctor: An Unfinished Song* (London: Jonathan Cape, 1983), 150.

6. Reinaldo Ruiz, "Los fundamentos económicos del programa de gobierno de la Unidad Popular: A 35 años de su declaración," *Revista Universum* 1, no. 20 (2005): 153–167. See also Luis Corvalán Lépez, *El gobierno de Salvador Allende* (Santiago: Lom Ediciones, 2003), 275–302.

7. Vuskovic, challenging liberal preferences for "efficiency" and the operation of market forces, commented that "the principal problem is not efficiency but power; that is, who controls the economy and for whom? . . . What is in play is the ownership of the means of production by a small minority. . . . To center the discussion in efficiency is to avoid discussing who really determines economic power and why a small minority that owns the means of production is capable of subordinating the majority": quoted in Ruiz, "Los fundamentos económicos del programa de gobierno de la Unidad Popular," 165.

8. Ibid., 163.

9. Unidad Popular, "Programa, las 40 medidas," http://www.abacq.net/imagineria/medidas.htm.

10. For in-depth analyses of Allende's economic program by former economic officials, see, among others, Sergio Bitar, *Chile: Experiment in Democracy* (Philadelphia: Institute for the Study of Human Issues, 1986); Edward Boorstein, *An Inside View: Allende's Chile* (New York: International Publishers, 1977).

11. For the section of the UP program on culture, see http://www.abacq.net/imagineria/frame5b.htm#07.

12. Quoted from http://www.memoriachilena.cl/temas/index.asp?id_ut=editoranacionalquimantu.

13. José Seves, interview with the author, August 11, 2011, Santiago.

14. Contreras was speaking at an event to commemorate the forty years since the 1973 coup on June 12, 2013, in Santiago.

15. Ricardo Venegas, interview with the author, June 27, 2012, Santiago.

16. Horacio Salinas, interview with the author, July 8, 2013, Santiago.

17. Corvalán Lépez, *El gobierno de Salvador Allende*, 190–193.

18. Chonchol wrote, "I believe in what the Chilean revolution claims to demonstrate, that it is possible to make a profound change toward socialism without the necessity of a violent confrontation. . . . We believe in the current context that in Chile it is possible to advance toward a socialist society without direct confrontation": quoted in Esteban Valenzuela Van Treek, "Cristianismo, revolución y renovación en Chile: El Movimiento de Acción Popular Unitaria (MAPU) 1969–1989,"Ph.D. thesis, University of Valencia, Spain, 2011), 155–156.

19. Robert N. Pierce, *Keeping the Flame: Media and Government in Latin America* (New York: Hastings House, 1979), 57.

20. Fabio Salas Zúñiga, *La primavera terrestre: Cartografías del rock chileno y la nueva canción chilena* (Santiago: Editorial Cuarto Propio, 2000), 83.

21. Pierce, *Keeping the Flame*, 58, 62.

22. *Miami Herald*, September 20, 1970, cited in Pierce, *Keeping the Flame*, 58.

23. Ibid., 59.

24. The commission stated that *El Mercurio* had received almost $2 million in U.S. funding in 1971 and 1972. Moreover, up to $1 million was spent to manipulate the 1970 election. "The large-scale propaganda campaign which was undertaken by the U.S. was similar to that of 1964: an Allende victory was equated with violence and repression": Church Commission Report, 20.

25. Pierce, *Keeping the Flame*, 56, 64; Hernán Uribe, "Prensa y periodismo político en

los años 1960–70," in *Morir es la noticia*, ed. Ernesto Carmona (Santiago, 1997), http://www.derechos.org/nizkor/chile/libros/reporter.

26. Max Berrú, interview with the author, July 11, 2012, Santiago.

27. Uribe, "Prensa y periodismo político en los años 1960–70."

28. Jara, *Víctor*, 158.

29. Venegas interview (June 27, 2012).

30. José Seves, interview with the author, June 26, 2012, Santiago.

31. Leonard Kósichev, *La guitarra y el poncho de Víctor Jara* (Moscow: Editorial Progreso, 1990), 150–151.

32. Colin Henfrey and Bernardo Sorj, *Chilean Voices: Activists Describe Their Experiences of the Popular Unity Period* (Atlantic Highlands, NJ: Humanities Press, 1977), 156–157.

33. Jan Fairley, "La Nueva Canción Latinoamericana," *Bulletin of Latin American Research* 3, no. 2 (1984): 113.

34. Fernando Barraza, *La nueva canción chilena* (Santiago: Quimantú, 1972), 61.

35. Casa de las Américas, *Habla y canta Víctor Jara* (Havana: Casa de las Américas, 1978), 23–24.

36. Mario Salazar, interview with the author, August 23, 2012, Santiago.

37. Nano Acevedo. *Los ojos de la memoria* (Santiago: Cantoral Ediciones, 1995), 110–111.

38. For a compact history and analysis, see Carolina Olmedo Carrasco, "El muralismo comunista en Chile: La exposición retrospectiva de las Brigadas Ramona Parra en el Museo de Arte Contemporáneo de Santiago, 1971," in *1912–2012: El siglo de los comunistas chilenos*, ed. Olga Ulianova, Manuel Loyola, and Rolando Álvarez (Santiago: Instituto de Estudios Avanzados, Universidad de Santiago de Chile, 2012): 299–314.

39. César Albornoz, "La cultura en la Unidad Popular: Porque esta vez no se trata de cambiar un presidente," in *Cuando hicimos historia: La experiencia de la Unidad Popular*, ed. Julio Pinto Vallejos (Santiago: Lom Ediciones, 2005), 166–168.

40. Eduardo Carrasco, interview with the author, July 26, 2012, Santiago.

41. Roberto Márquez, interview with the author, July 20, 2012, Santiago.

42. Jara, *Víctor*, 197–198. Jara organized similar spectacular shows to celebrate the fiftieth anniversary of the PC and the fortieth anniversary of La Jota.

43. Kósichev, *La guitarra y el poncho de Víctor Jara*, 144; Osvaldo Rodríguez, *La nueva canción chilena: Continuidad y reflejo* (Havana: Ediciones Casa de las Américas, 1988), 99.

44. Jara, *Víctor*, 198.

45. Raúl Encina T. and Rodrigo Fuenzalida H., *Víctor Jara: Testimonio de un artista* (Santiago: Centro de Recopilaciones y Testimonio, 1987), 24.

46. Cecilia Coll, interview with the author, August 27, 2013, Santiago.

47. Max Berrú, interview with the author, June 14, 2011, Santiago.

48. Seves interview (June 26, 2012).

49. *Ramona* 1, no. 23 (April 4, 1972): 38–39.

50. Berrú interview (July 11, 2012).

51. Ibid.

52. Miguel Davagnino, interview with the author, July 26, 2012, Santiago.

53. Albornoz, "La cultura en la Unidad Popular," 151.

54. Jorge Coulon, interview with the author, July 7, 2011, Santiago.

55. Seves interview (August 11, 2011).

56. Horacio Durán, interview with the author, June 13, 2011, Santiago.

57. Juan Valladares, interview with the author, July 23, 2012, Santiago.

58. Jara, *Víctor*, 150–151.

59. José Manuel García, "La Unidad Popular," www.cancioneros.com.

60. Rolle, "La nueva canción chilena," 3.

61. The historian Claudio Rolle has observed that "a strategy was developed with a certain trivialization of the music as a way of reaching a broader public and capturing the attention of young people who were colonized musically by foreign music": ibid.

62. Horacio Salinas told Marisol García that "there was a lively debate about the limits between song and pamphlet, which was something we discussed a lot": Marisol García, *Canción valiente 1960–1989: Tres décadas de canto social y político en Chile* (Santiago: Ediciones B, 2013), 129.

63. Fernando Barraza, for example, did so, and wrote that the "creativity [of New Song] seemed at times to be exhausted. The frankly propagandistic song, pamphlet songs, often replaced quality themes": Barraza, *La nueva canción chilena*, 59–62.

64. Juan Pablo González, Oscar Ohlsen, Claudio Rolle, *Historia social de la música popular en Chile, 1950–1970* (Santiago: Ediciones Universidad Católica de Chile, 2009), 266.

65. Berrú interview (June 14, 2011).

66. Seves interview (August 11, 2011).

67. *Ramona* 1, no. 33 (April 1972): 39. The individual speakers were not identified.

68. Interview with Manns in *Ramona*, no. 31 (n.d.), reproduced in José Osorio, ed., *Ricardo García: Una obra transcendente* (Santiago: Editorial Pluma y Pincel, 1996), 195.

69. Ricardo García, "La nueva canción chilena perdió el ritmo," *Ramona* 1, no. 8 (n.d. [1972?]): 12–14; see also Osorio, *Ricardo García*, 107–109. García's daughter, now in charge of the record company Alerce, confirmed that her father had been critical of the quality of some of the songs during this period: Viviana Larrea, interview with the author, July 25, 2012, Santiago.

70. Rodríguez, *La nueva canción chilena*, 89–90; Osvaldo Rodríguez, *Cantores que reflexionan* (Madrid: Ediciones LAR, 1984), 220–221.

71. Carrasco interview (July 26, 2012). See also Eduardo Carrasco, *Quilapayún: La revolución y las estrellas* (Santiago: Ediciones de Ornitorrinco, 1988), 227–228.

72. Horacio Durán, interview with the author, July 9, 2013, Santiago; Horacio Durán, e-mail communication to the author, July 9, 2013.

73. Rolle, "La nueva canción chilena," 4.

74. Casa de las Américas, *Habla y canta Víctor Jara*, 24. See also Claudio Acevedo, Rodolfo Norambuena, José Seves, Rodrigo Torres, and Mauricio Valdebenito, *Víctor Jara: Obra musical completa*, 2d ed. (Santiago: Fundación Víctor Jara, 1999), 46–50.

75. José Seves, interview with the author, August 21, 2012, Santiago.

76. José Seves, "Víctor Jara en la Peña de los Parra," 2010, https://www.facebook.com/jose.seves/notes.

77. Casa de las Américas, *Habla y canta Víctor Jara*, 29.

78. Kósichev, *La guitarra y el poncho de Víctor Jara*, 155. For Seves's account of discovering Jara's travel to Lonquimay during his own trip with La Jota in 1973, see Moisés Chaparro, José Seves, and David Spener, *Canto de las estrellas: Un homenaje a Víctor Jara* (Santiago: Ceibo Ediciones, 2013), 39–48.

79. Jara, *Víctor*, 163.

80. Albornoz, "La cultura en la Unidad Popular," 170.

81. See Isabel Parra's website, http://www.isabelparra.cl/mi_trabajo.htm.

82. Horacio Salinas, e-mail communication to the author, October 9, 2013.

83. Daniel Party, "Beyond 'Protest Song:' Popular Music in Pinochet's Chile (1973–1990)," in *Music and Dictatorship in Europe and Latin America,* ed. Roberto Illiamo and Massimiliano Sala (Turnhout, Belgium: Brepols, 2010), 671. For an encyclopedic review of many forms of popular music in Chile, see González, Ohlsen, and Rolle, *Historia social de la música popular en Chile.*

84. Rodolfo Parada-Lillo, "'La nueva canción chilena' 1960–1970: Arte y política, tradición y modernidad." *Patrimonio Cultural,* no. 49 (January 30, 2009), http://www.generacion80.cl/noticias/columna_completa.php?varid=3882.

85. Horacio Durán, interview with the author, July 31, 2012, Santiago.

86. Berrú interview (July 11, 2012).

87. Carrasco interview (July 26, 2012).

88. Juan Carvajal, interview with the author, August 15, 2012, Santiago.

89. For an article analyzing "hypermobilization" in Chile and the difficulty in controlling or channeling it, see Henry A. Landsberger and Tim McDaniel, "Hypermobilization in Chile, 1970–1973," *World Politics* 28, no. 4 (July 1976): 502–541. For a case study, see Peter Winn, *Weavers of Revolution: The Yarur Workers and Chile's Road to Socialism* (New York: Oxford University Press, 1989).

90. Van Treek, "Cristianismo, revolución y renovación en Chile," 47.

91. Henfrey and Sorj, *Chilean Voices,* 164–165.

92. Church Commission Report, 53.

93. Brian Loveman, *Chile: The Legacy of Hispanic Capitalism* (New York: Oxford University Press, 1988), 304.

94. Jorge Coulon, *La Sonrisa de Víctor Jara* (Santiago: Editorial USACH, 2009), 73.

95. For in-depth statements of the various positions, see Henfrey and Sorj, *Chilean Voices.*

96. Loveman, *Chile,* 305.

97. Berrú interview (June 14, 2011).

98. Eduardo Carrasco, interview with the author, August 9, 2011, Santiago. Patria y Libertad used the term "Jakarta" as a code to stoke fear. An anticommunist massacre of more than half a million people had taken place in Indonesia in 1965. The CIA helped compile death lists: see, e.g., http://www.indonesia-digest.net/3200genocide.htm.

99. Carrasco, *Quilapayún,* 225.

100. Carlos Valladares M. and Manuel Vilches P., *Rolando Alarcón: La canción en la noche* (Santiago: Quimantú, 2009), 164.

101. Albornoz, "La cultura en la Unidad Popular," 173.

102. Carrasco, *Quilapayún,* 225–226.

103. Lawner interview (August 26, 2011).

104. A group of well-known writers produced a document in 1970 titled "Por la creación de una cultura popular nacional" (Toward the Creation of a National Popular Culture) that supported the formation of an institute of culture but warned that a top-down government policy or any sort of orthodoxy might be counterproductive and overly bureaucratic. In the Padilla case, the Cuban government had arrested and mistreated the Cuban poet Heberto Padilla after he wrote several works that seemed to criticize the government (although he argued that they were directed at Stalinism). The episode created a stir among intellectuals and artists worldwide: Albornoz, "La cultura en la Unidad Popular,"151–152. See also Alfonso Calderón, "1964–1973: 'La cultura ¿El horror de lo mismo de siempre?'" in *Cultura, autoritarismo y redemocratización en Chile,* ed. Manuel Antonio Garretón Merino, Saúl Sosnowski, and Bernardo Subercaseaux, University of Maryland, College Park, Latin American Studies Center: (Mexico City: Fondo de Cultura

Económica, 1993), 25–26; Germán Alburquerque Fuschini, "El caso Padilla y las redes de escritores latinoamericanos," *Revista Universum*, no. 16 (2001): 307–320; Enrique Lihn, Hernán Valdés, Cristián Huneeus, Carlos Ossa, and Mauricio Wacquez, *La cultura en la vía chilena al socialismo* (Santiago: Editorial Universitaria, 1971).

105. Jara, *Víctor*, 195.

106. Encina and Fuenzalida, *Víctor Jara*, 27.

107. Memoria chilena, "La Quinta Rueda (1972–1973)," http://www.memoriachilena .cl/602/w3-article-3534.html.

108. Ibid.

109. Carlos Maldonado, *La revolución chilena y los problemas de la cultura: Documentos de la Asemblea Nacional de Trabajadores de la Cultura del PC* (Santiago: Horizonte, 1971), quoted in Albornoz, "La cultura en la Unidad Popular," 164–165.

110. Church Commission Report, 31.

111. Ibid., 27.

112. Jara, *Víctor*, 221–222.

CHAPTER 5

1. Eduardo Carrasco, interview with the author, June 12, 2012, Santiago.

2. William G. Roy, *Reds, Whites, and Blues: Social Movements, Folk Music, and Race in the United States* (Princeton, NJ: Princeton University Press, 2010), 2.

3. Ibid., 16.

4. Ibid., 2.

5. Eduardo Carrasco, interview with the author, August 9, 2011, Santiago.

6. Max Berrú, interview with the author, June 14, 2011, Santiago.

7. José Seves, interview with the author, July 27, 2011, Santiago.

8. Berrú interview (June 14, 2011).

9. Horacio Durán, interview with the author, July 31, 2012, Santiago.

10. José Seves, interview with the author, August 11, 2011, Santiago.

11. Seves interview (July 24, 2012).

12. Ángel Parra, interview with the author, January 24, 2013, Santiago.

13. Ricardo Venegas, interview with the author, February 1, 2013, Santiago.

14. Eduardo Carrasco, interview with the author, January 29, 2013, Santiago.

15. Carrasco interview (August 9, 2011).

16. Mario Salazar, interview with the author, August 23, 2012, Santiago.

17. Ibid.; see also the website at http://www.escritormariosalazar.cl.

18. Carlos Zarricueta, interview with the author, August 3, 2011, Santiago.

19. Héctor Salgado, interview with the author, May 24, 2012, San Francisco.

20. See Mark Mattern, *Acting in Concert: Music, Community, and Political Action* (New Brunswick, NJ: Rutgers University Press, 1998); Mark Mattern "Cajun Music, Cultural Revival: Theorizing Political Action in Popular Music," *Popular Music and Society* 22, no. 2 (Summer 1998): 31–48.

21. Mattern, "Cajun Music, Cultural Revival," 32.

22. John Street, book review in *Popular Music* 19, no 2 (2000): 258; emphasis added. For a sharp critique of Mattern's argument as reflecting naïveté and U.S. bias—e.g., assuming that exploited people can "act in concert" with oligarchies that despise them—see Martha Nandorfy, "The Right to Live in Peace," in *Rebel Musics: Human Rights, Resistant Sounds, and the Politics of Music Making*, ed. Daniel Fischlin and Ajay Heble (Montreal: Black Rose Books, 2003), 172–209.

23. Joan Jara, *Víctor: An Unfinished Song* (London: Jonathan Cape, 1983), 67.

24. Ibid., 195.

25. Horacio Salinas, interview with the author, July 26, 2011, Santiago.

26. Ibid.

27. Jorge Coulon, interview with the author, July 7, 2011, Santiago.

28. Seves interviews (July 27, 2011, and August 11, 2011).

29. Venegas interview (February 1, 2013).

30. "A Conversation with Horacio Salinas," newsletter, Center for Latin American Studies, University of California, Berkeley, October 6, 1999.

31. Eduardo Carrasco, interview with the author, July 26, 2012, Santiago; Horacio Salinas, interview with the author, August 26, 2011, Santiago; Rodolfo Parada, "Mucho le debemos a Sergio," *Revista Musical Chilena* 58, no. 201 (January–June 2004): 123.

32. Carrasco interview (January 29, 2013).

33. Ibid., Carrasco interview, August 14, 2013, Santiago.

34. Venegas interview (February 1, 2013).

35. Ricardo Valenzuela, interview with the author, August 21, 2012, Santiago.

36. "Quilapayún: 'Durante la Unidad Popular hasta los momios cantaban 'La batea,'" *La Nación*, January 12, 2012.

37. Max Berrú, interview with the author, July 12, 2011, Santiago; Seves interview (August 11, 2011).

38. Salinas interview (August 26, 2011).

39. Interview with Inti-Illimani (individual speakers not identified), in "Inti-Illimani: La vuelta a América," *Ramona* 2, no. 23 (1972): 39.

40. Inti-Illimani, "¿Terrorismo musical?" *Quinta Rueda*, no. 4 (1973).

41. Horacio Durán, interview with the author, July 9, 2013, Santiago.

42. See the exchange of letters between Quilapayún and Inti-Illimani in 1983, Eduardo Carrasco archives, Archivo de Música Popular Chilena, Universidad Católica, Santiago. See also Any Rivera, "Inti-Illimani en Italia: El canto de lejos, el canto de cerca," *La Bicicleta*, March–April 1980; Patricio Krebs, "No nos exilien de nuevo," *La Bicicleta*, June 1983.

43. Carlos Maldonado Prieto, "Militarización de la policía: Una tendencia histórica chilena," adapted from "Orden público en el Chile del siglo XX: Trajectoria de una policía militarizada," in *Justicia en la calle: Ensayos sobre la policía en América Latina*, ed. Peter Waldman (Buenos Aires: ISLA-Universitat Augsburg-Buenos Aires-Medellín, 1996), 73–97.

44. Jara, *Víctor*, 120–121.

45. Iván Ljubetic Vargas, "Morir en Puerto Montt," *Punto Final*, no. 568 (May 28, 2004), http://www.puntofinal.cl/568/puertomontt.htm.

46. Jara, *Víctor*, 122.

47. Ibid., 123–124.

48. Carrasco interview (July 26, 2012). For more detail on the genesis of "La Cantata," see Ricardo García's interview with Luis Advis in José Osorio, ed., *Ricardo García: Una obra trascendente* (Santiago: Editorial Pluma y Pincil, 1996), 185–187; Eduardo Carrasco, *Quilapayún: La revolución y las estrellas* (Santiago: Ediciones de Ornitorrinco, 1988), 149–163.

49. Berrú interview (June 14, 2011).

50. Patricio Manns, interview with the author, August 6, 2011, Concón.

51. Marisol García, "El blog de Spartakku: Patricio Manns 1971," http://spartakku.perrerac.org/chile/patricio-manns-patricio-manns-1971/46.

52. Javier Osorio Fernández, "Canto para una semilla: Luis Advis, Violeta Parra y la modernización de la música popular chilena," *Revista Musical Chilena* 60, no. 205 (June 2006): 37.

53. This story is told in the beautiful French documentary film by Mélanie Brun, *No habrá revolución sin canción* (There Will Be No Revolution without Song; 2013). Max Berrú said that while he had never heard about this episode directly from Ortega, he understood that Ortega had been walking by the Music Conservatory where he taught classes when he heard a group of workers in the street chanting, "El pueblo unido jamás será vencido." When he arrived at the conservatory, he began writing the song: Max Berrú, e-mail communication to the author, September 1, 2013.

CHAPTER 6

1. Joan Jara, *Víctor: An Unfinished Song* (London: Jonathan Cape, 1983), 190.

2. R. Keith Sawyer, *Explaining Creativity: The Science of Human Innovation* (New York: Oxford University Press, 2006).

3. Ibid., 32.

4. Ibid., 20, 122.

5. Steven Johnson, "The More We Get Together," *New York Times Magazine*, September 23, 2012, 48–49.

6. José Seves, "Puentes Musicales," blog entry, http://joseves.blogspot.com/2006/12/puentes-musicales.html.

7. Walter Isaacson, "Inventing the Future: Review of *The Idea Factory*," *New York Times*, April 6, 2012, 20.

8. Horacio Durán, interview with the author, June 13, 2011, Santiago.

9. Ángel Parra, interview with the author, January 24, 2013, Santiago.

10. Horacio Durán, interview with the author, July 9, 2013, Santiago.

11. Patricio Manns, interview with the author, August 6, 2011, Concón.

12. Volodia Teitelboim, *Neruda: An Intimate Biography*, trans. Beverly J. DeLong-Tonelli (Austin: University of Texas Press, 1991).

13. José Ignacio Silva A., "La nueva canción chilena," *Librínsula* 2, no. 73 (May 27, 2005); Karen Kerschen, *Violeta Parra: By the Whim of the Wind* (Albuquerque: ABQ Press, 2010), 120.

14. Osvaldo Rodríguez, *La nueva canción chilena: Continuidad y reflejo* (Havana: Ediciones Casa de las Américas, 1988), 46.

15. Joan Jara, interview with the author, June 8, 2011, Santiago.

16. Jara, *Víctor*, 45–46.

17. Ibid., 47.

18. José Seves, interview with the author, August 11, 2011, Santiago.

19. Jara interview (June 8, 2011).

20. Eduardo Carrasco, interview with the author, January 29, 2013, Santiago.

21. Parra interview (January 24, 2013).

22. See two art books with text and color reproductions of the posters and album covers: Antonio Larrea and Jorge Montealegre, *Rostros y rastros de un canto* (Santiago: Nunatak, 1997; Antonio Larrea, *33 ⅓ RPM* (Santiago: Nunatak, 2008).

23. Vicente Larrea, interview with the author, August 22, 2011, Santiago.

24. Antonio Larrea, interview with the author, August 16, 2012, Santiago.

25. Vincente Larrea interview (August 22, 2011).

26. Antonio Larrea interview (August 16, 2012).

27. Ibid.

28. Larrea, *33 ⅓ RPM*, 52.

29. Vicente Larrea interview (August 22, 2011).

30. Antonio Larrea interview (August 16, 2012).

31. Vicente Larrea interview (August 22, 2011).

32. Antonio Larrea interview (August 16, 2012).

33. Vicente Larrea interview (August 22, 2011).

34. See the Facebook page, http://www.facebook.com/pages/Colectivo-Brigada-Ramona-Parra/127151717319073?sk=info.

35. Vicente Larrea interview (August 22, 2011).

36. Ernesto Saúl, "Brigadas Ramona Parra, Arte de la ciudad," in *Pintura Social en Chile* (Santiago: Ediciones Quimantú, 1972), http://www.abacq.net/imagineria/arte.htm#top.

37. Larrea, *33 ⅓ RPM*, 52.

38. Alejandro González, "El arte brigadista," August 2000, http://www.abacq.net/imagineria/arte4.htm.

39. Horacio Salinas, interview with the author, July 26, 2011, Santiago; Seves interview (August 11, 2011).

40. Ricardo Venegas, interview with the author, February 1, 2013, Santiago.

41. Salinas interview (July 26, 2011). See also Horacio Salinas, *La canción en el sombrero* (Santiago: Catalonia, 2013), 124–125, 194–195.

42. Seves interview (August 11, 2011).

43. On the same subject, see José Seves, "En busca de Cándidos," May 26, 2010, https://es-es.facebook.com/notes/jos%C3%A9-seves/en-busca-de-c%C3%A1ndidos/124422297581277.

44. Manns interview (August 6, 2011).

45. Any Rivera, "Inti-Illimani en Italia: El canto de lejos, el canto de cerca," *La Bicicleta*, March–April 1980, 32.

46. Eduardo Carrasco, *Quilapayún: La revolución y las estrellas* (Santiago: Ediciones de Ornitorrinco, 1988), 84.

47. Venegas interview (February 1, 2013).

48. Carrasco, *Quilapayún*, 85.

49. Ibid., 139.

50. Parra interview (January 24, 2013).

51. Carlos Valladares M. and Manuel Vilches P., *Rolando Alarcón: La canción en la noche* (Santiago: Quimantú, 2009), 83–84.

52. Seves interview (August 11, 2011); Carrasco interview (January 29, 2013).

53. Horacio Salinas, interview with the author, July 8, 2013, Santiago.

54. Eduardo Carrasco, interview with the author, August 14, 2013, Santiago.

55. Seves interview (August 11, 2011).

56. Ibid., August 21, 2012, Santiago.

57. Fabio Salas, interview with the author, August 12, 2011, Santiago. See also Fabio Salas, *La primavera terrestre: Cartografías del rock chileno y la Nueva Canción chilena* (Santiago: Editorial Cuarto Propio, 2000).

58. César Albornoz, interview with the author, August 10, 2011, Santiago; Salas interview (August 12, 2011).

59. Joan Jara, interview with the author, August 4, 2011, Santiago.

60. Durán interview (June 13, 2011).

61. Rodrigo Torres, *Perfil de la creación musical en la nueva canción chilena desde sus orígenes hasta 1973* (Santiago: CENECA, 1980), 37.

62. Eduardo Carrasco, interview with the author, July 26, 2012, Santiago.

63. Joan Jara uses the term "clones" in Jara, *Víctor*, 190. Ricardo Venegas, interview with the author, June 27, 2012, Santiago.

64. Juan Valladares, interview with the author, July 23, 2012, Santiago.

65. Thomas Turino, *Music as Social Life: The Politics of Participation* (Chicago: University of Chicago Press, 2008), 16–18.

66. Carrasco interview (January 29, 2013).

67. Patricio Manns, "The Problems of the Text in Nueva Canción," trans. Catherine Boyle and Mike Gonzalez, *Popular Music* 6, no. 2 (May 1987): 194.

68. Salas interview (August 12, 2011).

69. José Seves, interview with the author, June 26, 2012, Santiago.

70. Víctor Jara, interview with Televisión Panamericana, Peru, 1973.

71. Max Berrú, interview with the author, June 14, 2011, Santiago.

72. Rodríguez, *La nueva canción chilena*, 104.

73. Max Berrú, interview with the author, July 11, 2012, Santiago. See also Salinas, *La canción en el sombrero*, 45.

74. Berrú interview (June 14, 2011).

75. Horacio Durán, interview with the author, July 31, 2012, Santiago.

76. Horacio Salinas, interview with the author, August 26, 2011, Santiago.

77. Cecilia Coll, interview with the author, August 27, 2013, Santiago.

78. Max Berrú, interview with the author, July 12, 2011, Santiago.

79. Ibid. (July 11, 2012).

80. Several friends of Advis's told me this in Santiago in 2012.

81. Carlos Orellano, ed., "Discusión sobre la música chilena," 1978, http://www.quilapayun.com/indexesp.html.

82. Jorge Coulon, *La sonrisa de Víctor Jara* (Santiago: Editorial USACH, 2009), 47–49. For another example, see Salinas, *La canción en el sombrero*, 95–96.

83. Parra interview (January 24, 2013).

84. Seves interview (August 11, 2011).

85. Salinas interview (August 26, 2011).

86. Fernando Reyes Matta, "The 'New Song' and Its Confrontation in Latin America," in *Marxism and the Interpretation of Culture*, ed. Craig Nelson and Lawrence Grossberg (Champaign: University of Illinois Press, 1988), 448.

87. Berrú interview (June 14, 2011).

88. Seves interview (June 26, 2012).

89. Ibid. (August 11, 2011).

CHAPTER 7

1. Salvador Allende, Jane Carolina Canning, and James D. Cockcroft, *Salvador Allende Reader: Chile's Voice of Democracy* (Montreal: Ocean Press, 2000), 17.

2. For a fascinating review, see Jiřina Rybáček-Mlýnková, "Chile under Allende: A Bibliographic Survey," Discussion Paper no. 63, Woodrow Wilson School, Princeton University, Princeton, NJ, March 1976.

3. For an excellent collection of primary documents, see Centro de Estudios Miguel Enríquez, http://www.archivochile.com.

4. See the reports by the National Commission for Truth and Reconciliation (Rettig Commission), 1991, and the National Commission on Political Imprisonment and Torture (Valech Commission), 2004.

5. Patricia Díaz Inostroza, interview with the author, July 4, 2011, Santiago. For more analysis of the regime's cultural policies, see Rodrigo A. Henríquez Moya, "30 años de políticas culturales: Los legados del autoritarismo," *Sepiensa.boletin*, October 2004, http://www.sepiensa.cl/edicion/index.php?option=content&task=view&id=174.

6. Junta Militar, Bando [Decree] no. 15, "Censura y clausura de medios de prensa," September 11, 1973.

7. Patricia Díaz Inostroza, interview with the author, August 8, 2011, Santiago.

8. This section draws from J. Patrice McSherry, "The Víctor Jara Case: Justice in 2013?" February 2013, http://www.socialjusticejournal.org/SJEdits/McSherry_Victor_Jara.html.

9. For a wrenching description, see Joan Jara, *Victor: An Unfinished Song* (London: Jonathan Cape, 1983), chap. 11.

10. Max Berrú, interview with the author, June 14, 2011, Santiago.

11. See, e.g., Pamela Constable and Arturo Valenzuela, *A Nation of Enemies: Chile under Pinochet* (New York: W. W. Norton, 1991), chap. 4; Pablo Policzer, *The Rise and Fall of Repression in Chile* (Notre Dame, IN: University of Notre Dame Press, 2009).

12. J. Patrice McSherry, *Predatory States: Operation Condor and Covert War in Latin America* (Lanham, MD: Rowman and Littlefield, 2005), 71–73, 86–87.

13. See ibid. and my numerous articles on Condor.

14. Marco Fajardo, "Lanzan libro sobre el intento de resistencia armada al Golpe," *El Mostrador*, October 4, 2013. See also Ignacio Vidaurrázaga, *Martes once: La primera resistencia* (Santiago: Lom Ediciones, 2013); Mario Garcés and Sebastián Leiva, *El golpe en La Legua: Los caminos de la historia y la memoria* (Santiago: Lom Ediciones, 2005).

15. Ricardo Ahumada, "Especial Golpe: Las otras calles fachas y monumentos que mantienen viva la dictadura," *The Clinic* (Santiago), March 11, 2013.

16. Patricia Verdugo, *Chile, Pinochet, and the Caravan of Death* (Miami: North-South Center Press, 2001).

17. For chilling testimony, see Luz Arce, *The Inferno: A Story of Terror and Survival in Chile*, trans. Stacey Alba D. Skar (Madison: University of Wisconsin Press, 2004); Manuel Guerrero Ceballos, *Desde el túnel: Diario de vida de un detenido desaparecido* (Santiago: Lom Ediciones, 2008); Hernán Valdés, *Diary of a Chilean Concentration Camp*, trans. Jo Labanyi (London: Victor Gollanca, 1975).

18. U.S. Senate, *Covert Action in Chile, 1963–1973*, Staff Report of the Senate Committee to Study Governmental Operations with Respect to Intelligence Activities (Church Commission Report), December 18, 1975, 39–40, 54.

19. "Sepultan a José Tohá tras confirmarse su crimen en el Hospital Militar," *La Nación*, November 19, 2012.

20. See, e.g., the testimony of his widow: Matilde Urrutia, *My Life with Pablo Neruda*, trans. Alexandria Giardino (Stanford, CA: Stanford General Books, 2004).

21. Jorge Barreno, "El ex chófer de Neruda afirma que el poeta fue asesinado por Pinochet," *Elmundo.es*, May 11, 2011.

22. In 1982, former President Eduardo Frei—who had turned against the military regime—died at the same clinic after a routine hernia operation. In 2009, his death was ruled a homicide, and six people—including two doctors—were charged with poisoning him: "El juez del caso Neruda interrogará a los médicos procesados por muerte de Frei," *Público.es*, May 3, 2013.

23. Jara, *Víctor*, 248.

24. Jaime Esponda, e-mail communication to the author, October 4, 2013.

25. Rodrigo Torres, interview with the author, July 9, 2011, Santiago.

26. "Los 'exonerados' de la guerra sucia," *El Mostrador*, July 15, 2013.

27. Luis Hernán Errázuriz, "Dictadura militar en Chile: Antecedentes del golpe esté-tico-cultural," *Latin American Research Review* 44, no. 2 (2009): 136–157.

28. See Arce, *The Inferno*; Rachel Field and Juan Mandelbaum, dirs., *In Women's Hands*, documentary film, WGBH Boston and Central Television for Channel 4 UK, PBS Americas series, 1992.

29. José Seves, interview with the author, June 26, 2012, Santiago.

30. Berrú interview (June 14, 2011).

31. José Ignacio Silva, "La nueva canción chilena," *Librinsula* 2, no. 73 (May 27, 2005), http://librinsula.bnjm.cu/1-205/2005/mayo/73/colaboraciones/colaboraciones520.htm.

32. René Largo Farías, *La nueva canción chilena* (Mexico City: Casa de Chile, 1977), 20.

33. Jaime Esponda, interview with the author, August 14, 2012, Santiago.

34. Ibid.

35. Ángel Parra, interview with the author, January 24, 2013, Santiago. For other testi-mony, see Jorge Montealegre, *Frazadas del estadio nacional* (Santiago: Lom Ediciones, 2003).

36. Ernesto Parra, interview with the author, August 23, 2012, Santiago.

37. Ernesto Parra interview (August 29, 2013).

38. Luis Alvarado, interview with the author, July 20, 2011, Santiago.

39. Torres interview (July 9, 2011).

40. Mariela Ferreira, interview with the author, August 13, 2012, Santiago.

41. Marisol García, "La música chilena bajo Pinochet," December 26, 2006, http://dicap.blogspot.com/2006/12/la-msica-chilena-bajo-pinochet.html.

42. Miguel Davagnino, interview with the author, July 26, 2012, Santiago. A number of Chileans referred to this meeting, and several said that no official decree has ever been found.

43. Laura Jordán, "Música y clandestinidad en dictadura: La represión, la circulación de músicas de Resistencia y el casete clandestino," *Revista Musical Chilena* 63 (July–December 2009): 90; Rodrigo Torres, interview with the author, July 9, 2011.

44. Karolina S. Babic, "La Cueca Sola: An Icon of Memory in Post-Authoritarian Chile," presentation at Latin American Studies Congress, May 30–June 1, 2013, Wash-ington, DC.

45. Torres interview (July 19, 2011).

46. Robert N. Pierce, *Keeping the Flame: Media and Government in Latin America* (New York: Hastings House, 1979), 69–70, 72, 78.

47. Henríquez Moya, "30 años de políticas culturales," 7, 9.

48. Ibid., 16.

49. Jordán, "Música y clandestinidad en dictadura," 84.

50. Constable and Valenzuela, *A Nation of Enemies*, 249.

51. Ibid., 223 and chap. 7.

52. Ibid., 231.

53. Much of Chile's industry collapsed, declining "from a high of 30% of GDP in the early 1970s to a low of 18% in 2000, taking the country back to pre–World War II levels of industrialization." After the collapse of the banking sector in 1982, the neoliberal model lost much legitimacy within Chile, and mass protests began to occur for the first time in years: see Public Citizen, "The Uses of Chile: How Politics Trumped Truth in the Neo-Liberal Revision of Chile's Development," September 2006, 9, http://www.citizen.org/publications/publicationredirect.cfm?ID=7460.

54. Under the Chicago Boys, 2,151 businesses declared bankruptcy between 1980 and 1983: Constable and Valenzuela, *A Nation of Enemies*, 208–209.

55. Harald Beyer and Carmen Le Foulon, "An Examination of Wage Inequalities in Chile," *Estudios Públicos* 85 (Summer 2002), http://www.cepchile.cl/2_3031/doc/an_exami

nation_of_wage_inequalities_in_chile.html#.VJstUBEBg. Since the 1960s, Chile has become one of the most unequal societies in the world; the richest 10 percent of the population now account for nearly half the country's income: Public Citizen, "The Uses of Chile," 6.

56. Church Commission Report, 54.

57. Babic, "La Cueca Sola."

58. Ricardo Venegas, interview with the author, June 27, 2012, Santiago.

59. Ibid.

60. "Barroco Andino 1974 (Chile)," blog entry dated 2009, http://rockchilelatino america.blogspot.com/2007/12/barroco-andino-barroco-andino-1974.html.

61. Torres interview (July 9, 2011).

62. Genaro Prieto and Jorge Calvo, "Nano Acevedo y la Peña 'Javiera,'" *Cactus Cultural* (May–June 2013), http://www.cactuscultural.cl/nano-acevedo-y-la-pena-javiera. For more on *Canto Nuevo*, see Gabriela Bravo Chiappe and Cristian González Farfán, *Ecos del tiempo subterráneo: Las peñas en Santiago durante el régimen militar 1973–1983* (Santiago: Lom Ediciones, 2009); Patricia Díaz Inostroza, *El canto nuevo chileno* (Santiago: Editorial Universidad Bolivariana, 2007); Marisol García, *Cancion valiente 1960–1989: Tres décadas de canto social y político en Chile* (Santiago: Ediciones B Chile, 2013), chap. 6; Javier Osorio Fernández. "*La bicicleta*, el canto nuevo y las tramas musicales de la disidencia: Música popular, juventud y política en Chile durante la dictadura, 1976–1984," *A Contra Corriente* 8, no. 3 (Spring 2011): 255–286.

63. Davagnino interview (July 26, 2012).

64. Torres interview (July 9, 2011).

65. Viviana Larrea, interview with the author, July 25, 2012, Santiago. See also José Osorio, ed., *Ricardo García: Una obra transcendente* (Santiago: Editorial Pluma y Pincil, 1996), 52.

66. Roberto Garretón, interview with the author, August 13, 2012, Santiago.

67. Patricia Díaz, interview with the author, August 8, 2011, Santiago.

68. Jordán, "Música y clandestinidad en dictadura," 89–90.

CHAPTER 8

1. Víctor Jara, interview with Televisión Panamericana, Peru, July 1973.

2. Mariela Ferreira, interview with the author, August 13, 2012, Santiago.

3. Edward J. McCaughan, *Art and Social Movements: Cultural Politics in Mexico and Aztlán* (Durham, NC: Duke University Press, 2012), 6.

4. Rodrigo Torres, *Perfil de la creación musical en la nueva canción chilena desde sus orígenes hasta 1973* (Santiago: CENECA, 1980), ii.

5. Miguel Davagnino, interview with the author, July 24, 2013, Santiago.

6. Horacio Salinas, interview with the author, July 8, 2013, Santiago.

7. Max Berrú, interview with the author, August 28, 2013, Santiago. According to Aparcoa member Julio Alegría, the formation of that group was different because young people in La Jota created it to have a political function, performing in PC events and tours: Julio Alegría, interview with the author, August 19, 2013, Santiago.

8. Eduardo Carrasco, interview with the author, July 26, 2012, Santiago.

9. Roberto Márquez, interview with the author, July 20, 2012, Santiago.

10. Miguel Davagnino, interview with the author, July 26, 2012, Santiago.

11. Salinas interview (July 8, 2013).

12. Joan Jara, *Víctor: An Unfinished Song* (London: Jonathan Cape, 1983), 156.

13. Mario Salazar, interview with the author, August 23, 2012, Santiago.

14. Salinas interview (July 8, 2013).

Index

Acción Mujeres de Chile, 81
Acevedo, Nano, 94, 177
"A Cuba," 73
Adorno, Theodor, 17
Advis, Luis, 13, 172; *Cantata Santa María de Iquique,* 13, 30, 61, 105, 136; *Canto al Programa,* 61, 160–162; *Canto para una Semilla,* 13, 61, 138
Aguirre Cerda, Pedro, 7, 23, 33
"Ahora Sí el Cobre Es Chileno" (Now Copper Is Really Chilean), 102
Alarcón, Rolando, 6, 33, 56, 59; "Canción para Pablo," 110; *refalosa* by, 59–60; "Se Olvidaron de la Patria," 59; "Si Somos Americanos," 57
Albornoz, César, 100
Albornoz, Luis, 75, 145
Aldunante, Isabel, 176
Alerce, 177–178
Alessandri, Arturo, 31–32
Alessandri, Jorge, 43, 83
Allende, Andrés Pascal, 49
Allende, Beatriz, 49
Allende, Salvador, 1; as Aguirre Cerda's health minister, 33; coup against (*see* Military coup [1973]); cultural presentations and, 77, 82, 86; economic model of, 88–89; Forty Measures of, 13, 88, 89, 160–162; New Song performances for, 15–16, 77, 82; presidency of, 86–114 (*see also* Unidad Popular [UP]

government); presidential candidacy of (1952), 38–39; presidential candidacy of (1958), 42–43; presidential candidacy of (1964), 24–25, 44, 47; presidential candidacy of (1970), 13, 77, 79, 82, 83–85, 86; Senate election of (1953), 39; Socialist Party and, 32; on Soviet invasion of Czechoslovakia, 79; Statute of Constitutional Guarantees of, 87; U.S. opposition to, 45–46, 80, 81, 83–85, 113
Alliance for Progress, 43–44, 45
Altamirano, Carlos, 79, 114
"A Luis Emilio Recabarren," 31
Alvarado, Luis, 173
Ambrosio, Rodrigo, 51
"América Insurrecta" (America Rebelling), 60
Anaconda Company, 22, 31
Andalién, 81–82
Andean music, 4, 40–41, 153
Ángel Parra Canta a Pablo Neruda (Ángel Parra Sings to Pablo Neruda), 144
Anita y José duo, 76, 122
Anticommunism, 36–37, 44, 46
Aparcoa, 6, 34, 68
"Aquí Me Quedo" (Here I Stay), 144
Araníbar, Eliana, 109
Araucanians, 28
Araya Peters, Arturo, 110
Arbenz, Jacobo, 22
Argentina, folk music in, 8, 55–56

"Arriba en la Cordillera" (High in the Mountain Range), 57, 62
"Arriba Quemando el Sol" (Above the Sun Is Burning), 133
Arte de Pájaros (Art of Birds), 144
Autores Chilenos (Chilean Authors), 105
Autumn of the Patriarch (Márquez), 149–150
Aymara, 41

Balmaceda, José Manuel, 28–29
Baño, Rodrigo, 27
Barroco Andino, 176
Bass, Saul, 145
Batista, Fulgencio, 22
Battle of the *refalosas*, 59–60
Bay of Pigs invasion, 22
Beatles, 70, 153–154
Becerra, Gustavo, 13, 34
Berkeley, California, La Peña in, 126
Berrú, Max, 58; on *Canto al Programa*, 160–161; on Inti-Illimani's 1988 return, 159–160; on La Jota, 184; on La Peña de los Parra, 66–67; on Latin American music, 118–119; on military coup, 171–172; on National Organization of Shows, 99; on New Song's creative crisis, 102, 107; on political involvement, 118, 120–121; on record production, 71; on Salvador Allende's election, 83; on State Technical University cultural outreach program, 97, 163–164; on Unidad Popular government media access, 92; on Víctor Jara's murder, 168; on Violeta Parra, 10
Bitar, Sergio, 27, 169
Blest, Clotario, 45
Bombo legüero drum, 4
Braden, Spruille, 35
Braden Copper Company, 35
Brazil, 23; folk music in, 8; U.S. covert intervention in, 46–47
Brun, Mélanie, 213n53
Buarque, Chico, 8
Bunster, Patricio, 34, 105

Caffarena, Elena, 30
Cajón, 153
"Camelot" project, 46–47, 199n95
Canciones contingentes (contingent songs), 74, 102, 130–132, 139, 161
Canciones de Patria Nueva/Corazón de Bandido (Songs of the New Homeland/Heart of a Bandit), 154, 159
"Canción Fúnebre al Che Guevara" (Funeral Song for Che Guevara), 73

"Canción para Pablo," 110
"Cándidos," 149–150
Cantamaranto, 105
"Cantantes Invisibles," 149
Cantata Santa María de Iquique, 13, 30, 61, 82, 105, 136
"Canto a la Pampa," 30
Canto al Programa (Song to the Program), 61, 105, 158–159, 160–162
"Canto al Trabajo Voluntario" (Song to Volunteer Work), 102
Canto General (Neruda), 31, 34, 60, 144
Canto Nuevo, 176–177
Canto para una Semilla (Song for a Seed), 13, 61, 105, 138
Canto por Travesura (Mischievous Song), 105
Cardoso, Fernando Henrique, 21
Carrasco, Eduardo, 8, 70–71; on contingent songs, 130–131; creative process of, 150–151; life of, 117–118; on New Song, 184; on New Song's creative crisis, 103–104, 107; on 1960s generation, 115–116; on poetry, 144; on political involvement, 117, 124–125, 157; on Quilapayún groups, 155; on Quilapayún threats, 110
Carrasco, Julio, 70–71
"Carta al Che" (Letter to Che), 73
Carter, Jimmy, 178
Carvajal, Juan, 72
Casa de las Américas, 77
Castillo, Fernando, 50, 78
Castillo, Patricio, 172
Castro, Fidel, 73, 91, 95
Catholic Church, 44–45, 61, 63
Catholic University: Federación de Estudiantes of, 78; Festival of New Song and, 78–79, 82; Office of Communications of, 78; student movement at, 50
Central Intelligence Agency (CIA): anti-Allende propaganda and, 81, 92, 113, 199n88; Bay of Pigs invasion and, 22; Christian Democrat Party support from, 45; creation of, 21; Dirección de Inteligencia Nacional and, 168; General Schneider's assassination and, 84–85; ITT relationship with, 83; Operation Condor and, 168–169, 174; truck owners strike and, 113
Central Única de Trabajadores de Chile (Unified Workers' Central of Chile; CUT), 39, 45; *Por la CUT* for, 72; State Technical University's relationship with, 99; strikes by, 78; Unidad Popular government agreement with, 89
Chacabuco, 172–173

"Charagua," 106–107

Charango, 4, 41, 70, 153

Chile: Balmaceda period of, 28–29; Cold War period of, 21–22, 35–38; democracy of, 14, 23–24, 26–27; early history of, 28–30; education in, 24; geographical isolation of, 28; indigenous peoples of, 28; labor movement beginnings in, 30–32; 1950s in, 14, 23, 38–43; 1960s in, 1–2, 14–15, 24–25, 43–51, 53–54; Partido Demócrata in, 29; Popular Front period of, 32–35; poverty in, 1–2, 41–42, 175; social divisions in, 1–2

Chilean Development Corporation (CORFO), 33

Chilean economy: during Alessandri's presidency, 43; export orientation of, 29, 31; after military coup, 175; during Popular Front period, 33; during Unidad Popular government, 27, 88–89, 107–110, 113

Chilean military, 24; in presidency, 31–32; songs about, 59–60; Tacna uprising by, 80; in Unidad Popular government, 108–109; U.S. power over, 46, 113; U.S. training for, 38. *See also* Military coup (1973)

Chile en Cuatro Cuerdas, 72

ChileFilms, 33

Chile Joven, 81

Chile Ríe y Canta, 65, 95

Chonchol, Jacques, 51, 91, 207n18

Christian Democrat Party (Partido Demócrata Cristiano; DC), 42, 44, 45; Unidad Popular relationship with, 87, 90–91, 108, 110; U.S. support for, 45

Christian Democrat Youth (Juventud Demócrata Cristiana; JDC), 49

Church Commission Report, 45, 81, 92, 113, 199n88, 205n111

Class: culture and, 6, 18–19, 182; in traditional songs, 29

Class consciousness, 27–28

Classical music, 13, 60–61, 152–153, 176

Coal mines, 36

Coercion vs. hegemony, 18–19

Cold War, 14, 21, 35–38

Coll, Cecilia, 97, 161, 187

Colombia, U.S. covert intervention in, 47

Comité de Cooperación para la Paz en Chile (Committee of Cooperation for Peace in Chile), 170

Conciliatory music, 127

Confederation of Truck Owners, strike by, 108–109, 113

Conferences of American Armies, 37

Confrontational music, 127

Contingent songs (*canciones contingentes*), 74, 102, 130–132, 139, 161

Contreras, Colonel Manuel, 168

Copper mines: nationalization of, 27, 44, 48; strikes at, 109; U.S. corporate interests in, 2, 22, 31, 35, 48, 88

Correa Sutil, Sofía, 26–27

Corvalán, Luis, 73–74, 169, 204n86

Costa Rica, 1948 revolution in, 22

Coulon, Jorge, 12, 52–53, 75, 100; on artistic process, 128; on contingent songs, 161–162; creative process of, 150; on instruments, 69–70

Counterhegemony, 19–21; of New Song, 3, 5–6, 20–21, 52, 141, 158–159, 162–163, 181–183, 188–189

Creativity: artists' processes of, 148–152; from "below," 9–11, 14, 159; networks and, 141–142; social nature of, 140–142

Crehan, Kate, 18, 20

Cuarteto Chile, 72

Cuatro, 70

Cuatro Alamos, 178

Cuba: First Conference on Protest Song in, 77; folk music in, 8

Cuban Revolution, 14, 22, 43–44, 73

Cueca, 7–8, 29, 174

"Cueca de la CUT," 76

Cueca sola, 176

Cultural Antifascist Offensive, 111

Cultural change, 14–15; institutions and, 99–100, 183–185; musicians and, 12–15, 34, 100–101, 156–160, 181–183

Culture: class and, 18–19, 182, 183; hegemonic-counterhegemonic struggle and, 17–21; military repression of, 170–175; popular, 9–11, 12–13, 159, 163; under Unidad Popular government, 89–90, 110–114

Cuncumén, 8, 39, 42; on radio, 55; Víctor Jara's relationship to, 143–144

Czechoslovakia, Soviet invasion of, 79

Davagnino, Miguel, 57, 99, 173, 177, 184

Dawson Island, 169–170

Daza, Fernando, 95

"De Aquí y de Allá" (From Here and There), 106

Decree Law 77, 167

Deliberative music, 127

Democracy, 14, 23–24, 26–27; arts and, 34

Democratic Party (Partido Demócrata), 29

De Ramón, Raúl, 61

Desdicha obrera (Recabarren), 30

Díaz Inostroza, Patricia, 52, 167, 178

Dirección de Inteligencia Nacional (National Intelligence Directorate; DINA), 168
Discoteca del Cantar Popular (Discothèque of Popular Song; DICAP), 17, 71–75, 185, 186; album covers for, 75, 145, 146–147; Illapu recording by, 72, 96; internal politics of, 73–74; military raids on, 173
Domination, culture of, 18–19
Dominican Republic, 23
Doña Javiera *peña*, 177
Durán, Horacio, 4, 12, 41, 62; on *Canto al Programa*, 161; on instrumental music, 154; La China *peña*, 68; in Los Dos Horacios, 75; on New Song's creative crisis, 104, 107; on Partido Comunista Chileno, 121–122; on State Technical University support, 100

Economic Commission for Latin America and the Caribbean (ECLAC), 88
Ecuador, 8, 98
Editorial Zig-Zag, 89
Edwards, Agustín, 92
"El Alma Llena de Banderas" (Soul Filled with Flags), 133
"El Aparecido" (The Apparition), 73
"El Arado" (The Plow), 67
"El Bandido," 56
El Derecho de Vivir en Paz (The Right to Live in Peace), 101, 154
"El Desabastecimiento" (The Shortage), 104
El Despertar de los Trabajadores, 31
"Eleanor Rigby," 176
"Elegía para una Muchacha Roja" (Elegy for a Red Girl), 102
El Folklore No Ha Muerto (Folklore Has Not Died), 144
Elgueta, Luis Enrique "Kiko," 172
El Mercurio, 31, 46, 78, 81, 91–92, 207n24
El Nuevo Cancionero, 56
El Nuevo Canto, 77
"El Pueblo Unido Jamás Será Vencido" (The People United Will Never Be Defeated), 60, 139
"El Rock del Mundial" (World Cup Rock), 55
"El Rojo, Gota a Gota, Irá Creciendo," 144
El Sueño Americano (The American Dream), 60, 61–62
El Teniente mine, 35
El Trabajo, 31
EMI, 93, 186
Enríquez, Miguel, 49, 81
Entre Mar y Cordillera (Between Sea and Mountain Range), 62
Errázuriz, Luis Hernán, 171

Esponda, Jaime, 44, 48, 172
Ewing, Colonel Pedro, 173
Export-Import Bank (Eximbank), 35, 36

Falabella, Roberto, 34
Faletto, Enzo, 21
Fascism, 32–33
Federación de Estudiantes (Student Federation) of Catholic University, 78
Feminist movement, 30
Fernández, Camilo, 55, 62, 65
Fernández, Tito, 6, 172
Fernández Zegers, Salvador, 81
Ferreira, Mariela, 55; on *Neofolklore,* 57–58; on New Song, 181; on Víctor Jara, 62–63
Festival at Viña de Mar, 110, 111
Festival of the Huaso, 110–111
First Conference on Protest Song, 77
First Congress of Popular Poets and Singers, 39
First Festival of Committed Song, 78
First Festival of New Song, 57, 59, 78–79
Florence, Italy, 141
Folk music: in Argentina, 55–56; commercialized, 5; Latin American revival of, 8–9; *Neofolklore,* 54–60; traditional, 7–8, 29, 33, 55, 154–155; in United States, 8, 126. *See also* New Song (*la Nueva Canción*)
Ford, Gerald, 178
Forty Measures program, 13, 88, 89, 160–162
Fourth Festival of Committed Song, 110
Frei Montalva, Eduardo, 14, 42, 44, 113; death of, 216n22; election of, 24–25, 47–49
Frente de Acción Popular (Popular Action Front; FRAP), 42–43, 44, 45
Fresno, Ana, 174
Friedman, Milton, 175
Fuentes, José Alfredo "El Pollo," 55

Galtung, Johan, 46
García, Charly, 74
García, Fernando, 13; "América Insurrecta," 60; on democracy and art, 34
García, Ricardo, 40, 55, 57, 59, 62, 176–177; Alerce establishment by, 177–178; Caupolicán Theater folk music festival organization by, 177; First Festival of New Song organization by, 78–79; on New Song's creative crisis, 103; Second Festival of New Song organization by, 82
García Lorca, Federico, 33
García Márquez, Gabriel, 149–150
Garretón, Roberto, 178
Garrido, Celso, 13, 105

Geografía, 63
Gertner, Jon, 142
González, Alejandro "Mono," 147–148
González, Juan Pablo, 30
González Videla, Gabriel, 35, 36
Goulart, João, 23
Gramsci, Antonio, 14–15, 17–21, 182
Graphic art, 145–148; in Allende's campaigns, 80; after Allende's election, 95; for DICAP albums, 75, 145
Grondona, Payo, 6, 68; "Ahora Sí el Cobre Es Chileno," 102; exile of, 172
Group of Relatives of the Detained and Disappeared (Agrupación de Familiares de Detenidos Desaparecidos; AFDD), 176
Grove, General Marmaduke, 32
Grupo Abril, 178
Grupo Lonqui, 68
Grupo Móvil, 133
Grupo Raíz, 126
Guatemala, 1944 revolution in, 22
Guevara, Ernesto "Che," 50, 73
Guillén, Nicolás, 144, 151
Guitarrón, 153
Gutiérrez, Julio, 59

Hegemony: vs. coercion, 18–19; contested process of, 19–21; elite, 18–19, 182. *See also* Counterhegemony
"Herminda de la Victoria," 135
Hilo de plata, 129–130
Hinchey Report, 38, 84
Historical-structural analysis, 21
Huamarí, 68
Huaso music, 5, 54, 174
Huneeus, Carlos, 36

Ibáñez, Colonel Carlos, 31–32, 38
Illapu, 6, 72, 95–96
Industria de Radio y Televisión, 93
Institute of Musical Extension, 33
Instrument(s): ancient/indigenous, 4, 70, 153, 176; of Inti-Illimani, 69–70; military ban on, 173
Instrumental music, 116–117, 154
Intellectuals: organic, 19–20, 29, 104; traditional, 19
Inter-American Defense Board, 37
Inter-American Treaty of Reciprocal Assistance (1947), 37–38
International Telephone and Telegraph (ITT), 81, 83
Inti-Illimani, 6, 68–71, 75–77; albums of, 76, 105; artistic collaboration and, 143, 148;

Autores Chilenos, 105; *Canto al Programa,* 105, 158–159, 160–162; *Canto para una Semilla,* 13, 61, 105, 138; "Carta al Che," 73; collective ethos of, 12–13; contingent songs and, 132, 161–162; "Cueca de la CUT," 76; early years of, 75–76; exile of, 171–172; instruments of, 69–70; international tours of, 76, 98–99; members of, 75; New Song's creative crisis and, 102–103, 104; 1988 return of, 159–160; popular classes' interaction with, 163–165; "Samba de los Humildes," 76; songs of, 69, 76; during Unidad Popular government years, 90, 109. *See also specific artists*
"Inti-Illimani," 105
Iquique massacre, 29–30
Isaacson, Walter, 142
Iturra, Claudio, 137
Izquierda Cristiana (Christian Left), 91

Jara, Joan, 9, 27, 170; on First Festival of New Song, 79; on Luis Emilio Recabarren, 31; on New Song, 127–128; on Pablo Neruda, 34–35; on Salvador Allende's election, 87–88; voluntary training by, 92
Jara, Víctor, 5, 6, 12; "A Cuba," 73; "A Luis Emilio Recabarren," 31; *Canto por Travesura,* 105; "Charagua," 106–107; creative process of, 150–151; on cultural policy, 111–112; Cuncumén involvement of, 143–144; "El Alma Llena de Banderas," 133; "El Aparecido," 73; "El Arado," 67; *El Derecho de Vivir en Paz,* 101, 154; "El Desabastecimiento," 104; *Geografía,* 63; "La Beata," 63; "La Partida," 117; at La Peña de los Parra, 66–67; *La Población,* 61, 104–105, 158; "Las Casitas del Barrio Alto," 104; life of, 62–63; "Los Siete Estados," 105; "Luchín," 93, 133, 135; "Manifiesto," 41; murder of, 167–168; on New Song, 53, 63–64, 97, 180; in 1973 parliamentary elections, 109; "Obreras del Telar," 102; Pablo Neruda's relationship to, 34, 144; on people's musical participation, 94; "Plegaria a un Labrador," 79, 135; *Pongo en Tus Manos Abiertas,* 31, 146; "Preguntas por Puerto Montt," 79–80, 133–135; "Qué Lindo Es Ser Voluntario," 101–102; Quilapayún directorship of, 70–71; "Samba por Che," 73; songs of, 64, 133–135; Violeta Parra's relationship to, 143; voluntary work by, 110
JotaJota, 17, 71, 186
Juntas de Abastecimientos y Precios (Boards of Shortages and Prices), 110

Juventudes Comunistas (Young Communists;
    La Jota), 4–5, 17, 184; Andalién break-in
    by, 82; National Organization of Shows
    of, 72, 99–100; New Song members of, 17,
    120–125; nitrate mine strike support by,
    35–36; protest march (1967) by, 78; Ramona
    Parra Brigade of, 95, 96, 147–148; record
    label of (see Discoteca del Cantar Popular
    [Discothèque of Popular Song; DICAP])

Karaxú, 126
Kennecott Company, 22, 31, 35
Kennedy, John F., 23, 43–44
Kirberg, Enrique, 50, 78, 97, 169, 187
Kissinger, Henry, 85, 113, 178
Korry, Edward, 84

"La Batea" (The Washing Tub), 132
"La Beata" (The Blessed), 63
La Carpa de la Reina, 41, 67
"La Carta" (The Letter), 41
La China, 68
"La Cueca de la Organización," 102
"La Exiliada del Sur" (The Exile from the
    South), 106, 138
Lafferte, Elías, 162
La Fragua (The Forge), 61, 105–106
La Jota. See Juventudes Comunistas (Young
    Communists; La Jota)
La Legua Nueva, 42
"La Marcha de la Producción" (The March of
    Production), 101
"La Merluza," 131
"La Muralla," 151
La Nación, 92
Landowners, 2; huaso music and, 5; peasant
    relationship to, 2
Land reform, 43, 44, 48, 89
La Nueva Ola (New Wave), 54–55, 56
La Nueva Trova, 77
"La Pajita" (The Little Straw), 144
"La Partida," 117
"La Patria Prisionera" (The Imprisoned
    Homeland), 144
La Peña de los Parra, 41, 65–68, 142–143
La Población (The Shantytown), 61, 104–105,
    158
"La Producción" (Production), 102
La Quinta Rueda (The Fifth Wheel; Spare
    Tire), 112
"La Respuesta del Soldado" (The Soldier's
    Response), 59
Largo Farías, René, 65, 95
Larrea, Antonio, 16, 75, 145, 146

Larrea, Vicente, 75, 145, 146, 147
Larrea, Viviana, 178
"Las Casitas del Barrio Alto" (Little Boxes),
    104
Las Cuatro Brujas, 56, 58, 59
"Las Ollitas" (The Little Pots), 131
La Vanguardia, 31
La Victoria, 42
Lawner, Miguel, 86
Law of Defense of Democracy (Ley Maldita),
    35, 36
Leighton, Bernardo, 174
Letelier, Orlando, 169, 174
Lihn, Enrique, 111
"Little Boxes," 104
Lonquimay, 6, 68
Lonquimay massacre, 105
"Lo Que Más Quiero" (What I Love Most), 65
Los Amerindios, 6, 70, 125; "La Producción,"
    102
Los Blops, 74, 154
Los Blue Splendor, 12–13
Los Chalchaleros, 56, 70
"Los Colihues," 125
Los Cuatro Cuartos, 56, 58, 59, 62, 82
Los Cuatro Huasos, 5
Los Curacas, 6, 68
Los de Ramón, 70
Los Fronterizos, 56, 70
Los Guaranís, 40
Los Huasos de Chincolco, 54
Los Huasos Quincheros, 5, 59
Los Incas, 40
Los Jaivas, 74, 93
Los Ramblers, 55
"Los Siete Estados" (The Seven States), 105
Los Trovadores, 56
Loveman, Brian, 33
Loyola, Margot, 8, 39, 42, 55, 162
"Luchín," 93, 133, 135

Makeba, Miriam, 110
Maldonado, Carlos, 112
Manguaré, 95, 106
"Manifiesto," 41
Manns, Patricio, 6, 58; "Arriba en la
    Cordillera," 57, 62; creative process of,
    150; "El Bandido," 56; "Elegía para una
    Muchacha Roja," 102; El Folklore No Ha
    Muerto, 144; El Sueño Americano, 60,
    61–62; Entre Mar y Cordillera, 62; exile
    of, 172; on Illapu, 95–96; "La Exiliada del
    Sur," 106, 138; on Los Huasos de Chincolco,
    54; on New Song's creative crisis, 103; "No

Cierres los Ojos," 106, 137; *Patricio Manns*, 106, 138; on political involvement, 157; "Valdivia en la Niebla," 106
Mapuche, 10, 28, 30, 64, 105, 125
Marcha de la Patria Joven (March of the Young Nation), 45
March of the Pots, 91, 131
Marginalization in culture of domination, 19
Marín, Gladys, 109
Márquez, Roberto, 58, 95–96
Matta, Roberto, 95, 147
Mattern, Mark, 127
McCaughan, Edward J., 182
McCone, John, 83
Milanés, Pablo, 8, 110
Military coup ("El Tanquetazo"), 111
Military coup (1970), 84–85
Military coup (1973), 114, 166–179; anticommunism of, 167; Caravan of Death of, 169; censorship by, 173–174; cultural blackout with, 167–169; cultural repression by, 114, 170–175; dance instruction and, 174; economic program of, 175, 217n53; electoral policy of, 175; Operation Condor of, 168–169, 174; press closures by, 174; resistance after, 176–179; shantytown occupation by, 169; Víctor Jara's murder and, 167–168
Millaray, 8, 39
Miranda, Hugo, 169
Misa Chilena (Chilean Mass), 61
Mistral, Gabriela, 95, 143, 144
Moffitt, Ronni, 174
Montealegre, Jorge, 81
Montes, Jorge, 46
Moren Brito, Marcelo, 177
Morton, Adam David, 18–19
Movimiento de Acción Popular Unitario (Unitary Movement for Popular Action; MAPU), 48, 51, 80, 91
Movimiento de Izquierda Revolucionaria (Revolutionary Left Movement; MIR), 48–49, 90, 108; direct action by, 80, 81
Murals, 80, 95, 147–148
Museum of Contemporary Art, 95
Museum of Popular Art, 40
Music: creative sources of, 127–130; as political instrument, 127–130; precommunicative aspects of, 116–117, 127. *See also* New Song (*la Nueva Canción*); *specific artists and songs*
Music Conservatory of the University of Chile, 50
Musicians, 181–183; collaboration among, 16, 64, 65–68, 141–144, 150–152, 155–156; cre-

ative processes of, 148–152; cultural change and, 12–13, 15, 34, 181–183; as leaders, 162–163; as organic intellectuals, 19–20. *See also specific artists and groups*

National Intelligence Directorate (Dirección de Inteligencia Nacional; DINA), 168
National Organization of Shows (Organización Nacional de Espectáculos, ONAE), 72, 99–100
National Party, 50–51, 109
Natural resources, U.S. corporate interests in, 2, 22, 31, 35, 48, 88
Nazoa, Aquiles, 144
Necochea, Carlos, 177
Neofolklore, 55–57; *la Nueva Canción* and, 56–60
Neruda, Pablo, 5, 7, 33, 34–35, 36; on anticommunist violence, 46; *Canto General*, 31, 34, 60, 144; death of, 170; homage to (1972), 96; Víctor Jara's relationship to, 144; Violeta Parra's relationship to, 143
New Song (*la Nueva Canción*): artistic collaboration and, 16, 64, 65–68, 141–144, 150–152, 155–156; classical music and, 13, 60–61, 152–153; contemporary continuation of, 189; contingent songs and, 74, 102, 130–132, 139, 161; counterhegemonic nature of, 3, 5–6, 20–21, 52, 141, 158–159, 162–163, 181–183, 188–189; creative crisis in, 87, 101–107; creative process and, 148–152; cultural change and, 12–15, 34, 100–101, 156–160, 181–183; emblematic songs of, 133–139; First Festival of, 59, 78–79; graphic art and, 145–148; innovative nature of, 7, 13, 64, 69–70, 104–105, 152–156; institutional support for, 183–185; internationalism of, 67, 69, 95, 98; international performances of, 15–16, 97, 98–99; La Peña de los Parra and, 65–68; military censorship of, 173–174; after military coup, 176–179; musicians of, 3–5, 181–183 (*see also specific artists*); *Neofolklore* and, 56–60; origin of, 2–9, 11–12, 53–55, 56, 57–58, 63–64; people's culture and, 9–11, 12–13; phases of, 52; political nature of, 3, 4–5, 7, 8–9, 11–13, 15–16, 117–130, 156–163; precommunicative aspects of, 116–117, 127; during Salvador Allende's presidency, 96–101, 109, 110–111, 125; Second Festival of, 82; State Technical University support of, 97–100; Third Festival of, 102. *See also specific artists and songs*

Newspapers: military closure of, 174; popular, 93; under Unidad Popular government, 91–92; workers', 31

New Wave (*Nueva Ola*), 9

Nicaragua, folk music in, 8

Nicola, Noel, 110

Nitrate mines, 28–30, 31; strikes at, 35–36

Nixon, Richard, 84, 113, 178

"No Cierres los Ojos" (Don't Close Your Eyes), 106, 137

No habrá revolución sin canción (There Will Be No Revolution without Song), 213n53

Non-Aligned Movement (NAM), 22–23

Nouzeilles, Rubén, 65, 72

Nueva Ola (New Wave), 9

Nueva Trova, 110

Nuevo Cancionero, 56

Numhauser, Julio, 70–71, 93

Núñez, Guillermo, 95

"Obreras del Telar" (Workers of the Loom), 102

Oddó, Willy, 156

"Oiga Usted, General" (Listen, General), 59

"Ojos Azules" (Blue Eyes), 176

Opera, 153

Operation Condor, 168–169, 174

Operation Winter, 93

Oratorio para el Pueblo (Oratory for the People), 60

Organización Nacional de Espectáculos (National Organization of Shows; ONAE), 72, 99–100

Ortega, Sergio, 13, 34, 60; *Canto al Programa*, 61; contingent songs of, 130, 131, 161–162; "El Pueblo Unido Jamás Será Vencido," 139; exile of, 172; *La Fragua*, 61; "La Marcha de la Producción," 101; "Las Ollitas," 131; Pablo Neruda's poetry and, 144

Ortiga, 100, 176

Padilla, Alfonso, 57

Padilla, Heberto, 210–211n104

Paris, Andean music in, 40

Parra, Ángel, 6; *Ángel Parra Canta a Pablo Neruda*, 144; *Arte de Pájaros*, 144; Atahualpa Yupanqui's relationship with, 144; *Canciones de Patria Nueva/Corazón de Bandido*, 154, 159; creative process of, 151–152; "La Cueca del la Organización," 102; La Peña de los Parra, 41, 65–68, 185; on lyrics, 4; military imprisonment of, 172–173; *Oratorio para el Pueblo*, 60, 61; on political involvement, 123, 162; Quilapayún directorship of, 70; recordings of, 106

Parra, Ernesto, 16; on La Peña de los Parra, 67–68, 185; military imprisonment of, 172–173

Parra, Isabel, 6, 64–65; "De Aquí y de Allá," 106; exile of, 172; international travel of, 106; La Peña de los Parra, 41, 65–68; "Lo Que Más Quiero," 65; "Póngale el Hombro Mijito," 102; "Recopilaciones y Cantos Inéditos de Violeta Parra," 106; recordings of, 106

Parra, Nicanor, 5, 39, 143

Parra, Ramona, 35–36

Parra, Violeta, 5, 6, 8; "Arriba Quemando el Sol," 133; awards to, 40; *Canciones Reencontradas en París*, 201n21; "Canto a la Pampa," 30; *Canto para una Semilla*, 13, 61, 105, 138; international travels of, 40; La Carpa de la Reina, 41, 67; "La Carta," 41; life of, 39–40; Margot Loyola's relationship to, 42; in origin of New Song, 7–8, 10–11, 53, 63–64; Pablo Neruda's relationship to, 143; radio show of, 40; songs by, 41; Víctor Jara's relationship to, 143; "Yo Canto la Diferencia," 41

Partido Comunista Chileno (Communist Party of Chile; PC), 4–5, 31, 32, 186–187; artistic openness and, 73–74, 121–122, 128–129, 163, 184; *Canta al Programa* and, 160–161; Commission of Culture of, 187; First Congress of Popular Poets and Singers and, 39; Law of Defense of Democracy and, 35, 36; membership of, 5, 80; National Assembly of Cultural Workers of, 112; U.S. opposition to, 38

Partido Demócrata (Democratic Party), 29

Partido Demócrata Cristiano (Christian Democrat Party; DC), 42, 44, 45; Unidad Popular relationship with, 87, 90–91, 108, 110; U.S. support for, 45

Partido Socialista (Socialist Party; PS), 32, 125; on Soviet invasion of Czechoslovakia, 79

Party, Daniel, 107

Patria y Libertad (Fatherland and Liberty), 81, 84, 91, 108, 205n111; truck owners strike and, 113

Patricio Manns, 106, 138

Pavez, Héctor, 8, 39, 172

Peasant Confederation of Ranquil, 105

Peasant Councils, 76

Peñas, 41, 65–68, 142–143, 177, 184–185

Peralta, Eduardo, 176
Pérez Zujovic, Edmundo, 90, 134–135
Perón, Juan, 55–56
Peru, U.S. covert intervention in, 47
Pierce, Robert, 92
Pinochet, Augusto, 36, 113, 159, 167. *See also*
    Military coup (1973)
Pisagua, 36
Pizarro, Gabriela, 8, 39
"Plegaria a un Labrador" (Prayer to a Farmer),
    79, 135
Poetry, 29, 143–144; of Pablo Neruda, 31, 34,
    60, 144; of *payadores*, 29, 39; of Violeta
    Parra, 13
Political consciousness, 157
"Polo Doliente," 144, 154
Ponchos, 12
"Póngale el Hombro Mijito" (Lend Your
    Shoulder, My Son), 102
Pongo en Tus Manos Abiertas (I Place in Your
    Open Hands), 31, 146
Popular Action Front (Frente de Acción
    Popular; FRAP), 42–43, 44, 45
Popular Front (Frente Popular), 32–35; arts
    and, 33–34
Por la CUT, 72
Por Vietnam, 71, 145
Posters, 146–147
Power, Margaret, 82
Pragmatic music, 127
Prats, General Carlos, 38, 85, 108, 111; assas-
    sination of, 174; protests against, 113
Prebisch, Raúl, 88
"Preguntas por Puerto Montt" (Questions
    about Puerto Montt), 79–80, 133–135
"Preguntitas sobre Dios" (Little Questions
    about God), 47
Prieto, Joaquín Alberto, 59
Proyección folklórica (folk projection), 42
Puebla, Carlos, 8
Puerto Montt massacre, 48, 79–80

"Qué Lindo Es Ser Voluntario" (How
    Beautiful It Is to Be a Volunteer), 101–102
Quena, 4, 41, 70, 153
Quezada, Carlos, 145
Quilapayún, 6, 7, 68–71; albums of, 105–106;
    artistic collaboration and, 142, 148, 150–
    151; audience relationship with, 129–130;
    Canciones folklóricas de América, 145;
    "Canción Fúnebre al Che Guevara," 73;
    Cantata Santa María de Iquique, 13, 30, 61,
    82, 105, 136; "Canto a la Pampa," 30; clones

of, 155–156; collective ethos of, 12–13; con-
    tingent songs of, 130–132; exile of, 171–172;
    international tours of, 71; *La Fragua,*
    105–106; members of, 70–71; opera by, 153;
    Partido Comunista leadership on, 73–74;
    Por Vietnam, 71, 145; songs of, 69; threats
    against, 110; *Vivir como Él,* 105
Quimantú, 89, 112

Radical Party, 32, 33, 35
Radio, 40, 91; Cuncumén on, 55; military
    closure of, 174; New Song on, 106–107;
    "Nuestro Canto" on, 177; rock-and-roll on,
    55; Unidad Popular government support
    by, 92
Radio Chilena, 40
Ramona Parra Brigade, 95, 96, 147–148
Ramos Rodillo, Ignacio, 39
Ranquil massacre, 105
RCA, 93
Recabarren, Luis Emilio, 24, 29, 30–31, 122
"Recopilaciones y Cantos Inéditos de Violeta
    Parra" (Compilations and Unpublished
    Songs of Violeta Parra), 106
Refalosa, 59–60
Revolutionary Left Movement (Movimiento
    de Izquierda Revolucionaria; MIR), 48–49,
    90, 108; direct action by, 80, 81
Reyes Matta, Fernando, 163
Reynolds, Malvina, 104
Rio Pact (Inter-American Treaty of Reciprocal
    Assistance [1947]), 37–38
Ríos, Fernando, 40
Rock, Peter, 12–13
Rock-and-roll music, 5, 54, 153–154;
    apolitical nature of, 74; "Chilenized"
    (*La Nueva Ola*), 54–55; DICAP recording
    of, 74; U.S. Information Agency sponsor-
    ship of, 52
Rodríguez, Osvaldo "Gitano," 6, 47, 160;
    "Canto al Trabajo Voluntario," 102; on con-
    tingent songs, 103; on *El Sueño Americano,*
    61–62; exile of, 172
Rodríguez, Silvio, 8, 110, 177
Rojas, Julio (*Canto al Programa*), 61
Rolle, Claudio, 104, 209n61
Roosevelt, Franklin D., 21–22
Roy, William G., 116–117, 139, 158

Salas Zúñiga, Fabio, 74, 153–154, 158
Salazar, Gabriel, 24
Salazar, Mario, 16, 94, 112, 125, 188
Salgado, Héctor, 126

Salinas, Horacio, 16, 75; on Andean music, 41; on *Canto al Programa*, 161; on Communist Party, 163, 184; on contingent songs, 132; creative process of, 148–149; "Inti-Illimani," 105; "La Pajita," 144; on *Neofolklore*, 58; on New Song, 64, 128, 132, 152–153; on protest songs, 77; "Tatatí," 105, 107
"Samba de los Humildes," 76
"Samba Landó," 149
"Samba por Che," 73
Santa Cruz, Domingo, 34
Santa Cruz, Nicomedes, 162
Santiago del Nuevo Extremo, 176
Sawyer, R. Keith, 8, 140–141
Schneider, General René, 38, 84–85
Schwenke y Nilo, 176
Second Festival of New Song, 82
Self-consciousness, 20
"Se Olvidaron de la Patria" (They Forgot the Nation), 59
Seves, José: Anita y José duo, 76, 122; on artistic process, 128–129, 149–150; "Cándidos," 149–150; "Cantantes Invisibles," 149; creative process of, 149–150; on Cuncumén, 143–144; on "El Rock del Mundial," 55; on La Peña de los Parra, 65–68; on *La Población*, 105; life of, 119–120; on military-forced exile, 171; on musical styles, 3, 4, 16; on *Neofolklore*, 56, 58; on New Song, 3; on New Song's creative crisis, 102–103; on political involvement, 122–123, 158, 162, 164; "Polo Doliente," 144; on Quimantú, 89; "Samba Landó," 149; on State Technical University cultural outreach program, 97–98; on State Technical University initiatives, 9–10, 164–165; on Víctor Jara, 64; on voluntary work projects, 93
Shantytowns (*las poblaciones*), 2, 41–42; *La Población* about, 61, 104–105, 158; military occupation of, 169; Operation Winter in, 93
Shaw Moreno, Raúl, 56
Sicus, 4, 41
Sieveking, Alejandro, 104; "Herminda de la Victoria," 135
Silva Henríquez, Cardinal Raúl, 110, 170
Singing in unison, 116
"Si Somos Americanos" (If We Are Americans), 57
Socialist Party (Partido Socialista; PS), 32, 79, 125
Socialist Workers Party, 30–31
Social relationships, music and, 116–117, 139
Sol y Lluvia, 176

Sosa, Mercedes, 8, 65, 67
Soto León, Jaime, 176
Soublette, Luis Gastón, 72
Souper, Lieutenant-Colonel Roberto, 111
Spain, fascism in, 32–33
Special Operations Research Organization (SORO), 46–47
State Technical University (Universidad Técnica del Estado; UTE), 185, 187, 204–205n102; cultural outreach program of, 97, 163–164; seasonal schools of, 9–10, 164–165; student movement at, 49–50, 78, 118
Statute of Constitutional Guarantees, 87
Street, John, 12, 15, 127
Student Federation of Chile (Federación Estudiantil de Chile; FECH), 49; military ban on, 175
Student movement, 2, 49–51, 78, 118; voluntary work projects and, 92–93
Student *peñas*, 68, 76

Tacna uprising, 80
"Tatatí," 105
Teitelboim, Volodia, 46, 102, 121; on cultural policy, 112
Tejada Gómez, Armando, 8
Tejas Verdes, 168
Television, 14, 106–107
Third Festival of New Song, 102
Tiempo Nuevo, 6
Tiple, 70, 153
"Todos Juntos" (All Together), 74
Tohá, José, 169, 170
Tomic, Radomiro, 51, 83
Torres, Rodrigo, 3, 64, 69, 170, 183
Townley, Michael, 174
Trabajos voluntarios (voluntary work projects), 92–93
Train of Popular Culture, 94–95
Turino, Thomas, 6, 7, 157

Unidad Popular (UP), 26, 27, 28; formation of, 79; internal divisions in, 108, 109; military decimation of, 169–170 (*see also* Miliary coup [1973]); in 1971 municipal elections, 28; in 1973 parliamentary election, 109; "Venceremos" song for, 82, 86, 105
Unidad Popular (UP) Committees, 80
Unidad Popular (UP) government, 86–114; anti-Allende propaganda and, 91–92, 113, 199n88; book publishing under, 89; cultural policy of, 89–90, 110–114; economy under, 27, 88–89, 107–110, 113; first year

of, 87–90, 101–102; Forty Measures of, 13, 88, 89, 160–162; mass media and, 91–92, 112; military ministers in, 108–109, 113; mural arts under, 95; New Song movement and, 86–87, 95–101, 158, 188; political parties' relationships with, 90–91, 108; record industry under, 93–94; songs for projects by, 101–102; Train of Popular Culture initiative of, 94–95; voluntary work projects and, 92–93

Union movement, 24, 30–31, 35–36, 39, 122

Unitary Movement for Popular Action (Movimiento de Acción Popular Unitario; MAPU), 48, 51, 80, 91

United Fruit Company, 22

United Nations Economic Commission for Latin America and the Caribbean, 88

United States: anticommunism of, 36–37, 38; Christian Democrat Party support from, 45–46; covert interventions by, 22–23, 45–47, 81, 84–85, 199n95; folk music in, 8, 126; foreign policy of, 37–38; Jimmy Carter's presidency of, 178; military training by, 37, 38; mining interests of, 2, 22, 31, 35–36; opposition to Salvador Allende by, 45–46, 81, 83–85; rock-and-roll music of, 5; Vietnam War of, 23. *See also* Central Intelligence Agency (CIA)

Universidad para Todos (University for Everyone), 50

Universidad Técnica del Estado (State Technical University; UTE), 185, 187, 204–205n102; cultural outreach program of, 97, 163–164; seasonal schools of, 9–10, 164–165; student movement at, 49–50, 78, 118

University of Chile: military closure of, 174–175; Music Conservatory of, 50; student *peña* at, 68

University reform movement, 49–51, 78

Urbina, Silvia, 39, 42; *El Folklore No Ha Muerto*, 144

Uruguay, folk music in, 8

U.S. Army Caribbean School (USARCARIB), 37

U.S. Army School of the Americas (SOA), 37, 38

"Valdivia en la Niebla" (Valdivia in the Fog), 106

Valenzuela, Arturo, 32

Valenzuela, General Camilo, 84

Valenzuela, J. Samuel, 32

Valenzuela, Ricardo, 71, 72, 74, 131

Valladares, Juan, 100–101; on Quilapayún groups, 155–156

Vanguard of the People (VOP), 90

Vatican II, 44–45

Veinte poemas de amor y una canción desesperada (Twenty Love Poems and a Song of Despair), 144

"Venceremos" (We Will Win), 82, 86, 105, 137

Venegas, Ricardo: on artistic process, 129, 148, 151; on contingent songs, 131; on cultural expression, 90; on La Jota, 17; on musical styles, 4, 7; on political involvement, 123–124; on Quilapayún groups, 155; voluntary work by, 92–93

Viaux, General Roberto, 80, 84

Vicaría de Solidaridad, 170, 172, 178

Vietnam War, 23

Viglietti, Daniel, 8, 65, 67

Vilches, Manuel, 57

Villa Grimaldi, 178

Vivir como Él (To Live like Him), 105

Voces Andinas, 62

Voluntary work projects (*trabajos voluntarios*), 92–93

Vuskovic, Pedro, 88, 207n7

War of the Pacific (1879–1883), 28

White songs, 173

Women: *Desdicha obrera* and, 30; military torture of, 171; right-wing, 81, 91, 131

Woodstock, 15

Workers Confederation of Chile (Confederación de Trabajadores de Chile; CTCH), 32; nitrate mine strike support by, 35–36

World War II, 21–22

"Ya Parte el Galgo Terrible" (The Terrible Hound Is Leaving), 144

"Yo Canto la Diferencia" (I Sing the Difference), 41

Yupanqui, Atahualpa, 6, 8, 56; Ángel Parra's relationship with, 144; "Preguntitas sobre Dios," 47

Zarricueta, Carlos, 125–126

Zitarrosa, Alfredo, 8

Zolov, Eric, 52

J. Patrice McSherry is a Professor of Political Science at Long Island University and a Visiting Professor at Alberto Hurtado University in Santiago. She is the author of *Predatory States: Operation Condor and Covert War in Latin America* and *Incomplete Transition: Military Power and Democracy in Argentina* and a co-editor (with John Ehrenberg, José Ramón Sánchez, and Caroleen Marji Sayej) of *The Iraq Papers*.